A Scandinavian Story

A Scandinavian Story

TWO FAMILIES ALLIED IN ART AND MARRIAGE

Teresita Sparre Currie

To order additional copies of this book, contact:
Xlibris Corporation
1-888-795-4274
www.Xlibris.com
Orders@Xlibris.com
31342

Contents

I should like to dedicate my book to Marketta Tamminen,
my Finnish friend, who has been so helpful in
correcting historical errors in my text;
to my children Julie, Frank, Patrick and Peter, and with
special thanks to my daughter, Teresita C. Schaffer; and
to the memory of Louis Connick, my first editor.

The cover of this book shows a portrait of
Eva Mannerheim Sparre,
"Summer Evening," painted in 1906 by her husband,
Louis Sparre.
This book tells their story.

Chapter 1

PRELUDE IN FINLAND

Seven children were born to Count Carl Robert Mannerheim and his wife, Helene, within ten years, 1863 to 1873. To all outward appearances the couple was a 19th Century idyll, eagerly expecting a bright future in Imperial Russia's Grand Duchy of Finland. Both had inherited land and houses, and Helene had an ample income. He was handsome and gifted, heir to the castle Villnäs. Like her husband, she had grown up in a manor, Fiskars, admired for her independence and quick wits.

Carl Robert, elegant, clever and instinctively calculating, married Helene von Julin, the daughter of a recently ennobled industrialist who had made a fortune. Helene was an accomplished girl but difficult to win; she had already refused several offers. Carl Robert was polished and urbane, with a sardonic tongue and the languages expected of his class: he translated French, German and English poetry, and his verses were published.

His rebellious attitude stayed with him for decades. In later life, he championed radical causes and had been openly contemptuous of the anti-Semitism of the Dreyfus affair which was the focus of controversy in France at the time. Captain Albert Dreyfus, an Alsatian Jew, had been sentenced for treason to Devil's Island by a French court-martial in 1894. He claimed innocence, but the French military were riddled by anti-Semitism. In Paris, Emile Zola, one of the best known writers of the day, wrote an open letter accusing the military of influencing the judges. The case inflamed all Europe, divided along class lines: royalists, military, clergy were anti-Dreyfusards; socialists, republicans and anti-clericals joined to defend Dreyfus. The affair concerned the discovery of a handwritten schedule listing secret French documents, sent to the German military attaché in Paris. Evidence was later discovered that Major Ferdinand Esterhazy was author of the schedule. Esterhazy was tried and acquitted instantly. In 1898 it was found that much evidence against Dreyfus had been forged by a French intelligence officer, who committed suicide. Esterhazy fled to England. In a new court-martial Dreyfus was again found guilty by a court unable to admit its error. The President of France issued a pardon and in 1906 the Supreme Court of Appeals found Dreyfus innocent.

In his university years, it pleased Carl Robert to know that his advanced views reached conservative friends and family. He had published a journal of controversial arguments called "The Basilisk". Despite polite society's disparaging view of the acting profession, he had been on the stage and had written plays, acted at the university. Its president had to leave his post for having failed to censor his latest play, "Dramatic This and That," which pointed fingers at the Russian-appointed Governor General, and characterized Finland as oppressed and poverty-stricken. Carl Robert was expelled from the university for six months, ostensibly for failing to wear the student's uniform.

In short, Carl Robert was an aristocrat with a fetchingly notorious reputation. At twenty, Helene was smitten.

Their engagement was announced at the stately manor of Fiskars, her childhood home. Helene's father, who began as an apothecary and built a fortune from iron mines, had bought Fiskars in 1822. Its ironworks factory has been preserved, and the mansion is much as it was, an early 19th Century building with a central gable and four pillars forming a portico at the entrance.

In August, 1862, after a walk in the park and garden, a radiant Helene, holding Carl's hand, declared "now I am engaged!" Helene's young friends sewed her white dress in the ballroom while poetry was read aloud. A wreath of cornflowers adorned the bride's hair, and after dinner relatives and friends dressed up, as the custom was, to pose as famous figures from poetry and history.

The wedding was held on New Year's Eve of 1862 in the style of their time, with days and nights of feasting and dancing, but it did not take place without controversy. Concerned about Carl Robert's unwelcome views, Helene's family had sent her to a family manor to think things over first. Carl Robert won the day, but at the wedding one of the guests remarked acidly that the groom had made Helene a Countess while she had made him a rich man. My 90-year-old cousin, Louise Ehrnrooth, granddaughter of Carl Robert and Helene, told me that the wedding dinner itself was delayed for an hour; a crystal chandelier had plunged from the ceiling to the bridal couple's table smashing glasses and china. Was it an omen?

In a letter of January 1863, to her sister Hanna in Stockholm, Helene describes her homecoming to the castle Villnäs. The happy bride describes the castle staircases decorated with garlands of evergreens and colored lanterns, and flowers from the greenhouse in the drawing room, to honor the newlyweds. Carl and his bride spent joyful hours at dancing parties, riding together on their horses, skating and sleighing.

Fortunately, Hanna kept her sister's letters, a reflection of the times, and a unique account of Helene's preoccupations and opinions. Writing letters and news articles became a solace to Helene, an escape from her bitter life later on.

Perhaps there was some momentary disappointment that the first child was a girl, Sophie, born in 1863, but she was soon followed by four brothers and two sisters. One of those sisters, Eva, was my grandmother. She and her family were all influenced by their country's history, and in turn one of her brothers, Gustaf, profoundly helped bring about Finland's emergence from Russian domination. Yet he himself, like other young men of his time, had made his careeer in the Russian military. Gustaf dealt with and served Russia, while maintaining his patriotism. This was not always understood, and caused consternation in his family.

But Helene and Carl Robert's marriage, despite the early joy, was not a happy one. Carl Robert, uninterested in agriculture and the running of his estate, was drawn to a life in Paris, leaving his wife and children behind in their cold stone castle. In a letter to the then eight-year-old Sophie, in 1872, her godfather, Hugo von

Becker, congratulates her on the birth of a little sister. At the time, Carl Robert Mannerheim was far from home, in Munich, when his wife Helene must have wanted him at her side. Sophie's godfather also asked if Sophie has been brave enough, in the icy weather, to go down to the beach and boat house and watch the carpenters build her father's steamboat. Life was still luxurious.

From their earliest years, these children cherished Villnäs, standing like a sentinel on Mynälahti bay in southwest Finland, where the waters of the Baltic Sea lap at the shores. It lies in the hamlet of Askainen, west of Turku, capital of Finland when Villnäs was built, and just northwest of Naantali, the site of an ancient cloister. The main house is a white three-story building crowned by a high flared roof. Two low one-story wings with tiled saddle roofs complete the complex. It was completed in 1655. An avenue lined with birches, two kilometers in length, runs from the castle courtyard to a little white stone chapel with a cupola-capped bell tower, built in 1653 over the foundation of an earlier wood church. In the 1870's, when my grandmother Eva was a small child, her widowed grandmother lived nearby in a separate mansion called Hannula, with land and steamboat. Hannula and the chapel were all part of the Villnäs estate.

The Grand Duchy of Finland, ruled from the Swedish throne for 600 years, became Russia's in a war trade in 1809, with the Tsar ruling as Grand Duke. But the Swedish language remained official. The Mannerheim children grew up speaking only Swedish. The upper class considered it sufficient to command only enough Finnish to communicate with the "outside servants," if they lived on estates, generally those hired as farm workers and fishermen. The "inside servants" of the larger places—tutors and governesses, ladies' maids and valets, the cook, the housekeeper in charge of house servants—spoke Swedish and were usually descendants of Swedish farming families who had come to Finland in the 13th Century to consolidate the Swedish King's title to his Finnish lands.

The children's second language was French. They had the privileges of an aristocratic family with an historic name, but were given spartan discipline and reminders that they must be self-sufficient and expect no favors. The norms of both the family and the Victorian era decreed that one should not reveal fears or feelings. The children's mother, the Countess Helene, was careful to train steely nerves and toughened bodies in her children. Her seven sons and daughters slept on hard mattresses with horsehair pillows and took cold baths in the English fashion. Nevertheless, they had a joyous childhood, the girls urged by their mother to be as daring as the boys, to ride and sail and climb trees, to swim each day in their icy waters at a time when swimming was not the usual sport of females, to figure skate, ski and sled in the winter.

On the few occasions when he was home, the children's father, Count Carl Robert Mannerheim, wrote plays for his children in French, one of them to celebrate their mother's name-day. (That is the day, dedicated since Medieval times, to the saint whose name one bears, and is celebrated much as a birthday.) All the children adored theatricals, and each one had a role to play. Grownups danced the "gallopade", and parties, even for the children, were held in the banquet hall.

In her correspondence with her sister Hanna, Helene wrote that she was teaching her children herself, Bible and gymnastics in the mornings. Helene Mannerheim had a modern outlook despite a male-dominated society. She was concerned that her daughters' education should be as competent as that of her sons. At the time, needlework, playing an instrument and social conversation were generally considered as important as learning to read. In Helene's view, Governesses for the girls had to be more than adequate in teaching languages and mathematics, as well equipped to do so as the boys' tutors. But they were hard to entice to the cold winters of Finland. In the long, dark months it was a remote and insular land, isolated from other European centers of culture.

It was an era when travel was primitive. Mail, if weather permitted, was delivered by horse and buggy. The family traveled by phaeton; in winter by horse-drawn sleighs with bells. Such luxuries as sugar were kept under lock and key; sugar granules were given in small packages as special Christmas presents.

The children's upbringing and isolation in the country put the seal on their lifelong covenant with one another. The mutual trust was sometimes strained when differences in politics or points of view came between them, but it was never broken.

Living in an ancient castle, their country's history woven into its tapestries and painted on its vaulted ceilings, these children had from childhood absorbed the tales and poetry of wars against an ancient foe, their Russian overlord. Their own great-grandfather Carl Erik Mannerheim had come from Sweden, provided with money from his parents, a university education from Uppsala and a baron's title. He bought the Castle Villnäs in 1793, while Finland was still ruled from the Swedish Throne. When Finland was traded to Russia by Sweden in exchange for Norway, he played an important role in establishing Finland's autonomy. Though some considered him treasonous to have treated with the enemy, he met with the Tsar of Russia to ensure that Finland's ancient western laws would be upheld: freedom of religion, their language, lives and property secure, their army units commanded by Finns. The Tsar made Carl Erik a Count in 1824, the title passing to the eldest son. Younger sons were barons; daughters were baronesses.

Finland's last war under Swedish banners was chronicled by the national poet, Johan Ludvig Runeberg, a contemporary of the Mannerheim children's grandparents. The verses were learned by heart in Eva's childhood. It was both entertainment and a lesson in history, as the children sat by the lamp's rosy glow in their drawing room. On black winter evenings, warmed by the Dutch-tiled stove, grownups read them the verses. The poet's subject was Finland itself, its thousand lakes and forests, its proud poverty, its hardy sons and harsh history. His heroes were the Finnish foot soldier fighting for king and country, and the Russian, far from his homeland; the peasant girl whose love has deserted his post; the young recruit "whose wits were weak though his heart was strong", alone defending the bridge.

Carl Robert seldom wrote his wife, but she tried to maintain an official belief in his fidelity as husband and father. Slowly her letters to her sister Hanna in Stockholm reveal a growing anxiety and loneliness, with mounting bills and no money. Her lively brood by turns delighted and enraged her. Her oldest child Sophie is unusually obstinate at 13, irritating to her mother as one reads in her letters of 1876. Certainly there is no inkling of the woman she will become, a pioneer in nursing, the architect of Finland's health care and hospitals. There is no hint that Gustaf, Helene's third child, will one day become a national hero and the founder of his country's independence. He is, in fact, his family's bête noire. Helene writes in May, 1877, that Gustaf couldn't bear the slightest opposition. He had announced one day that he would throw himself out the window.

Helene could see the humor in it, but knew her son meant what he said, and feared the day would end "in a terrible way". Gustaf was always in trouble, falling from the barn roof in August, 1877. She wrote her sister that Gustaf had failed his exams in June 1878, but "he's been much better" and one could reason with him "when his wild temperament shows." But from Carl she heard nothing.

Helene's joy in learning that the family planned to surprise her with a party was tempered by her own suspicious thoughts, unspecified in her letter to Hanna. Rumors reached her of Carl's infidelity in Paris with a blue-blooded mistress, whom he later married. But life at the castle continued normally. On October 4 Helene wrote, "We had a visit from hunters, who harried more than they hunted. There was clatter and hullabaloo getting everything ready . . ." In November, she learned to her distress that their sons might have to spend the winter in the town house without her, while she felt marooned at Villnäs.

Helene was conscious of the difference between her sister Hanna's happy marriage and her own. In May 1878 she wrote that "even if one feels useless it is a great joy to follow one's husband and be at hand for him." However, she sadly added that Carl needed her care and presence "more out of habit than desire."

She had to keep up appearances, and had difficulty attracting good domestic help. Others had the same problem: "Rosina has a kitchen maid who has never roasted a pig . . ." In May 1879 she wrote: "My two new maids are unaccustomed geese, and Carl is coming home tomorrow." Nevertheless, there was no lack of entertainment, for she wrote, "I had promised my children they could dance in the Church Room [a banquet hall]." There was the annoying fact that she has no maid for the winter.

In a rare political comment, she wrote about one of the attempted assassinations of Tsar Alexander II. "One sees with horror how tottering and ruined this great empire is, which our conscripts now must protect and defend." If plays were censored, were letters opened? If so, this was a daring thing to write.

By the end of October Helene had to dismiss the cook. Financial problems were forcing a rearrangement and separation of the children; Eva and her governess Elisa went to Fiskars, their uncle's manor, while Helene moved to Villnäs, leaving the boys in town with a servant.

In a letter of November, 1879, she broke the news. Her son Gustaf had been expelled from school for heaving rocks through a neighbor's windows, a prank with comrades "whom he lured," as the angry headmaster told her. Gustaf had to bear the whole punishment while the original rock-thrower got only a beating. She took her boy home to Villnäs with her, understanding his pride and silent shame.

Helene wrote that she could not understand how Carl could arrange his "tangled skeins," and she had no idea how he would deal with Gustaf's predicament. Her husband's family criticized her with bitter words, she reported to her sister. "The boy should have been taken away from me from the moment he was born, and come into good hands," she lamented. Helene was neither supine nor helpless. Gustaf was her big worry, though what he did was usually "just mischief." But he had given her "a great sorrow" which she did not care to mention even in a letter. Had Gustaf said, in a moment of anger, hard truths about his parents' relationship? She felt that Gustaf must get away from all schoolmates and be at home where he was liked and would have no reason to become bitter.

Hannula, her mother-in-law's dower house, was being sold, including steamboat, harvest and inventories. (A "dower house," part of an estate, is lived in by the owner's widow—the dowager—when the oldest son takes over the manor or castle.) Helene lacked the courage, she wrote, to tell her mother-in-law the news. She hoped Carl would inform her himself. On December 6 she had a chilling telegram from Carl, which read: "Will put my affairs in order before year's end. Cannot return without losing the earnings of important undertaking. Inform the family." At home, there was still enough domestic help for routine chores, the slaughtering, washing and baking.

It seemed they would be at Villnäs for Christmas, though no one knew it would be the last time. On December 18 Helene was still hoping Carl will come home for the holiday. She has, she wrote, only "good wishes" to give for Christmas presents. Gustaf had been reasonably good, but still lazy and listless about work. However, their life at home sounded cozy, for in the evenings they took turns reading aloud. Carl wrote more encouragingly that despite his worries, he hoped everything would turn out well, so that they could "live calmly and happily together," but there was no word about his trip home or advice about how they should manage their lives.

In late January of 1880, Helene thanked her sister for a present of money to pay for Sophie's music and drawing lessons. What worried her most was the thought of sending her youngest daughters to boarding school in Russia. On March 12 she wrote from Villnäs, "Probably I must put my little girls in the Institute ["Smolny" in St. Petersburg] because there is no chance to have them educated at home as all the boys still need schools." She had written to Carl about this important subject, but he had been "mute."

Helene prayed for some possibility of paying all the debts, but "I see everything so sorrowfully and understand nothing." She continued to be haunted about her girls, insistent on their schooling. She knew that the boarding school Smolny in Russia would provide free education for the girls, but was reluctant to send them so far from home—and to a country so foreign to them. All the boys would incur expenses for a long time. Boys still came first when it was a question of money. At last she reported in March, 1880, that Carl had written, "What you do is right and will always so be considered by me," words that she treasured as protection against fault-finding by his family. He acknowledged that he had compromised his family's future and asked his wife to do "what necessity demands." But she could no longer show the shabby Villnäs to friends traveling through Finland.

In April, the resourceful Helene had asked for canning jars to sell preserved cranberries, and in June she was translating articles from French newspapers to earn money. "Work is a blessing, not handwork but thought work." She wondered if her translations would be published, which they were, in a Gothenburg newspaper, among others. On June 21 there was the usual refrain: "We'll see when Carl can come, now I have peace enough to wait when I know he's on the way . . ." In July, Sophie had a pair of new shoes made for her trip to Stockholm, but the boys' new strong boots were made partly with leather from the old ones.

Helene's faith remained strong: "God watches over all our days, the happy as well as the sad." But from Carl she had heard nothing, and she prayed he hadn't become sick.

Aunt Hanna remembered Gustaf's behavior from this time, when she was visiting Sällvik, Helene and Hanna's stepmother's home. Gustaf was there, rough-housing with other boys. He had driven his own "puukko" knife into his leg, between knee and hip. Hanna found him resisting her attention and impossible to keep still. At last, in her efforts to keep him prone on a sofa, she gave the boy a violin and bow. It didn't take long before Gustaf was snapping the strings and trying to produce sound in the instrument. He was so preoccupied that he stayed still and was amused to show his cousins that he could make the violin quaver.

The historian Stig Jägerskiöld, whose eight-volume life of Gustaf Mannerheim is essential to any student of the subject, has written sharply of Carl Robert Mannerheim's attitudes and behavior. By a combination of flawed business ventures and an addiction to gambling, he had lost his own fortune and that of his wife, her considerable income in rubles, her houses and land. It is clear that after their marriage Helene's husband had been able to do as he pleased with her inheritance, a commentary on that era's view of women's property rights.

Carl did not join Helene to deal with the results of his extravagance. Alone, she had to sell their home with all its treasures. She described her last day at the castle to her sister in a letter: the heartbreak lies in the calm cataloging of details. She was permitted to claim the dining room furniture and kitchen pots, linen sheets, homespun curtains, and her clothing. She outlined articles she might save for her sister Hanna, including wedding linens that had belonged to their mother. For each child she could take a bed with bedclothes, one suitcase and clothing, for that was usually allowed, she wrote from Villnäs on September 15, 1880, twelve days before the auction.

She moved back to the protection of her own family, into the manor of Sällvik. The four youngest children went with her. The oldest, 17-year-old Sophie was with her Aunt Hanna in Stockholm to finish her education and find employment; 16-year-old Carl, called Calle, was preparing for university in Helsinki. Gustaf, at 13, was sent to a school to prepare for the Cadet Corps. Thus they were both joined and scattered, all of them torn from their beloved home, their ghost-haunted castle with its spacious grounds, park and gardens, beach and waters.

There was only one more letter, dated January 22, 1881, a short note reporting on the horrendously cold weather, and saying "don't be anxious about me, it will surely be possible to live again if only I get good work and spare time." Eva remembered going to her mother's room and bursting into tears at finding her so frail, lying on the blue silk sofa. Helene gently admonished her child not to weep, for "to speak of death is as commonplace as talking of morning, noon and night," and gave her comforting thoughts of how Sophie and Calle would look after the younger ones when she was no longer there. Early the next morning their grandmother summoned the children. Their 38-year-old mother Helene was dead of a heart attack.

There were those who felt she was lucky. Carl Robert Mannerheim returned from Paris for the funeral. His brother-in-law, Albert von Julin, found him deeply moved; he remained a long time in the room where Helene lay. He is remembered to have put a flower and small note in Helene's coffin, according to his grandson Carl Erik. Helene's brother Albert von Julin wrote about the funeral to his sister Hanna on February 5, 1881. After the funeral, when he and two sons, Carl and Gustaf, had carried the coffin with other family members, Carl Robert stayed at Sällvik only two days, leaving his son Johan there to be cared for by his maternal grandmother.

Carl Robert did not return to Paris immediately. Exactly one month after Helene's death, on February 23, 1881, he wrote 12-year-old Johan from Helsinki. He called his wife a "guardian angel," and urged Johan to let him know if he had all he needed. Carl Robert had visited Villnäs, and forwarded Gustaf's greetings to his particular friends, the gardener and blacksmith. Carl Robert encloses a five-mark note to buy goodies for Johan and the youngest ones. His words give us a warmer, gentler portrait of this man, whose abandonment of wife and children is hard to forgive.

Helene's memory was preserved by her children. Sophie left a picture of a young mother who knew more than anyone else how to cast a magic shimmer over whatever plans and games she invented. She remembered her mother's ski trip with her, writing of a sunny and happy woman early in her marriage. Eva wrote of her mother's calm courage, her stoic resolve, her sheltering embrace. Various biographers of Sophie and Gustaf have added their own impressions of Helene. Berta Edelfelt, childhood friend and biographer of Sophie Mannerheim, writing only four years after Sophie's death, quotes a letter describing Helene in her young girlhood as much sought after, known as a merry girl at parties in Turku, selective with her many swains. Sophie herself was described as devastated by her mother's death, mourning the date each year. Sophie's more recent 1948 biographer, Tyyni Tuulio, never knew her subject personally but explored Sophie's own writings of childhood incidents. This biographer saw Helene as making a mother's benign mistakes, but keenly aware of her child's oversensitive reactions to the death of a family dog and the loss of a doll, wondering how such a delicate sensibility would survive in the cruel reality of life. Stig Jägerskiöld, with his insight and careful research of Helene's background, has sketched an independent and self-critical woman whose memory was a lodestar for her children.

Only one biographer has taken a negative view of Helene. Veijo Meri, drawing on material from other books rather than primary sources, twisted his interpretation of the childhood events to suit his dark psychological theories. He cast Helene as a mother who had little interest in her children's psychology or spiritual capacity; he called Sophie the main victim of her mother's harsh upbringing. He could not have read Helene's letters and they are not listed in his bibliography. But he probably correctly points out Helene's situation as a "social death." In her day bankruptcy was equated with character flaws and a wife's abandonment by her husband cause for her ostracism. Two of Helene's letters hint with a trace of bitterness at her isolation from those who never made visits any more, small treacheries which are universal and timeless. Helene herself did not make much of this. Far from calling herself a victim or casting herself as a tragic stereotype, she emerges from her still breathing letters as a quick-witted, resolute and modern mother. Her priorities are clear. Only at the end are there signs of collapse amidst the chaos, but there is no hysteria.

Soon after her mother's death, Eva was not happy to learn that Villnäs would once again become their home. Although her temperamental grandmother and namesake, Countess Eva Mannerheim, now presided over the castle, the actual owner was the children's paternal aunt Wilhelmina, "Aunt Mimmi," an unsmiling, strict and unloved lady. Reluctantly, harboring her bitter feelings, Eva returned with her two youngest siblings, Annicka and August. As shattering as their mother's death had been, as little as they could bear their new standing in the old home, as unwelcome as they felt, their haunts in the park, their climbing trees, their boats at the dock, the old staircase to the attic secrets, drew them in again.

It is from this time that we have letters from Eva to her favorite brother, Calle. She remembered when they all had been at Villnäs as children, while Calle and Gustaf still wore knee pants, how Annicka had sewn royal costumes and a crown for her boy doll, how Eva herself had built her a dollhouse. Sometimes a childhood detail points the way to the future. Eva's carpentry for Annicka foreshadowed her own woodworking skills. As an adult, Eva earned her keep by designing and perhaps carpentering the delicate furniture that still exists, carving elaborate frames and a chest of pear wood decorated with sculpted Renaissance-style fruits.

His children learned in 1883 that Carl Robert had married again. Baroness Sofia Nordenstam became the new Countess Mannerheim, half Russian, a lady-in-waiting to the Tsarina. When he returned to Finland with her in 1887, Sophie and Gustaf were the two who showed him particular understanding.

In 1884, Aunt Mimmi made a fateful decision, one that would mark all their lives and memories. She revived an old and dreaded idea: to send the two youngest girls to boarding school in St. Petersburg, to Smolny Institute, the school for the daughters of Russian nobility also open to Finnish girls. Its chief charm was that the girls would be educated at no cost. Eva was rejected as being too old. She was dispatched to Stockholm to finish her schooling.

But Annicka was accepted at Smolny. The child, speaking no Russian, never before separated from her family, was sent off without any family member to ease her into a harsh new life. She was 12 when she left for Russia, and in the spring of 1886, barely 14, she died from pneumonia following an attack of typhus. Her brother Carl rushed to her side, but arrived too late. One family member had come in time, Aunt Mimmi, perhaps prodded by a guilty conscience. Sophie and Eva met the boat from St. Petersburg carrying Carl with Annicka's coffin. They and Carl attended Annicka's funeral in the Villnäs chapel, and buried their young sister in the family's churchyard crypt. Her longing to come home had been fulfilled, exactly as she predicted. Annicka's pencil drawing on school notebook paper is preserved: a coffin on the farm wagon, pulled by Villnäs horses, waits for burial outside the little chapel gate.

The story of the Villnäs children's young adulthood begins at this time, though Eva and August were still adolescents. Their losses of home and money, their mother's death and their sister's, the absence of their father—these traumas suffered in so short a time made them grow up too early. For all of them it was the end of innocence.

Papa, Count Carl
Robert Mannerheim

Mama, Countess Helene Mannerheim

The 7 Mannerheim children:
from left, Johan, Carl, August, Sophie
(seated in middle), Eva
(seated in foreground), Annicka, Gustaf

Villnäs Castle

Smolny Institute

Bell tower and church in Askais,
built 1653

Chapter 2

EVA'S CAREER BEGINS AND SHE FINDS A HUSBAND

The Mannerheim men had known from childhood that inherited money and land with a family manor, the usual expectation of male children of the aristocracy, were not their lot. But the end of the 19th century was called a golden time for women's careers.[1] Marriage for a young girl was not the only goal. Eva and Sophie Mannerheim grew up with no feelings of inferiority to men; they were liberated young women with confidence and what we would call job skills.

Letters to young Carl Mannerheim from his 15-year-old sister Eva in Stockholm in 1885, living with her Aunt Hanna, give a picture of a lively girl with a critical approach to her studies and friends. She had been sent to Stockholm for her schooling, joining her youngest brother August and her oldest sister Sophie. In the letters to her brother, Eva is a typical Mannerheim, with a tart approach. Her caustic tongue mocks a French teacher who knows less than his student and she calls most of her classmates "too sweet". In time, as she adjusted, she loved her studies, turning often in letters to her favorite brother to overcome the loneliness she felt when Sophie left Stockholm for Finland to start a new career.[2]

Eva was expected to come home and support herself. Sophie had started out like Jane Eyre, as a governess; Eva, at 19, returned to

Finland with a diploma from the industrial arts school in Stockholm. Education was not a social embellishment but necessary and practical.

One of her wishes was fulfilled almost at once: a place of her own. Michael Street Number 7 was the proudly independent Eva's new address in Helsinki, though it wasn't altogether hers, because Sophie and Calle shared it with her. Every morning as they left for their work Eva cleaned house and turned the living room into a studio and classroom. At home she had pupils taking classes in wood carving and handcrafts. But her specialty was leather tooling, which happened at that moment to be at the height of fashion. The Ateneum Industrial Art School in Helsinki was already planning to give a new course in it and needed a teacher. Eva turned up and filled their need. She could hardly compete with Calle's law practice and Sophie's bank job, but money was the least important worry. She was in charge of her life.

Her delicate designs in acanthus leaves had caught somebody's eye. The Danish community in Helsinki was to present the King and Queen of Denmark with an Address to be given their Majesties on their golden wedding jubilee. Eva won the commission to create a suitably elegant leather binding for the Address, designed in Neo-Renaissance style. It was finished in 1892. Her artist's career was launched.

In Finland in the fall of 1892, Albert Edelfelt, an old family friend and the foremost painter in the country, asked Eva to show her wood carvings in an exhibit of Finnish artists. He was eager to promote crafts, to give them a place with paintings and sculpture. Would she help? Of course she would. She was the first in her family to be a professional artist.

And what an evening the exhibition opening turned out to be! Arm in arm with her father, she stood before a landscape called "Spring Stream". Its rippling dark water, tender birches and melting snow were enchanting, she thought, and noticed the signature. It was a name she had heard from Edelfelt and her own father. Louis Sparre, a Swedish count living in Paris, had been invited earlier to her father's home. He had been lured to Finland by a close friend and fellow-artist, Axel Gallén, already famous in Helsinki for his gigantic canvasses inspired by Finnish mythology. Sparre had fallen in love with their country, and returned so often that he was accepted as a Finnish artist. During the previous three summers with Gallén he had explored the pristine wilderness of Karelia, not yet visited by western man, stretching across eastern Finland and over the border into Russia. Louis had even learned the Finnish language, almost a foreign tongue to Eva.

One can imagine Eva on the evening of the opening, her hair bobbed unfashionably short with bangs, taking the measure of strangers. Which of the artists circling the gallery was the Swedish one? As if in answer to her thoughts, even as she was admiring his painting, a young man with black hair and eyes like coals bounded up the stairs with a fencer's grace. Louis did not look like a typical Swede, for his Italian mother had given him a Mediterranean coloring. Eva's father made the introductions and the evening grew long and late as they wandered home to Count Carl Robert's apartment to continue their conversation.

Weeks went by without a sign of Count Louis. But then one evening, at a "Popular Concert," he appeared from nowhere and settled at Eva's table. The orchestra was playing the work of a young Finnish composer, Sibelius, who was in the audience. A friend of Louis's, he was introduced to Eva. The table was enlarged, and Louis played jester. He was a clown, a mimic. He aimed his darts around the table and told funny stories until his audience was limp. Eva was in heaven, and could hardly bear to leave for Christmas at Villnäs.

Early in the new year, Eva came back to her lessons and commissions. Now in 1893 she was busy tooling the calfskin binding of the Finnish poet Runeberg's epic Elgskyttarne (The Elk Hunters). But while her art work was flourishing, and the new order exciting and flattering, Eva was restless. Perhaps something was amiss. Was Count Louis neglectful? Eva hid her feelings. Disappointments would not control her life; no man or event would dominate her. Only she could set a new course. Trained since childhood to be resourceful, she looked for a new challenge. Perhaps she could escape from her familiar routine to a new life. Boldly, impulsively, Eva decided to emigrate to Argentina. For an upper class young woman of the 1890s, single, without financial resources, it was a daring plan. She took lessons in Spanish as a serious step toward her goal. But something unexpectedly changed her plans.

Her brother Carl had made it a habit to invite a certain young singer home to the Michael Street apartment. She was the lovely Aina Ehrnrooth, already preparing to go to Paris to study voice, against the best advice of her relatives. She had a weekend party at her house to say good bye to all her friends, and Carl took Eva along. Louis was there.

Outside in a flurry of snow, their skis strapped on, Eva and Louis decided before the evening had ended that they must spend the rest of their lives together. Louis's broad gold wedding band bears the inscription On Skis, 5 February, 1893.

Eva's coming marriage was announced in the old Villnäs church and Louis was introduced to Grandmama Eva at the castle. The Countess was still a beauty, her fair skin and dark blue eyes framed by the starched white muslin cap with its ribbons. It was the last time Eva saw her, and the first time Grandmama had thought Eva worthy of hearing her views on the art of cuisine. Louis had made a good impression.

Eva and Louis were parted for some months before the wedding, but kept in touch by mail. Eva's stepmother promised to give her a bridal gown, so she would look as elegant as Louis in his English tailcoat. "Good Lord! How snobby we'll be!" Eva wrote. But she also confessed that her temper was tried whenever she heard wedding vows. "It's really uncomfortable to have to go through it oneself. It exasperates me and my feeling of independence! Now I can see you laughing!" She reported that Villnäs looked shabby, which explains why their wedding took place in Helsinki. She also made sure to tell Louis that her friends felt sorry for her lonely state, but "I answer rudely that I seldom have had such fun!"[3]

In her spare time she was studying Finnish, which she found difficult. One piece of advice from her father on another matter was that she should learn something about food "to avoid many disagreeable quarrels." (Eva would later write a famous cookbook.) Looking into the future, Eva remarked that it would be an interesting project to develop Finnish native crafts: something that became Louis's passion.

There was much to keep her busy in the months before her wedding. From her letters to Louis during their engagement, one learns that Eva, although not musical, loved trying to tease tones from Louis's kantele, an ancient Finnish stringed instrument. She reported dancing the "Boston" and organizing her part of an exhibit at the Ateneum gallery. Her brother Johan had persuaded her to go riding with him and though she'd never mounted a horse before, she pretended she had never done anything else. In May of 1893 she proudly wrote that she had given her last lesson at the Ateneum as Eva Mannerheim.

All the brothers and Sophie gathered for the July wedding, the first time they had all been together in a long time. Gustaf came from Russia with his bride and August from Stockholm. No one worried about the weather. Swedish brides wear small crowns over their veils, and it was a tradition that some drops of rain in the bride's crown brought good luck. On Eva's wedding day her ancient relative, Tante Aurore Karamsin, formerly a lady-in-waiting to the Empress of Russia, had given her a silver purse filled with gold coins.

Aurore and her sister Emilie Stjernvall had been presented at court in St. Petersburg, to Tsar Nicholas I and Empress Alexandra. Both became ladies-in-waiting to the Empress in the 1830s. Emilie made a brilliant marriage to Count Mussin-Pusjkin. They were first cousins to Eva Mannerheim Sparre's grandfather Carl Gustaf Mannerheim, who was said to have once asked Aurore's hand in marriage. Aurore instead married the fabulously rich Paul Demidoff. His great-great grandfather Nikita, a blacksmith and gunsmith, owned iron and gold mines in the Urals. He was ennobled by Peter the Great. Nikita's son secretly struck coins in his mines, whose workers, being escaped Siberian convicts, were not in a position to tell tales. He reigned over tens of thousands of serfs and a personal army. Nikita's great-grandson Nicholas bought the cloister of San Donato near Florence, building a magnificent mansion and park, decorating his rooms with malachite and filling glass cases with jeweled treasures. He made huge donations to the poor of Florence, and left his vast fortune to his two sons, Anatol and Paul. Anatol, married to Napoleon's niece Princess Mathilde, was made an honorary citizen of Florence and the Grand Duke of Tuscany named him Duke of San Donato. Paul, the younger brother, gave his bride Aurore a gold case holding a four-string necklace of pearls as big as hazlenuts, and the "Sancy Diamond", seventh largest in the world. Paul was fat and obstinate, with a limitless sense of his own importance and little regard for the feelings of others. He was not liked by the Tsar, who, rumor had it, was himself more than a little interested in the very beautiful Aurore. Anatol had no children, but adopted Paul's and Aurore's only child, their son Paul, who thus inherited the San Donato title and wealth. Young Paul, married to Princess Hélène Troubetskoy, also inherited some of the less attractive traits of his forebears. Through the marriage of one of his daughters, Aurore became the great-grandmother of the regent of Yugoslavia, Prince

Paul. After Paul Demidoff's death Aurore married a Guards officer, Andrei Karamsin, who was killed in the Crimean war.[4]

Eva's and Louis's wedding ceremony took place on July 19, 1893, in her father's apartment in Helsinki. Carl Robert Mannerheim had returned to Finland six years earlier with his new wife Sofia and small daughter Marguerite. Although initially only Sophie and Gustaf openly supported their father's decision to remarry, his wife in time was well liked by them all, and Marguerite, called Kissie, a great favorite.

At the reception in the Opera Cellar restaurant after the wedding, Gustaf had too much champagne and sat on a trayful of glasses. A festive dinner followed. The groom's best man, the young artist Gunnar Berndtson, presented a handsome menu cover he had designed of a mediaeval bridal couple gracefully turning toward each other. Louis with his Mediterranean looks is drawn from life; the bride is in a wimple, a fair young northern noblewoman. The new twenty-three-year-old countess gave the signal to end the toasts and music only when she had changed her clothes to a well cut sand colored traveling suit.

Eva was relieved that she had changed her mind about what she should wear. While Louis was in Paris she had woven a coarse red and white tweed for a suit to be made by a local seamstress. This would really impress her new husband, she thought, with his love of the Karelian wilderness, and the native women's weaving skills. But when Eva went to meet Louis on his return from Paris, she found a Parisian boulevardier in a dark blue coat with a foulard silk scarf around his neck. Suddenly she felt he would not be an admirer of rough country outfits—especially if worn by his bride! She hastily got rid of the hand-woven and ill-fitting tweed, and ordered a suit of beautiful English wool from the best tailor in Helsinki.

The young pair started the first leg of their honeymoon journey by train, at first, but had planned a long camping trip to the wilderness of Finnish Karelia to the east and north, and further eastward into Russian Karelia.

There were two other family weddings in that century. Three years after Eva's marriage, Carl married Aina Ehrnrooth, in whose home Eva and Louis had met. The same year Sophie, in an announcement that surprised her family, became engaged to an old family friend whom she had known since childhood. Socially it was a most acceptable match.

Louis accepted as Finnish Artist

Louis Sparre, self portrait

Grandmama Eva Mannerheim

Menu from Louis and Eva
Mannerheim Sparre's Wedding

Chapter 3

LOUIS'S SWEDISH BACKGROUND AND HIS

GRANDMOTHER CAROLINA'S 1863 JOURNAL

When Eva married Louis in 1893 she probably had no more idea than any other young bride what sort of man the bridegroom was. They shared the same career; they were both at home in the same landscape; they were from the same social class. But Louis was the product of several cultures, an exotic man among the homogeneous Scandinavians, and no doubt this added to his attraction. He was a Swede whose forebears had served early Swedish kings; he was half Italian by birth; he had the taste of a Frenchman, having grown up in Paris. Eva was smitten with his charm and idealism, and with the romantic in him that was so attractive to other women. As time went on she was puzzled by other aspects of his nature. Any bride in love will be optimistic about dealing with known or future problems. Eva surely was. But for his open show of emotions, joy, rage, love and despair, for his tears, she may have been ill prepared.

Louis's family was rooted in Swedish history.[5] The first Sparres were known by the name of Tofta, a manor on the island of Adelsö about 20 miles west of Stockholm. (In early times, the names of family seats and patronymics were used to identify families and their members.) The Tofta men were appointed to the nation's highest offices, and their dynasty was recorded as the most illustrious in Sweden. The early records, perhaps little better than conjectures, list Chancellor Abjörn Sixtensson, who died in 1310, as the first noteworthy ancestor. He was said to be the grandson of Lord Nils of Tofta, and of Princess Martha, King Erik Knutsson's daughter. The heraldic symbol was a spar, a "sparre" in the Scandinavian tongues, signifying the rafters of a roof, a chevron, a common device on coats of arms.

Before being ennobled, the Sparres belonged to the earliest class of knights.[6] Louis's forebears were introduced to the nobility under the name Sparre af Rossvik, one of several family seats. This is the oldest branch of the family. Sparres cannot be traced with certainty farther than to Sigge Larsson, who was deeded a manor in 1396 by Queen Margareta, ruler of the three Scandinavian lands of Sweden, Norway and Denmark. Sigge Larsson is the direct ancestor of all the Sparre branches including the Sparres af Söfdeborg, to which Louis belonged.[7]

Sparres served their monarchs as statesmen. Such a man was Lars Siggesson of Sundby Castle, friend and chancellor of King Gustaf Vasa in the early 16th Century, the first King of a united Sweden. Erik Sparre, great-great grandson of Sigge Larsson, was Chancellor of the Realm. As Sweden's Ambassador to the Court of James VI of Scotland (James I of England), he was created a Scottish baron in 1583 by King James at Holyrood Palace in Edinburgh, and kept his old coat of arms, a golden spar in a blue field. Erik was Ambassador also to England and to Poland. There he made the mistake of giving his allegiance to King Sigismund III of Poland, hereditary and legitimate King of Sweden as well, and a Roman Catholic. Sigismund's uncle, the Swedish Duke Charles, was a strong contender for the Swedish crown, and had the support of the commoners who had become Lutherans and wanted no Catholic ruler. After a battle in which the Swedish Duke had the advantage but no clear victory, Erik Sparre and several other important men were handed over to the Duke as hostages by the Polish King. The treacherous Sigismund fled the country, leaving the hostages to their fate. Erik and the others were beheaded in 1600 and the Duke ruled Sweden as Charles IX.

Louis's grandfather's grandfather, Paul Pihlgard, was the son of a blacksmith. Called "the man of iron", he was one of the family's most remarkable men. He was so poor that when he left home to seek his fortune his only shoes were a pair of shabby wooden clogs. He took his name from the family croft, Pihlgarden, educated himself, started a small shop that thrived and grew. He was later chosen mayor of the port city of Karlskrona. Paul died a rich and influential man, a member of Parliament, head of the board of trade, the outspokenly liberal upholder of the rights of common people. But though he was generous to hardworking artisans, he was unforgiving if they were lazy or drinkers. When he found them lacking, his fearful Spanish cane came out to deliver a bastinado with a shout for the miscreants: "I won't force a pledge on you to repay your loan for that will only harm your wife and children! But you'll get a beating because you've behaved like a dog!" All this Eva told in her biography of Louis.

But at home the liberal in politics was a tyrant who expected blind obedience. When young Count Erik Sparre, Louis's great-grandfather, asked Pihlgard for his youngest daughter Ulrica Regina's hand in marriage he was turned away with the comment that neither counts nor barons need apply. Young Erik had no support from his parents, Admiral and Countess Erik Arvid Claesson Sparre, who felt their favorite son had destroyed their dreams of a splendid career for him at Court. But in the end the lovers won the day. The Admiral and his lady gave their blessing, and Ulrica, a true daughter of the "man of iron" declared that though the law was in her father's favor, nothing could prevent her from rejecting an unwanted bridegroom at the altar. Pihlgard had to promise that she might choose her own husband.

Things did not go well for young Erik Sparre and his bride. Though Erik, a major at 24, had proved his worth in the regiment, an illness destroyed his chances for a military future and he had to turn in his commission. His Pihlgard family looked out for him, made him a deputy in their copper and iron mines and their paper-making business, and he took care of their farm. But at 38 he left his wife Ulrica Regina a widow. She was fearless, and though virtually penniless managed to educate her two oldest sons.

The little one, Pehr, only one year old when his father died, was given his first education at home. His mother encouraged his practical nature, his craving for learning, and gave him a strong sense of patriotism with the maxim that each man must forge his own happiness. Pehr remembered in his memoirs how he had looked up to his grandfather, old Pihlgard "with his well-powdered wig, blue-grey dress coat, embroidered silk vest, ruche, cuffs, black watered silk breeches, striped silk stockings, shiny shoes with gleaming buckles." Smoking his clay pipe, he welcomed the leading citizens of the town for discussions of current events and card games. Young Pehr was always encouraged to ask his grandfather questions until the guests arrived, and then listen to their tales—especially those of an old war hero admiral. The vision Pehr had of this Swedish flagship commander surrounded by dead and wounded, calmly ordering maneuvers while his servant curled and powdered his wig, fed his dreams of romance and adventure. As a small boy Pehr had witnessed a ship of the line blown up. He never forgot the earsplitting explosion, the black column of smoke, lightning flashes, the pieces of wood and bodies.

For lack of funds, the solitary young dreamer could not get the education he longed for, but joined the military, as was the custom of penniless noblemen. As a young sub-lieutenant he was sent on expeditions to root out Russians on Swedish and Finnish soil. In the winter campaign of 1809 his regiment had to retreat across the ice to Sweden. He was wounded and won a gold medal for courage. Later he commanded the 1813 siege of Glückstadt and painted it and the battle of Leipzig from memory. (The paintings are now owned by his great-great-great-grandson.) All these memories and experiences fueled his future writing of the historical novels that reminded readers of Sir Walter Scott.

In 1824 Pehr married his cousin, Carolina Pihlgard, and had three children with her. Their second son, Ambjörn, born in 1828, would become the father of Louis Sparre. In his turn, Ambjörn found home too confining and set out to make his way in the world. Ambjörn figured largely in his son Louis's shaping, perhaps more as an example to be avoided than one to copy.

Count Ambjörn Sparre was an eccentric inventor and civil engineer, completely absorbed by his work, certain that millions would be his, never disheartened by failure. But he was a tinkerer, unable to refrain from changing his design, wearing out the patience of those who were interested in his clever inventions.

Ambjörn had originally studied medicine at Uppsala in 1847 to cure his own deafness. He had no ambition to become a doctor. But at medical school he practiced in the dark to remove ear drum membranes from corpses retained for postmortems. When he considered himself sufficiently expert, he operated on himself. This is described in the June 12, 1955 issue of the Stockholm newspaper Svenska Dagbladet. Ambjörn cut out his own eardrums and replaced them with loose membranes of deerskin. He was able to hear quite well for many years after that.

The thought of flying interested him. On July 13, 1851, Ambjörn became the first Swede to fly by balloon, in a Royal park with an Italian, Giuseppe Tardini, who had once flown for the Imperial Russian Court. Tardini had advertised his plan in a local newspaper. Sparre flew once more, this time promoted to "scientist" by Tardini, to make astronomical observations, "for which such a trip gives abundant cause." This is recounted by the historian of the Sparre family, Baron Per Sparre.[8] Later, when over 80 and half blind, Ambjörn returned to his interest in air travel. He worked on an aircraft that could lift off vertically from the ground. It was, as Pehr Sparre writes, a technical challenge which was solved only much later, through the invention of the gyroplane in 1923. The helicopter evolved from this.

When Swedish authorities announced in 1854 that they would introduce postage stamps, they learned that Ambjörn had created a machine for perforating, printing and gumming stamps (the first one to perforate a whole sheet at once). Eva Mannerheim Sparre wrote that Ambjörn successfully contracted with the Swedish postal authorities for the engraving, production, perforation, and gumming of the first Swedish postage stamps in 1855, and that the perforation machine, "unlike the English one," perforated the entire sheet at once. She also writes that he probably designed the stamps, taking his sketch from a 200-year prototype. The contract specified the date of first delivery, the design to be engraved with special safety measures to avoid forgery, the machines to be in Sparre's care. Someone was appointed to prevent unofficial use of the machines and type presses, also invented by Ambjörn and purchased by the postal department along with an explanation of his method of reproducing the stamps. The contract was to run from 1855 to 1858, but was renewed several times and actually continued after his move to Paris in 1861. It was annulled in 1871, when Ambjörn had definitively settled in Paris. Sveriges Frankotecken 1855-1905 (Swedish Postage Stamps 1855-1905) gives information about his contract and machines. An article in the Swedish journal of the Post Museum, Nyheter från Post Museum, Stockholm, February, 1954 finds the work in 1855 accomplished with amazing speed and expertise, the stamps delivered exactly on time. The contract stipulated that no more than 12 million stamps were to be printed in any year.

Half a century later, in 1905, a scandal surfaced—allegations in a Swedish philatelic journal of a forgery of the 1858 issue of the stamps. The article's author asserted that he was on the tracks of the most dangerous type of forger. "Judging by the precision with which the forgeries are done and the expense connected therewith, it is not impossible that somewhere outside the country there exists a whole printing establishment with extensive activity . . . . all the stamps except the black local stamps are printed on horizontally or vertically grooved paper." One year later, in the same journal, more news amazed the readers: the forgeries appeared to have come from the postal printing establishment in Stockholm! They had probably been provided from concealed printing plates. Fifteen years later, in June, 1921, a known expert, writing in his own philatelist newsletter about the 1858 counterfeit Swedish stamps, reported that he had been sent, by a "foreign dealer," the same 1858 stamps printed on "strangely grooved paper."

The story continued to reverberate around the philatelic world. In an article in Svensk Filatelistisk Tidskrift of April, 1944, Nils Strandell reports on the foreign dealer, M. Th. Lemaire, whose shop he visited in Paris. It seems that Count Sparre had been in regular communication with the Frenchman, who had bought his collection in 1905. Lemaire had sold a few of the stamps to an American dealer. Still later, a Belgian dealer had come across several Swedish proofs of the stamps, which had been given by Sparre to a friend in France. Strandell examined the authenticity of the proof printing, and with a strong magnifying glass determined that they had been made from the original engravings of 1858. In 1935 the owner placed the collection with a Danish collector, whose heirs planned to sell the stamps. The heirs were said to have fled to Sweden during the Second World War, and there the tracks come to an end, unless they have been unearthed in post-war Sweden. Wherever the stamps ended up, it seems clear that no forgeries had been made.

Ambjörn was honored in 2005 by the Swedish Post Office. Stamps were issued bearing his image, celebrating his work of 150 years earlier, in designing the first Swedish stamps. Ambjörn sold his machinery to the postal authorities in 1858 but the money was soon swallowed up by new inventions. If only he had thought to save a few stamps for himself he might have died a rich man.

Though he moved permanently to Paris in 1861, Ambjörn remained a loyal Swedish subject. Eva Sparre writes that he was said to have been repeatedly summoned to the Emperor's court at the Tuileries and received at the English court.

In Switzerland, in 1862, Ambjörn met and fell in love with an 18 year-old Italian girl, a relative of the postmaster general with whom he probably had business dealings. Teresita Adele Josefa Gaetana Barbavara, 16 years younger than Ambjörn, was of a noble family, daughter of the Chevalier Luigi Barbavara di Gravellona and Countess Constance de Maria de St. Dalmazo. She and Ambjörn were married in Ouchy, Switzerland on September 10, 1862, "and from that day I have been yours for always," Teresita later wrote. A week later, from Turin, Teresita wrote her new sister-in-law Ada a warm note in French on the new stationery with her coronet. She wrote that Ada was greatly missed. The wedding day had been merry, the church service at noon and a dinner at 4 p.m. for 26, most of the guests Swedish. "To end a day so well begun, a charming ball" followed in the evening. Shortly after her marriage, Teresita converted to Ambjörn's Lutheran faith at the Swedish church in Paris.

Ambjörn's young wife was very much at home in Paris, speaking French as fluently as she spoke her own language. She was passionately fond of music. There is much in her letters about the piano's role in her life, and the music albums she asked for, usually Beethoven's. At their first home in Paris, 14 Rue Tronchet, Teresita's drawing room was the meeting place for "many of the Imperial court's best known personalities", including Massenet, composer of Manon, as Eva Sparre later wrote in her biography of Louis.

Teresita returned to her Piedmontese manor, Villa Teresita in Gravellona, near Turin, to spend the summer of 1863 while she awaited the birth of her baby. The little town of Gravellona had been ruled by her family for centuries; servants had watched over the family from father to son. In June, she learned that her new parents-in-law, Carolina and Pehr Georg Sparre, whom she had never met, had made a sudden plan to visit her at Villa Teresita together with their son Erik and daughter Ada. She was entranced to welcome a woman who would give her the guidance she had missed after the death of her own mother in her early childhood.

The elder Sparres embarked on the long voyage from Sweden to Turin. Carolina was conscious of her obligation to keep a journal. *My Travel Memoirs of 1863* is bound in red Morocco leather with gold trim, lined with French marbled paper. It has never been published, although Eva Mannerheim Sparre quoted a few phrases in her biography of her husband.[9]

The first entry is for June 15, 1863. "At 3:30 p.m. we left from the steamship dock in Carlskrona [Karlskrona, Sweden]." Their trip, hastily arranged, had left "no time for reflection," but alone in their roomy cabin they considered the journey ahead. Pehr Georg was 73 and his wife 67, in those days an advanced age. They were facing a trip of unforseeable length and danger, to a country whose religion and customs were foreign and forbidding. Nothing daunted them. To get there they would travel on steamships and trains, both new, mid-19th Century inventions, and at one terrifying point by horse and mule-drawn stagecoach.

The first steamship took them to Malmö where the Sparres decided to "try the Swedish railroad" for a trip to Lund, the old university and cathedral town. The Swedish railroad had only opened to the public in 1856, its tracks lengthened in 1860. It was a spur-of-the-moment decision, not typical of an elderly couple. Friends entertained them for dinner and recitals of singing and piano.

The following day the Sparres boarded the boat for Copenhagen. By the 1850s the steamboat had begun to replace the sailing ship. Carolina's and Pehr Georg's steamship to Denmark was still fitted with sails; Carolina commented on "our snorting steam horses with all their sails hoisted." In Copenhagen they saw the works of a contemporary sculptor, Bertel Thorvaldsen, whose workroom was a museum. Carolina was an inveterate visitor of museums, an intrepid tourist who left no sight undescribed and recorded her critiques on the considerable art she visited in the galleries of Copenhagen, Milan and Paris.

Carolina usually wrote on the train even as they were rushing past the landscape; there is a lively immediacy about her descriptions, often accompanied by her own pen-and-ink illustrations. From Copenhagen they took the train to Lübeck, then to Hamburg to meet Ambjörn. They gazed over the city in the evening from their hotel room, "just as all the gas lamps were lighted around bridges, houses, shops . . . it presented a magically lovely scene." Carolina was in raptures and could compare the sight only to the magic of Venice. In Heidelberg she noted without enthusiasm the "many student faces marked with scars and cuts . . . it's considered fashionable to duel and he who has the greatest number of marks from his battles earns the greatest merit."

They began to see grape plantings, and, "in the blue distance," the Alps. To the pragmatic Caroline the Rhine was "yellow-grey, brown and dirt-colored." Leaving Switzerland for Aarburg, she wrote in more lyrical praise of "sky-high mountains . . . deep valleys dressed in the freshest green . . ." But her thoughts were never far from Sweden. "Sometimes one place or another is reminiscent of our dear Blekinge [a Swedish province]." At Lake Bienne she saw "the first really beautiful clear water in transparent harness-green," she writes, using a familiar metaphor.

We travel with Carolina, living in her moment: "the whistle is blowing now, the train is stopping, the door opens, they're calling Neyville," with St. Gotthard in the distance, rushing past as swiftly as "sun-gleams." She lamented the passing of traditions: "One wants to see . . . the beautiful costumes of the valleys and mountains, but where are they now? Maybe at the bottom of a trunk." But practical Carolina could not waste time on regrets. Between trains at Culoz they made an excursion to see "the still inhabited old castle Landsberg, situated on a ferocious height." Now the train tunneled through the Alps. " . . . One feels a sort of relief . . . when daylight reappears through the mountains' black and never-disappearing night." At St. Michel the railroad stopped, "and we will ride in stagecoaches, drawn to begin with by 7 horses and mules . . ." She became almost speechless. "The higher . . . we came . . . the less could the field glasses turn from these enchanting sights." At last there were "13 mules and 2 horses driven by the walking muleteer with words, shouts and whip . . . Still I was not afraid, I think, besides there wasn't time, I had to look and admire . . . The road went into a steep zigzag with high mountains on one side and an abyss on the other . . . with shouts and whip harshly used, it went as fast as the poor creatures could run . . . At all changes the mules and horses were ready to go, and the whole team was hitched to the stagecoach with a hook . . ."

Finally came the descent. "It was off with flying swiftness, though the carriage's speed was restrained by a brake . . . then the poor horses had to run as fast as they could until a possible resting place . . . I was bound to hold fast to the carriage straps at the abrupt turnings downhill." By the light of stars they stopped at Susa, where the railroad again continued. Here the stagecoaches turned back to ascend the mountain at night: "We were happy not to sit there then. We saw their lanterns' play . . . peep out and disappear. At last they looked like little stars in the heights."

In Turin they were "welcomed in the most hearty and engaging way by our Teresita's kind father, who in two carriages brought us to Villa Teresita." Outside the property's gate, "there were pillars with golden letters: Villa Teresita, and there was our little beloved Teresita, glowing with happiness . . . We now went up to the castle through the long passageway lined by grape plantings. We came in through a long beautiful gallery to a dark room." Carolina, blinded at first, soon discovered that they were in an "elegant salon." She was pleased to call the castle magnificent, with many rooms in two storeys. The upper one where they lived was teeming with bedrooms and guests and on the ground floor was the "state apartment, where a large dance chamber rising through both stories has a mosaic floor with the inlaid Barbavara coat of arms." All the ceilings had paintings and the floors were of stone, the rooms high and rather large "with tall windows which in the upper story reached from floor to ceiling." She called the dinner awaiting them excellent. "The Italian cuisine is very different from the Swedish. It has such richness in the good vegetables and delicate fruits which we lack, that it both is and ought to be much better than ours." Teresita would discover this difference when she came for a long stay in Karlskrona.

Visits to neighbors began. Carolina called on Madame Ferraris on June 29, "to thank her for the carriage which she sent to meet us . . . The Countess was rather amiable but very much la grande dame, the gentleman never talked about though it's he who is the most important . . ." There was the fine park to see "with tall splendid beeches, lindens, elms . . . the most beautiful weeping willows whose fine, yielding branches hang down in the water. Alas! if this park had only belonged to Gravellona."

She described the surroundings: "Gravellona lies at one end of a big town of the same name. On its square the people gather every evening smoking cigars, talking, sitting . . . both men and women burned brown by the sun. Youthful beauty disappears early, and the old sometimes look horrid with large goiters." Carolina added that on the way home they were met by an elegant carriage, belonging to the "rich farmer Gastoldi's wife" who had noticed that Luigi Barbavara had no coach.

Members of their daughter-in-law's family turned up for inspection: "two Barbavara gentlemen came here, one a military, the other a Canon. Their dress was knee trousers, stockings and shoes, three-cornered hat, a long caftan . . . The Canon had the courtesy to invite us for luncheon . . ."

Carolina was charmed by the Canon, who she suspected had not willingly become a servant of the Church. "His house was shabby, many stairs up . . . high under the roof. After the food he showed us some quite lovely tapestry work that he had done himself . . . After coffee the Canon took us to the churches . . ." Carolina's Protestant spirit found her experiences of visiting church services disturbing. "Yesterday evening at 7 we went to church and visited the Friday Benediction. It was a highly peculiar service . . . 3 priests who looked like peasants in white shirts and black trousers made their peculiar curtseys, turns and bowings . . . Sometimes the whole congregation joined in the singing, if this screeching can be called that? During all this . . . we were on our knees on a hard wooden kneeler, while the crinoline wires bit into the knees . . . . the organ played a cheerful polka for leaving. The whole thing made a miserable impression."

She did not directly criticize, but made her point clear: "At an afternoon visit a whole group of neighboring ladies and gentlemen came, only one of them spoke a little French." She found everything interesting and removed from her own provincial life in Sweden, but the local clergy and church customs continued to repel her. "On a visit here yesterday came the village's 2 priests who looked repulsive . . . an expression of sensuousness in their prowling eyes. Luckily they only know their own dialect, which made conversation impossible . . ."

The weather was another unfamiliar trial. "Today as yesterday one of the most heavy heat, we went upstairs some hours to our rooms . . . . We wore the lightest possible negligee, only a loose dress over the crinoline." Suddenly she saw an astonishing sight: "I cried out in fear and surprise. From the sky to the earth there came . . . . a roar and howl . . . Earth, sand, gravel, roofing tiles and more flew into the air . . . . as if unseen giant hands had let them loose . . ."

Whole orchards of lemon and orange trees were uprooted but Carolina was fascinated. "I can't deny that it was very interesting to see a real hurricane."

Teresita's father, the Chevalier Barbavara, went once a week to "preside at the public works" in Turin. Swedish guests were expected at the end of the month, for Baron Gyllengranat, an admiral at home in Karlskrona had come with his wife, an Englishwoman, to visit the Sparres at the Barbavaras. They walked in the garden and ate "a big splendid dinner. Teresita lively, sweet and gracious, charming them." The baron "said he had never heard anyone who was not born English, speak the language as she does."

The Swedish visitors took "promenades" to visit the Barbavara rice fields, and Carolina carefully examined the plants, much like the "corn plant's spike." She was intrigued to visit the neighbor, "Madame Gastoldis, a rich farmer's wife (the same who sent us her carriage.) She took us into her fine rich vineyard and there I ate a sort of pink big grape cluster which I haven't seen before . . . Here we saw the cotton plant which grows low here and has lovely yellow flowers." The cotton plant's husk, likened to Spanish nuts, was illustrated.

It was time for the most exciting event, the birth of the Sparres' grandchild, Louis, on August 3, 1863. The young mother, only 19, was fragile, and afraid to be parted from Ambjörn, so often called away on business. "But daily letters came, and our dear little lively, beloved Teresita was better when her husband returned . . . and soon could do her walking in the afternoon." She was not well and in the fashion of the times leeches and "blood lettings" were the cure.

The christening of Teresita's baby was noted in Carolina's journal on September 7th. "Today an excellent . . . Protestant clergyman came from Turin . . . He baptized the little boy Pehr Louis, and churched Teresita . . . . the service [was] pure and lovely" and, she commented with relief, "it's just as with us." The clergyman refused Ambjörn's offer of payment. "No Catholic priest would have done this, they take with the hand what is offered and the eye asks more. I carried the little boy toward the Chevalier . . ."

The time had come to leave, though not before Pehr Georg had painted two watercolors of Villa Teresita, showing rice fields and snow-topped mountains in the distance. On September 19th Carolina wrote: "At 5 this morning in the company of our Ambjörn, we left Gravellona . . ." They were on their way to Milan, and "passed the famous Magenta and saw the great battle field . . . There were marks on many houses of Austrian bullets." Indeed, it was only a few years before the Sparres' trip that Napoleon III had met Cavour and promised the Italian leader military aid against the Austrians, the dominant power in Italy. War had broken out in 1859, and the French and Sardinians defeated the Austrian enemy at Magenta.

Milan impressed Carolina as no city had until then. She wanted to take her time, enjoying the park "but horses and coachman didn't agree, it went forward, forward and we stopped only in front of La Brera's wonderful museum." The tourists took in the portrait galleries and sculptures. Again Carolina was thunderstruck. The Danish sculptor Thorvaldsen had been surpassed. She stopped before a piece called the Marriage Destroyer "not knowing if it is a vision, a superhuman revelation . . . I thought she breathed, had life and feeling . . . . I must say that her eyelids were half closed so the otherwise cold, stony eye didn't show." Carolina had a pragmatic explanation for most phenomena.

By no means did great heights and a long climb deter them: the Cathedral in Milan "exceeded my greatest expectations . . . This admiration rises with each of the 501 steps which lead up and up all the way." Each of the two pulpits was "so large that a game table with 4 chairs would have room in it." She was dazzled by the riches in the Borromean sepulchre and the walls, worked in silver by Cellini.

La Scala was on their itinerary. They heard a performance of I Puritani, and found the tenor's voice "excellently beautiful," but, like many another opera-goer, found the singers' corpulence unsuited to their romantic roles. "Then if one adds the continuously flitting arm movements, which kept reminding me of a weather vane's wing, I didn't enjoy seeing as much as hearing. The ladies' dresses were elegant . . ." At La Scala the Sparres met Teresita's cousin Antoine Barbavara, "head of the railroads in Milan." He gave them valuable travel advice, and persuaded them to visit Lake Maggiore.

On September 20 they boarded the steamship to "the long, narrow charming lake, surrounded by the most beautiful shores . . ." One of Carolina's favorite memories was visiting a small island in the lake, the Isola Bella, and the Borromeo family castle. "Despite the fact that Count Borromeo lived there with his family, we still got the first and second floors in which there was no sign of their existence other than some Italian cats . . . The 2nd story exceeded the royal castles I've seen . . ." She was angered at the Austrians, thieving and vandalising the castle, whose owner had returned to restore it. "One forgot time and everything else until one saw the steamboat coming . . ." They had to press on. "On the return to Arona we were offered . . . grapes, peaches, figs, all sorts of delicate fruits in profusion . . . though it was late and we were tired, we couldn't rest because now the promenade time between 9 and 10 began for the beau monde . . ." One must do the fashionable thing.

They caught a glimpse of the Italian king. "At a station called Verecelli . . . we were informed they expected King Victor Emanuel there . . . alas, alack! He came and went with lightning speed, past the military standing by, the music and the station full of people, all with long noses, and we . . . felt it was a silly end to a hopeful beginning." The Sparres were aware of recent history: the Kingdom of Italy had been proclaimed in March 1861 under Victor Emanuel II, with Turin as the capital. Local European events absorbed their thoughts, but one can find no word about the distant, ongoing American Civil War.

In Turin "we made a promenade through the city in two carriages and stopped outside Ambjörn's studio, where it was a sad sight to see several of his rooms filled with machines, which stood there in silence, unreal and dispirited . . ." That was a look into the future which Ambjörn's son Louis would find all too familiar twenty years later, when living with his father in Paris.

Ambjörn rejoined his family for the trip from Turin to Paris. Again they made the stagecoach ascent over Mont Cenis, this time in lamplight. "Now the moon was obscured by dark clouds, and the rain . . . . turned into fat snowflakes . . ." They changed horses at 4 in the morning, and were welcomed at a resting place by "a crackling fire and coffee." There was little rest. "We again had to jump out in snow and dirt with our skimpy shoes, up the high exposed stairs which led us to the stagecoach. Now it was downhill again . . ." They made it down with less fear and took the train at St. Michel.

Early in the morning of September 23, they arrived in Paris. "We sat up in one of these [carriages], with all the baggage on the roof . . ." Carolina described their apartment, above Ambjörn's, as "rather nice and pleasant . . . The hostess's daughter . . . . came in and arranged things for us . . . . and had the goodness to follow us out to buy hats for Ada and me so we'd be like the others on the streets of Paris . . ." A chic hat was a must.

After a visit to the aquarium and the Bois de Boulogne they returned home, soaked to the skin after a rain storm, "tired and disgruntled." It is the only petulant note. The next day they inspected "the great panorama of Sevastopol, at the capture of the Malakhov fortress," a reference to the Crimean War of 1855, eight years earlier, when French capture of the fortress forced the Russians to give up Sevastopol. They were followed on their visit by "a young invalid soldier" who "described everything to us . . ."

The Invalides was an impressive sight, and they stopped in wonder before Napoleon's coffin. But however tired and hungry they were, they had to get to the Industrial Palace. On their way "we were met by the appetizing smell of waffles, and saw nearby a waffle factory, the smallest, cutest stove with its four waffle irons, a sugar bowl and a little nice madame with the ingratiating question, plaît-il monsieur?" This was too much of a temptation to Ada, and they ate in the open air. There was still time to see the Industrial Palace's "gewgaws and rarities . . . from jewels . . . to grains and foodwares . . ." They wandered under trees, by pools and water works, missing nothing under the high glass roof.

An exciting evening lay ahead at the "Théâtre Impérial Lyrique . . . to hear the Mariage de Figaro. No matter how much we hurried, the overture was over, the curtain had risen and the play begun . . . . The whole ceiling was frosted glass over which a lot of strong gas flames burned . . . . the most lovely glow illuminating everything . . ." The next day at Versailles, Carolina noted the room and "remarkable little hat" of the first Napoleon, whose defeat in 1815 was not far in the past. After a long train trip from Versailles they walked through the city to see it "by the brilliant gas lighting, it was enchantingly opulent and lovely." She added, "also this night it was one o'clock before we wandered up the long staircase to the 3rd floor of number 14 Avenue Tronchet."

Notre Dame looked shabby and was a disappointment, but the Louvre was a feast. "There the hours flew, one swam in an ocean of . . . treasures . . . Only with one painter's works was I unable to reconcile myself, that was Rubens. Of the many there were to see, there was not one beautiful or pleasant. His women were the coarsest, most disgusting barnyard wenches ever painted on a canvas . . . ."

Shopping was on the agenda, and a play. "We drove with Ambjörn to the silk merchants, bought beautiful black satin for a dress . . . At

6 we were to go to dinner, and from there to the theatre at Porte St. Martin where The Devil's Pills was playing, a real comedy with big magic acts . . ."

They parted with difficulty from Ambjörn at the railroad station on September 29. In Hamburg they stopped to see the Exchange, watching "the confusion from a balcony." The train took them to Kiel where "in the most heavenly moonlight" they once more boarded a steamship for Korsör. In Copenhagen the next afternoon they bought a portrait of the Danish Princess Alexandra, married that year to the Prince of Wales.

The next to last stop was Malmö, where they "were once more on our dear forebears' soil." From there the final journey took them on board the Carl IX, whose captain, Baron von Otter, had wife, children and sisters to keep him company. They landed at Karlskrona early in the afternoon on October 3, "where we were met at the steamship dock by all the dear ones we had said a last farewell to . . . . Happy and rich in memories we now entered the old friendly home, where all was bright and filled with flowers, and the cozy coffee table invited us to rest and conversation." The journal ended after three and a half months of arduous traveling and visiting described in 83 pages of observations and ink drawings. They are written in Carolina's neat and usually legible hand, evidence of her lively curiosity, zest for all that was new, sharp eye and sometimes biting views. But always she was conscious of being far from her dear Sweden and the cozy coffee table at home.

Count Ambjörn Sparre
Oil, by his son Louis.

Chevalier Luigi Barbavara
and
Teresita Barbavara

The first Swedish stamps
executed by Ambjörn Sparre

Villa Teresita in Gravellona, Provincia Pavia,
painted by Pehr Georg Sparre 1863

Chapter 4

AMBJÖRN AND TERESITA

After their marriage Ambjörn wrote from Paris to his "Poussy", begging her to write him every day and to continue with her study of Swedish. Teresita's letters to Ambjörn were carefully preserved by him and form a counterpoint to Carolina's contented, occasionally ebullient, sometimes sharply worded diary. Eva Mannerheim Sparre transcribed Teresita's handwriting, sometimes written vertically over the horizontal lines, to save paper. The stationery bears her coronet and initials. Teresita spoke little Swedish, and Ambjörn spoke no Italian. They corresponded in English and French.[10]

Teresita's first letters from Gravellona in June, 1863, speak of preparing for Ambjörn's return. "Tomorrow I shall have our beds prepared in the great room and I shall again be happy, morning and evening . . ." She imagined taking evening walks together, "accompanied by many kisses and also some Swedish." She hoped to learn her husband's language by the time their child could speak. In mid-June she knew that Ambjörn's parents, his brother Erik and his sister Ada were coming, and Gravellona was painted in their honor. Her own mother had died when she was four, and now she would have "really a mama that will love me and that I can love, and a young girl in whom I can confide without fears . . ." She was trying to be more like the Swedes: "I cannot kiss you before papa and mama, but as soon as we shall be in the house we go behind a door." Ambjörn's shaky finances must have intruded early in their marriage, for she guiltily confessed that she had bought a new tablecloth and 12 napkins.

One has a picture of happy activities. Ambjörn's father and his brother Erik visited the Barbavara rice fields while Teresita read Swedish and worked with her mother-in-law. There was no hint of anything amiss.

The letters began again in Sweden in the fall of 1865, when Teresita had traveled to Karlskrona with Louis, then two years old, his nurse, Hilda, a maid, her father, the Chevalier Luigi Barbavara, and Ambjörn, to have an extended visit with the Sparres in the port city of Karlskrona. Ambjörn left her there while he attended to his business.

But the solemn, pious Swedish attitude and the Italian spontaneity could not find room under one roof. Teresita's gaiety and impulsive ways charmed everyone except the family. Her mother-in-law, Carolina, misinterpreted her warmth as being unacceptably lacking in discipline. Swedish winters, with their short days and interminable nights, were hard for Teresita and her father to bear. Teresita found the Swedish ladies provincial, even stupid, hiding any talents they might have. Many, however, became her friends, particularly those who spoke languages and had worldly experience and interests like hers. Teresita's piano lessons, with a teacher who was enchanted with her playing, gave her a daily escape, and the piano itself became her most faithful companion.

She asked Ambjörn's manservant Alexandre in Paris to find her muff and pelisse, a fur lined cape. Her father, also miserable in the deep chill, found little diversion except an occasional game of whist with Carolina's family. Teresita's feelings about him were an uneasy mix of affection and exasperation at his constant depressions.

The culture shock Carolina experienced on her trip to Italy was repeated in reverse when Teresita came to Sweden. She describes the daily meals, so different from her own Italian cuisine. Carolina's soups were like "dirty water." Lamb was "of the worst sort . . . only skin and bones and not a centimeter of meat . . . . sour milk and old plättar [Swedish pancakes]." The young wife was ill at ease with the stiff, conventional attitudes of the household.

Teresita needed books and intellectual stimulation to keep her busy. Again, she asked Ambjörn's man Alexandre, in Paris, to send her albums of music, a history of Italian literature and some of Dante's works "for Papa gives me lessons." Papa Luigi gave Teresita´s sister-in-law Ada lessons, too, in Italian, while Teresita had lessons in Swedish from her father-in-law. On the surface, things were going well.

But time and again Teresita's letters reveal her boundless longing, her desperate attempts to wring a visit from Ambjörn, to share some news of his world of affairs, to win her place on his agenda. Her first letter ended by wishing she "could have jumped from the window and run after you but no, now there is all that ugly sea between us." In another early letter she signed off with words in Swedish: "[your] sweet, kind, obedient and dear wife Teresita—but not prudish, God knows!" She asked Ambjörn, if he had the money, to send her a subscription to the "Mode Illustrée."

Teresita quickly made friends. As was natural in that day, she met almost no one who was not of her class. She rarely mentioned first names. But she added enough details to make it possible to identify, in almost every case, the person she wrote of. Her friends were a reflection of her interests, and a picture of life in a Swedish port city of the 1860s.

Baroness Susanna Gyllengranat, who had visited Gravellona with her husband in 1863 and returned to Sweden a widow, was "the only lady worthwhile speaking to." Baroness Susanna was an Englishwoman in her 70s who let Teresita borrow her books. She invited her for long walks and home to drink wine and eat "sweetmeats." To put a stop to gossip that Ambjörn was using her fortune, Teresita planted a bit of information with the Baroness. She told her that she and her husband had decided on a "separation des biens," separation of their pre-marriage assets. She well knew how quickly this would travel through the social network. After Teresita had returned to Gravellona, she kept up with the Baroness, then old and ill, who had been so good to her.

One reads of parties and dinners, and young naval officers who admired Teresita. " . . . Yesterday I was out and I saw Mr. Pantzerhielm—only do not get jealous." Ludwig Pantzerhielm was in his mid-forties when Teresita knew him, and later would have a career as commandant of naval fortresses at Karlskrona. He danced beautifully, she wrote, so much so that he tempted her to dance a waltz and polka at the Admiral's ball. Another favorite young naval officer was Axel Lind af Hageby, who praised her English. She went to a "supper" and "a gourmet feast, with beautiful furniture," and she judged the society "rather pleasant though not of the finer sort." The ladies, she remarked after one of the balls, "are a little peasant-like." But "Mr. Lind is very pleasant, he has been in India and has brought back so many interesting things." He had served in the British Navy, and taken part in the 1857-59 campaign in India at the time of the Mutiny, earning recognition in the general's dispatch and a medal from the Swedish King. Teresita was painfully reminded of her single life when the Linds asked her to dine alone with them. Her eyes brimmed over when "he told [his wife] to sing, and he seemed so enchanted with what his wife did, and I poor solitary was there by myself."

She was a flirt. At the Freidenfelts, a naval commander whose wife was Carolina's sister, Teresita felt she had made a conquest. She wrote of a young naval officer's remarks to his sister, about Swedish ladies. They were "pedantic and affected," and now that he had met Teresita he preferred Italians. "I was so naive and had the sun playing in my eyes. You see it is quite dangerous."

Admiral Virgin gave balls of great elegance. His career had spanned the command of a frigate that had sailed around the world, and ambassadorships to England, Denmark and the Netherlands. One of his parties "was quite an affair in style, all the ladies in low dresses and as low as in Paris or Turin with all their prudery, and the men, except the officers of the Navy, as stupid as possible . . . . The service was very elegant also . . . Friday there shall be the famous ball and I shall go in my velvet dress, so gare au coeurs Suédois [beware, Swedish hearts]."

Teresita reported on a visit with friends in December to the John Ericsson, the first Swedish Monitor, built at the Motala shipyard, named for its inventor. The American Monitor's engagement with the Merrimac in 1862, three years earlier, was the first between ironclads, and changed the nature of sea warfare.

Countess Cronstedt was an older lady and a hostess with a name that resonates with Swedish history. She and her husband were "very kind to Papa." This was Beata, 20 years older than Teresita, married to a naval captain in Karlskrona. But there were many other women friends who earned her affection. Baroness Söster Peyron was typical of the popular young women drawn to Teresita. She was pretty and charming, speaking French "as a French woman of the meilleur ton [better class]". Teresita wrote of these women friends, "One can see so well that [they] have traveled" and lost "all their Swedish prejudices."

Teresita made an acid observation on a society beauty's jewelry. "Fancy, the article said that the most brilliant lady [at the ball] was a Mme. la Comtesse B., née de M . . . . I presume it is Mrs. Barke, for they say she is not Swedish. They say too she had the most brilliant diamonds. I think they were false." (Countess Barck, a French marquise in her first marriage, was born Claire-Marie Napoline de Marc.) Teresita's son Louis would meet Countess Barck as a young boy, in his first encounter with a classic beauty. She continued to charm men into her old age.

Teresita dreamed of returning to Italy to assume her rightful role. "We shall give a grand ball in Gravellona if our affairs do well, so those who said that we are ruined shall come and eat and dance, to see with their own eyes." But she could not feel close to her Swedish family. "I think here they think best of those who do not feel anything . . ." This would be her lasting impression of the humorless Sparre household. Ada was not the sister Teresita had hoped to confide in. "She is so majestic and pedantic that sometimes I want all my strength for not jumping in the air. Ada's singing teacher "told me that she sang so well and I expected to hear something beautiful. But I was quite disappointed, she sang so coldly and from the nose! But as everyone was so enchanted with her performance, I of course looked so too." Teresita could not resist a wicked touch. "Today is Ada's jour de naissance [birthday] and there is downstairs a troupeau de jeune filles un peu majeures [a bevy of somewhat mature young girls]." Ada was 26.

Teresita was suffering from an illness which led the doctor to believe she was pregnant. "I am already rather voluminous so that my stays hurt me. I ask you what a pleasure it is with my 22 years to go to a ball and to sit and see others dance. And even now I have had such dreadful convulsions . . ." She complained of a persistent cough, drenching sweat at night, and many of the other symptoms tied to tuberculosis. The capricious disease allows victims to enjoy reasonable wellbeing for periods of time.[11] Teresita wrote, between bouts, that she felt well.

She kept Ambjörn informed about their boy. "He gets so fat that when he walks it looks just as if he was rolling." Ambjörn must not forget a doll of papier mâché for Louis. "Fancy when I asked Louis what he would send to you he said, non papa est méchant, il a fait kaka dans les pantalons. [No, papa is bad, he's made a mess in his pants.]"

Teresita wrote that Ambjörn's refusal to take her away caused her great distress. Naturally she would "obey," as wives did then, but "many times I require a great courage to go on. Now here I am in a strange land without you, without any comforts and all my habits broken." All the relatives were good persons, "but can only speak of butter and fish and housekeeping." They thought her a frivolous spendthrift, but "I have done my duty as much as them, though I am not as icy."

At the end of January 1866, Teresita reported that illness had prevented her going to the Admiral's ball. The doctor was a "donkey," and she expressed her irritation with her mother-in-law and Ambjörn's brother. He had already been "enflamed" with her maid in October, continuing the habits Teresita had noticed on his visit to Italy. She could not write his name without a scathing comment.

There was little sympathy for Teresita's illness at home. The attitude was that "God had sent it and his will be done" and Teresita exclaimed to Ambjörn that such "cold people I have never been able to understand." Finally, in March, it was discovered that she was not pregnant, and "I can travel as quick as you like and whichever way you like." Despite coughing attacks, Teresita went dancing as she loved to do. She joined a sleighing party in the March snows, and took drives with a naval officer who had his own carriage and horses. But no matter how festive the invitations, Teresita longed for Italy. "I have such a longing after milder air and flowers and Poussy's kisses and these not the least of all."

At last Ambjörn must have come to take her home to Italy with "Bibi," as little Louis was called, for the next letter was from Gravellona in April. The boy was happy, "he springs, dances and sings the whole day . . . ." There was a bit of social news about the family, the engagement of "Miss Ferraris", presumably the daughter of the Countess, to the "Directeur des Postes," Barbavara. It was through him that Ambjörn, in his discussions of stamp manufacture, had met Luigi and Teresita.

In a letter from Gravellona in April, Teresita wrote about a pending court appearance, in which Papa Luigi must legitimize a child born to Maddalena, the maid. The girl had already engaged a lawyer to "summon Papa before the tribunal for the legitimization. All this is so dreadful that it makes me ill only to think of it . . ." Luigi's illegitimate son "has not the family name." For Teresita it was one more bit of suffering.

Teresita comforted herself with the thought that "the Queen wants your ringing appareils [apparatus]." Ambjörn had invented an aerial telegraph, of interest to the War Science Academy in Stockholm. It was shown to the King and two apparatuses were ordered. This was a forerunner of the electric bell system, and spread in Sweden on steamboats, railroad carriages, hotels and offices, even in prisons and private homes.[12] Abroad, Queen Victoria was an admirer. Ambjörn had less and less time to spend at Gravellona.

In early May, 1866, Teresita wrote "what a nice thing if you can sell the Italian patent . . ." Ambjörn started a lawsuit against the Italian State, which had broken a contract for the delivery of stamps and given it to an Italian firm. Ambjörn's machinery stood empty in Turin.

Teresita's piano continued to give her great pleasure. She asked Ambjörn to bring her "Beethoven's oeuvres . . . . for I cannot study any more all these insipid pieces." Teresita had acquired a pupil for English lessons, Marietta, the daughter of Countess Ferraris. Her lessons and the sale of asparagus and fruits helped pay the servants.

Teresita was caught up in the turmoil of Italy's unification struggle. In 1860, the provinces of central and northern Italy had voted to unite with Sardinia. Napoleon III, then ruling in France, was willing to recognize this union, but had his price: Nice and Savoy were to be ceded to France. The legendary leader Garibaldi, though he favored establishing a republic, supported the Italian King Victor Emmanuel II of Sardinia as the best unifying element for Italy. With Victor Emmanuel's tacit permission, Garibaldi and his Red Shirt volunteer army conquered the "Two Sicilies" (Naples and Sicily); Sardinia annexed Umbria and the Marches. By 1861 Italy was united under Victor Emmanuel, though the union did not include Venetia, Rome and part of the Papal States. In 1866, Garibaldi commanded a volunteer unit siding against Austria in the Austro-Prussian war; as a result, Venetia was won for Italy.

In a letter from Gravellona dated May 22, 1866, she wrote of the enthusiasm for Garibaldi's efforts, noting that "everybody here goes to engage himself for Garibaldi." She later wrote that 50,000 volunteers had signed up for the war. Garibaldi even affected fashions. In one letter Teresita asked Ambjörn to bring her a "Garibaldi," no doubt a red blouse. Little Bibi had his own checked Garibaldi shirt.

Though he was only three, Louis was to remember this time all his life. In these fevered weeks, just before the outbreak of war against the Austrians, tempers were frayed and there were quarrels within families. Louis watched one murderous scene, when the gardener Corsico's son pulled a knife on his father. Hilda, Louis's nurse, threw herself between the two Corsicos, and earned the admiration of the people on the place as "la Hilda", the brave Swedish girl.

Villa Teresita threw open its doors to military officers and their aides, and Bibi remembered the clinking of spurs and clatter of sabers against the steps at night. In the evening, from the dining room, he saw their lanterns like fireflies in the garden, and was awakened from his sleep by the noise of departing troops, wagons and ordnances.

The neighbors were beginning to notice Ambjörn's absence. " . . . Often people ask me with a funny expression if I received news of you." But the garden was beautiful. After a rain the nightingales sang "with such a clear voice" and "everything seems to ask me why you are not here."

Teresita wrote on June 10th that she was well enough to go to Novara for a new piano. "I have found one quite new and very good from Paris." Though she had invitations to go away with her friends, "I will not leave Bibi and also Papa." It was silent as a Trappist monastery, "and I am so desolate to see that I can never be well again." But the piano was coming, and "I shall learn nice things to play to you if ever you come."

In her next letter of June 16th Teresita worried about money again. She was fearful of quarrels between her father and Ambjörn, and made herself a buffer between them. But she dreaded her father's words about Ambjörn's debt, as Gravellona was mortgaged to pay for it. "Money is melting in my fingers," she wrote, and the government was demanding forced loans to pay for the war.

Teresita wrote Ambjörn the day after war was declared between Prussia, allied with Italy, and Austria. Of course the war was on everyone's mind. A group of ladies was organized to make bandages for the soldiers. Teresita had declined to join, not being well, though she made bandages at home every evening with the doctor. But the doctor, Teresita's only confidant, was leaving to join his regiment.

Even Countess Ferraris and her promised drives did not materialize. A new violin-playing friend who sometimes came to play duets with her had "engaged himself as a simple soldier, and fancy that so have done all the young men of the best families."

Now all the curtains were hung for Ambjörn's return, and Teresita made a compote of cherries "to have something good to give to my Poully when he comes home." But her health was fragile. "The fever came again. Last night I thought I should never see the light more. Tomorrow I shall have sangsues [leeches] and a good dose of China [quinine]." The danger passed, and she thought only of having Ambjörn "in my power, then I do not let you go."

These summer letters about daily chores and jam making, to "give you the illusion to think yourself in a Swedish home" end in July and do not begin again until December. Much happened in the intervening months. Teresita had the joy of Ambjörn's company. But an accident marred her happiness. Louis remembered it always.

Lt. Pippo Della Beffa, a favorite friend of the family, had come to call for Teresita and little Bibi, to drive them to Vigevano. Della Beffa was on the coachman's seat, driving. Louis had not been allowed, as he usually was, to sit with him and hold the reins. The little boy instead sat inside the carriage, between his mother and grandfather. Somewhere on the long, straight road between the rice fields, Bibi felt the carriage roughly knocked backwards, into the ditch. Teresita jumped out, but her foot was caught, pinched and crushed between the carriage step and the ground. For months Teresita lay in bed while the doctor came to remove splinters of bone with his dreaded knife.

Ambjörn did not join them for Christmas. Teresita wrote that she was better, and could sit up almost a whole day in bed. She encouraged Ambjörn about his business, but even if he should not succeed, "I would be as happy as a queen." She was isolated from all but Della Beffa and the farmer. The compound fracture was not healing, her foot was swollen and infected, and she was again helplessly in her bed. The doctor came with his terrible knife, and later in January "another bone is broken over the foot where the sore is open. I have cried a little as you may imagine." Between the miseries of her illness, she worried about payments on the piano. But she did not lose her humor or sharpness. When she reported the announcement of a friend's marriage, she remarked that "he did not forget to say that the bride-elect was rich."

Though she was in pain, Teresita looked forward to a visit by Pippo Della Beffa and his sister. On a beautiful day in February "I have had the window open the whole day. Mr. Pippo has come back with his sister. It seems music for my ears to hear a woman speak as a lady here that one only hears things that can best ornate the vocabulary of peasants."

Good news from Ambjörn was received with rapture: "I could have danced even with my foot which today feels well or without pains." But her anxieties intruded on her moment of joy. There was a threat of jailing Papa Luigi for non payment of a debt. Only a miracle, she wrote, could save them. Later the Chevalier was able to pay the "forced loan," perhaps the debt referred to.

The bone in her foot must be extracted and she must endure an operation. "I have promised to let him do it when you will be here, for only your caresses will give me the strength to support it."

Teresita had read in the papers about the French Government's order of 500,000 breech-loading rifles, but "perhaps it is not true." She hoped instead that Ambjörn's rifle would win the contract. He was reconstructing a rifle which experts believed would be widely bought. At the same time he was working on mines, cannons and a locomotive, and at the end of that year a telephone, described by a co-worker as "talking by telegraph."

Teresita tried to pass the time by reading, wrote letters to her friends in Sweden and studied the atlas on the pretext of taking a trip to Mexico. "I only wish I had your head hanging over mine seeking the places, but I am afraid that then we should only find what are called kisses." Why Mexico? It must have been much in the news in Italy, as the Austrian Archduke Maximilian, governor of Lombardo Venetia, had become Emperor of Mexico with the connivance of Napoleon III. In March of 1867, when Teresita was writing, Maximilian was under siege by the popular hero Juarez, and soon after was captured and shot.

In mid-March Teresita was still bedridden, unable to play her piano. "And I have also cried. You never will guess why? For Mr. Bibi . . . he profits of my immobility for to play me all sorts of tricks." She asked Ambjörn for toys, some balls and a game of ninepins.

Ambjörn came home briefly, and she was able to get up four hours and even play her piano. Countess Ferraris was a visitor, but otherwise her days were "monotonous, a succession of working now at stockings, now at tapestry and then a little playing and reading."

In early April Teresita was buoyed by news that Ambjörn had been to the "opening of the exhibition though fiasco it has been." Ambjörn won a medal at the world's fair, which opened in Paris in April, 1867. But it did little for him, as war rumors dampened the economy and business ventures. "I wonder how you have managed to see the Emperor [Napoleon III] or get in at all."

She became very ill in mid-April, with fainting fits and coughs. Ambjörn had just written, telling her to take pills for the coughing. Teresita pushed her limits, walking downstairs and into the garden with Della Beffa's help, for "it is so painful for the breast and under the arms to stand up on the crutches." But another ordeal lay ahead. "I told the doctor to operate my foot, and he said he will do it Saturday. I shall have courage for I think I have quite enough of this life . . . I want my Ambjörn and have him never."

In July, Teresita traveled to Paris with Bibi and Hilda to consult Ambjörn's doctor. From this moment all her letters are in French. She probably had no energy to spare for English. Her doctor recommended a cure at Allévard, a spa for asthma sufferers not far from Aix-les-Bains. From there, Teresita wrote short notes the first week of September. She wanted grapes from Gravellona, and her high-necked dress with long sleeves of antique watered silk. There were days when she could not "take the cure," and others when she could "take the air." But her constant refrain was "Write me often. I am so alone."

When Ambjörn came from Gravellona, she wrote, he should bring her black and red flannel to make skirts to wear under the crinoline in cold weather. In mid-September she wrote that she had no mail from anyone in her family—not even a wicked letter. She asked Ambjörn to buy her vanilla caramels and fruit-flavored gumdrops to help her cough, and wanted her skirt in white silk with the little black stripes.

Ambjörn had written from Turin on September 4 that he "pushed through" a storm on Mt. Cenis. "The railway there had been tried but is not yet open to public use, so I went as usual by diligence [coach]." He urges her to take her carriage out as much as she likes. In the same letter he reports that he has been offered 25,000 francs for half of his "English ringing patent." He will carry the basket of grapes from his darling "as cautiously as possible." His visit, judging by letters, was short. Teresita wrote that he had left her full of courage.

Ambjörn reached Paris by September 21, 1867, writing her from 88 rue Lafayette. He had talked to his doctor, M. Billard, who approved of her going to Pisa, where she would be more at ease and see friends. Teresita wrote back that she was "spitting like a locomotive."

Later, still hopeful that "cold inhalations" would help the increasingly terrible cough, she begged Ambjörn to write two words, and give her news of their boy. Ambjörn answered that he had taken a happy Bibi to the circus to see a troop of Japanese and Chinese acrobats show off their balancing acts. She would love to have seen Bibi at the circus, and begged Ambjörn to have a photo taken. As for dressing Bibi like a boy, there was time enough for that. Tell Hilda, she wrote, to put on him his pretty blue dress with matching padded jacket. She sent her boy chocolates, and Bibi wrote her back a note by himself.

Ambjörn wrote dutifully. Between questions about cushions and flannels, he urged her to "utilise as much as possible the cold inhalations, as it appears to do you some good." He worries about how to get Teresita over Mt. Cenis with the least risk, using a little apparatus he has from England to breathe through, tempering the cold, damp air. Best of all, for Teresita, he has ordered a photograph of Bibi, "such a little fine fox."

The doctor said that her husband must fetch her at the earliest moment because it was too cold in Allévard. It was decided that she should go to Pisa. She listed the dresses Ambjörn should bring: her skirt in antique silk, her silk dress with ruffles and the high neck, her velvet dress with high neck and belt, and the velvet coat.

Ambjörn wrote, on October 2, that he hoped to come and bring her to Pisa. He urged her to exercise her foot by walking. Bibi had posed "with aplomb" at the photographer's, and Hilda had made him a little Garibaldi shirt out of Teresita's wool morning coat.

At home in Gravellona, her Papa wrote in early October that he was in heaven because of her return to Italy, and would meet her in Genoa or Turin with grapes. For the joy of her news he had given a bottle of wine to each worker. But Teresita had to report "une fièvre de cheval" (a galloping fever), which left her no energy to cough, and gave her a convulsive trembling. She asked Ambjörn not to forget the stick of apple sugar for her poor chest, and she thanked him for the photograph of Bibi.

She wrote matter-of-factly that selling the piano might be a solution to paying off some debts. She had hinted at this earlier; now she was able to contemplate the loss of the piano for Ambjörn's sake. She was waiting for Ambjörn as though he were "the Messiah."

Ambjörn wrote from Paris October 8, that the shortage of money was only "momentary." He would leave for Turin within days, having done all her commissions; all the dresses were in the drawing room, "waiting to be packed."

Ambjörn moved her, in mid-October, to an establishment in Pisa that is not described, where she had a room, access to the doctor and a good cook. She wrote her last letters there. The first one was dated October 24th. There is a new note of relief, a sigh of joy. She was "gay and sensible" and felt so happy in the house. The cook had found her magnificent sweet grapes, two big bunches for 20 centimes. Despite suffering, her strength seemed to be returning. The doctor found her better and was very kind.

On the 30th, she wrote her last letter. While she had bad days and even worse nights, she felt that better times were coming. Her morale and courage were improving, though her physical strength was up and down. But the cook was a marvel and knew exactly what suited her. Her Papa wrote every day, and she asked Ambjörn in Turin to bring him a photo of Bibi. She would knit stockings for the poor, for it was the only work that did not tire her. Her last words were of Bibi, and that she would take charge of Ambjörn herself when he came. "Love me," she wrote at the end.

On November 4, from Paris, Ambjörn was happy that she was content with her kitchen maid, and was sure that her appetite would return. But in his self-absorbed delight at his own successes, he turned a deaf ear to Teresita's longing. He wrote her that Emperor Franz Joseph, who had granted him an audience and was interested in his new rifle, had asked for a model of it. The Emperor had given him a gold medal to wear on a red ribbon like the Légion d'Honneur. But, he added, he would "put everything in the fire" if only he could make her well. On the 8th he reported to her that "my gun makes quite a furor here . . . it has succeeded far beyond my best expectations." Just after Teresita's death, Ambjörn's cartridges were accepted for the Italian army.

There was no reply from Teresita. But on November 12th a thin grey telegram arrived in Paris. 'Condition of the Countess hopeless.

Come immediately. Professor Fedely.' This was soon followed by another from the same source: 'The Countess is dead. Hasten here. She died this morning.'

Louis, in Paris, remembered only a numbing, frightening feeling, and Ambjörn's tearful embrace.

Teresita was buried in the Protestant cemetery at Turin. To avoid offending her Roman Catholic relatives, few attended. In modern times her remains were moved into the Barbavara family plot.

Luigi Barbavara's grief was unrestrained. He moved to Paris to be near his little grandson, but in March, 1868, he followed his daughter in death and was buried in the Cimetière du Nord after a funeral mass in the Eglise St. Vincent de Paul.

Commemorative stamp
of Ambjörn Sparre

Count Pehr Georg Sparre   Countess Carolina Sparre

Their children, Ada, Ambjörn and Erik

Sparre family in 1860s

Chapter 5

LOUIS'S YOUNG YEARS

After Teresita's death, Ambjörn, Louis and his nurse Hilda lived in a spacious, sunny apartment two storeys up at Rue Lafayette 88. There they had a view from the balcony, a big drawing room, dining room and bedrooms. There were no bathrooms, but baths were taken in tin-lined copper tubs filled with pails of hot water, the whole ambulatory equipment carried up the kitchen stairs by men in blue uniforms. This was a highlight for Louis, something not to be missed, though in winter warm baths were considered risky for the health.

One of his dreams was to see the Emperor with his own eyes. From his father's balcony, one day, Louis was watching the soldiers from Napoleon III's guard of cuirassiers. Suddenly one of the men slipped and fell from his mount, his bright saber gleaming against the dark street. The Emperor's landau carriage stopped just below the balcony, and visible through the carriage windows was Napoleon himself, waiting for some time to learn the wounded man's condition. When the man was carried away, the Emperor gave a hand signal to continue. Louis told this tale of 1867 to his great-grandson who had come to see him on his 100th birthday in 1963.

Ambjörn won his lawsuit against the Italian state but his financial situation did not improve. The mortgage assumed in Gravellona to prosecute the lawsuit had to be repaid, as the estate was to be left to Louis Sparre. His Swedish grandfather Pehr Georg wrote Ambjörn that he must insure the little boy's inheritance. But Ambjörn, as always, was an unheeding optimist, particularly now when he had sold his cartridges to the Italian army. Gravellona was lost to Louis.

Ambjörn sent Louis to spend the summer of 1870 with "Oncle Antoine" Barbavara, Teresita's cousin, in his villa on Lake Como. The Prussian threat of war against France had become a reality, and little Bibi would be safe and happy with his kind Italian relative, jolly Don Antonio with his round cap and happy disposition. The two made train trips to Gravellona, where the servants still remembered Louis. They also crossed Lake Como by paddlewheel and rowboat. Louis stayed with his uncle for the duration of the Franco-Prussian war. The mimosa trees, the big shady garden with its peaches, apricots and cherries, the lake water clucking against the boathouse became enchanted memories. Later, in his young manhood, when discouraged by his father's demands on him and acutely depressed, Louis wrote his Italian kinsman. He longed for moral support, and wanted to move to Italy and live with this protective, affectionate man. Antoine had always been skeptical of Ambjörn's illusory, erratic way of life, and he feared for Louis' future. But his answer to Louis, written in sadness, was that he could not in conscience intervene between father and son. He advised the young man never to give way to temporary difficulties, and to heal the rift with the father who would always be his best friend. Antoine had planned to leave Louis his Villa Barbavara on Lake Como, but it was willed instead to another nephew. Antoine died soon after their correspondence, and Louis forever lost the connection with his Italian family.

In the summer of 1871 Louis learned at Oncle Antoine's that his paternal grandfather, Pehr Georg Sparre had died. This was a greater loss than he knew, for in the old man he had a protector and a home in Sweden. Louis hardly remembered him, having been only two when he left Karlskrona with his mother.

During the Franco-Prussian war Ambjörn, who had spent years studying artillery, gunfire and ammunition, put himself at the disposal of the French government. He was called to Lyon by the men who came to power in a bloodless revolution, toppling Napoleon III. The rifle he had been working on, patented and similar to the

Remington, was offered to the French defense but not accepted. They had their chassepot, also a breech-loading rifle.

During the same period, while making a trip between Paris and Bordeaux to see about an ammunition project, Ambjörn had been taken for a German spy and arrested because of his strong Swedish accent. His life hung by a thread: he would be shot! Ambjörn had been on his way to see Gambetta, the French statesman and minister of war, organizer of the French defenses against the enemy. Only a telegram from the great man saved Ambjörn.

The upshot of his relationship with Gambetta was characteristic of Ambjörn's roller-coaster-like career. Ambjörn set up a factory for producing cartridges with tubes made of paper rather than the more expensive metal. Ambjörn closed a favorable delivery contract with Gambetta, but "at his own risk." Until peace was declared he had the gratitude of French defense officials. The work was done under difficult conditions—the city could not fulfill its promise to deliver supplies to Ambjörn. Ambjörn himself undertook to obtain and pay for the materials he was using to make the cartridges. He was considered a savior.

At the end of the war, Ambjörn expected a large sum for the delivered ammunition, but was instead accused of having short-changed his client. After many years of litigation he won the case, but the sum of money he was awarded was 100,000 francs less than the legal expenses needed to recover it. Ambjörn was made a knight of the Légion d'Honneur by the President of the French Republic in December 1871.

But with the end of the war, everything changed. The city of Lyon, organized as the southern defense of the country, was in debt. It tried to cancel the contract. Ambjörn's furniture and machines were tossed out on the street and he was forced into bankruptcy. His work was interrupted, his letters searched. Eventually, he won the lawsuit against the city, though the money was less than the lawsuit had cost him.

His troubles were not over. The city appealed the high court's favorable decision on his lawsuit in March, 1872, and a further investigation ordered. Ambjörn was manhandled in the court chambers, and a threat was made to bring a judgment of treason against him. In a second judgment he was vindicated again, and his conduct was recognized as having been blameless and altruistic toward his second country, France. He wore his decoration with pride for the rest of his days.

Louis came home to the Paris apartment in 1871, after the second siege of Paris and the suppression of the workers' Commune, to find holes in the walls and ceilings from bullets. The balcony's iron railing was shot through. Alexandre was no longer there to look after Bibi: in fear of being called up by the Commune, he had hidden and left the city. It was at this period of Louis's life, while his father was entertaining guests for dinner, that Countess Barck, the mysterious "Madame B." of his mother's letters to Ambjörn, befriended him and aroused his undying affection—and a lifelong admiration for beautiful and amusing women. Countess Barck's charms were also said to have ensnared Emperor Napoleon III.

Louis's early years with his father were lonely, though the faithful nurse Hilda remained his protector and caretaker, and was the important person in his life. He had few playmates. Schooling in French and Swedish by various tutors was tolerated, but was hated when his own father became the teacher. The dreary hours of memorizing battles and dates back to Charlemagne were like a prison sentence. But Louis soon found his first art inspiration in battle scenes from the recent war. Taken to see a huge panorama in the "Cirque d'été" on the Champs Elysées, the small boy tried to copy it with crayon on glass. The artist, Detaille, known for his realism, had himself served in the Franco-Prussian war.

By the time Louis was ten, in 1873, Ambjörn decided that the little boy should grow up in his own country. He found a home for him with old friends in Stockholm, the Anckarswärds, whose own son was of the same age. Ellen Anckarswärd became a warm and loving mother for him. (She was later to win a gold medal for her work on women's causes.) His grandmother Carolina introduced him to the Swedish Christmas and other old-fashioned customs. A romantic longing to have a seafaring life led to a summer as a cadet on the corvette Eugenie—and memories of the ship under full sail, golden in the sun, in the Danish waters off Kronborg castle. Louis proudly wore his cadet uniform, and slept cheek-by-jowl with his mates in his hammock. He proudly described the diet to his father: peas and fried ham, brown beans and potatoes, and on Sunday a keg of beer. But the seaman's career was not to be. Louis collapsed after some weeks with measles and pneumonia.

Ambjörn did give some thought to a permanent home for his boy. He had started a weaving enterprise in Kalmar, Sweden, with French and Swedish workers. There he bought the old Bishop's house, and in a moment of feeling flush, provided tile stoves decorated with the Sparre coat of arms, the fashionable painted window panes of the period, and fine antiques. One detail that Louis loved was a feat of his father's engineering: from his bed Louis could push a button to open the front door.

Louis continued to love his lively life with the Anckarswärds, their son and all the cousins who gathered for Christmas and holidays. Even after the death of her husband, Ellen Anckarswärd insisted that Louis continue to live with them. It was the one safe place in Louis's life.

However, the home in Kalmar did not last long. By 1878, Ambjörn's silk-weaving mill was in distress. Silkworm and mulberry farming failed, and the board of directors panicked. Ambjörn had constructed a patented mechanical knitting machine for the jacquard looms in silk factories, but now the directors declared bankruptcy and the buildings and machines were put out at auction. The factory complex was sold for little. Ambjörn, in all his worry, at least knew that his boy was in school and in good hands.

Louis now began night school at the art academy in Stockholm. His first success was a difficult assignment: to draw a hussar leading a wild horse. After trying drawing lessons, he was considered mature enough to become a student of watercolor with Baron Hermelin, a landscape painter, who had recently been commissioner of Swedish art at the World's Fair in Philadelphia.

Louis spent the summer of 1879 with his father in Paris and took his first fencing lessons. He developed artistic taste in the museums of the Louvre and Luxembourg, and saw the latest in art at the Salon of the Industrial Palace. Louis pursued exhibits at the fashionable clubs to which Ambjörn belonged. All this exposure awakened his desire to become a painter.

In the 1880's Louis returned to Stockholm. There he combined the student's life with the season's balls, making an impression with his Italian looks and elegant evening attire, his top hat and patent leather boots. He saw something of the young architects of the day; several were beginning to make their mark. Ferdinand Boberg, just three years older, was one of his companions; he later designed Waldemars Udde, Prince Eugen's Stockholm home, now a museum, and the famous NK department store in Stockholm. Inspired by this man and others, Louis expressed his ardent wish to study architecture. But Ambjörn disagreed. His son's future was predetermined: he was to be educated in and give his talents to Ambjörn's school of inventions.

In 1884, after matriculation, Louis returned to Paris, to his father's new apartment at Place de la Madeleine 16, with a balcony and view of the church and the boulevards. Each day was spent at the workshop on a street nearby, drafting Ambjörn's machinery. Louis resented his captivity.

Paper was the stuff of Ambjörn's inventive dreams. He invented a forgery-proof paper for bank notes, and offered it to the Banque de France, saying that he could duplicate their notes in his bedroom. It was child's play! The gentlemen of the Banque told him that it would be impossible, but they allowed him to try his luck. This was in the mid-1880's; Louis recalled the event decades later. His father had sliced a bank note in two through the thickness. That way, the two sides could be laid on transparencies and photographed. The bank men were astounded when they saw the photographic replicas. But despite Ambjörn's success, the Banque de France challenged him on a vital point. Their water mark could not be forged. Louis later told the story in Svenska Dagbladet :

> 'Give me a kitchen and two hours' time, and I'll make your watermark,' answered Pehr Ambjörn Sparre. The Frenchmen agreed to his terms. We were given a kitchen with a gas burner, a pot and water . . . Father and I arrived with some sheets of white English paper . . . we were searched and locked in. The water mark consisted of a Republican head in profile; earlier I had made it in wax on a glass slide. We tore the paper into strips, and transformed them in the boiling water, shaking the pulp into a mold of the same size as the franc note. Inside the mold was the Republican head, of which I'd made the model [with a metal cast from the wax]. We made 10-12 samples, dried them on strings over the stove, and when they were dry, we knocked on the locked door and said: 'We are ready.'[13]

Once again the gentlemen of the bank were astounded. However, no French notes were ever printed on Ambjörn Sparre's paper, but he did gain official permission to copy French banknotes experimentally.

Ambjörn also received permission from the Bank of England to duplicate a five pound note. He copied their control (a tiny nick in the "i" of Five) as well as their watermark, both of which they had asserted made counterfeiting impossible. He added his copied note to a bundle of genuine banknotes, and asked the gentlemen to pick it out. They could not. He extracted the original from his pocket, and pulled out from the inspected bundle his counterfeit bearing the identical number. Unfortunately, the bank gentlemen's astonishment was not followed by an offer.

Louis, isolated in his life and daily work, became more and more depressed. His expectations for the future were extinguished, as every wish he expressed for a career of his own was turned away. He was offered a place in an engineering firm, but Ambjörn scotched the idea.

With his usual optimism, Ambjörn started a new weaving factory, this time assembled in Manchester. Money grew scarce; now there was only enough for one meal a day. Louis remembered the threatening tramp on the stairs of men coming to attach their possessions. But in an ecstasy after the sale of a patent, Ambjörn bought a shiny metal stand on which was mounted an ostrich egg. This amazing sight later inspired Louis to conclude that he must live independently.

It was at this time in 1886 that Louis wrote his uncle Antoine and tried to change his life. When rejected, he moved to the new workshops near the Arc de Triomphe. His lodging consisted of two rooms in a ramshackle house. He cooked meals himself at the workshop, or took them at a nearby coachman's pub. He joined Ambjörn for dinner, and helped him draw the mechanical works for one of several new dirigible balloons. Ambjörn remained deaf to proposals that Louis study art. Why should he risk years of an uncertain future when he would be earning millions as soon as the latest invention took hold?

Encouraged by Ellen Anckarswärd, his guardian angel, Louis decided to leave Ambjörn after a violent quarrel. Without any means but permitted to keep his rooms, he found a job as journalist and artist for an illustrated Swedish weekly. With his new journalist's card, he sent news from Paris. But his dreams of being discovered as a water-colorist remained unfulfilled and his wallet was empty. He renewed his relationship with Ambjörn, who, perhaps reflecting on his son's pride and ambition, approved his decision to become a student in the Académie Julian in 1887-88.

Ambjörn rented a large studio for Louis. It was so cold that the water in a basin turned to ice in winter, but the drafty, two-storey room was so spacious and bright that one of Louis's artist companions decided to share it with him. This was the Finn, Axel Gallén, who was to become his closest friend and have a defining influence on his future. (Axel was to change his name to a Finnish one in 1907, Akseli Gallen-Kallela). Gallén, a student of William Bougereau, Mary Cassat's contemporary, was even then, in the 1880's, working on his monumental and stark portraits from Finnish mythology. Louis's high studio ceiling with its excellent light was particularly suited to his needs.

Louis continued with his water-colors, struggled with oils and won his first portrait commission. The joys of painting and his new freedom were reinforced by the friendships among his new artist companions, some of whom became well known internationally. One was Pierre Bonnard, a painter with an impressionistic style, a lithographer and stage set designer. Another close friend was Paul Sérusier. With Bonnard and other artists, Sérusier started the Nabis2 group in the 1890's, influenced by Gaugin's bold swatches of color and outlined patterns, its name drawn from the Hebrew word for prophet. Louis's friendships with Finnish fellow students, the sculptor Emil Wikström and the painters Gallén and Eero Järnefelt, were to change his life.

Louis submitted a painting to the salon, La Société des Artistes Français. To earn a little money he found work drawing fashion pictures for l'Art de la Mode on the coast of Normandy. It was a short-lived enterprise, for Louis was overcome by hay fever, or rather, cat fever (his lady employer had a house full of cats to which he was allergic) and he could not continue. Instead, Ambjörn invited him to the Scottish highlands, where he was enchanted by the shifting colors, lakes, valleys, ruins and old castles, the white fishing huts in the north and black storm-swept cliffs.

In 1888 another important Swedish artist came into Louis's life via Gallén: Anders Zorn, whose artistry Louis had admired earlier. He and his wife lived in the stylish Quartier Monceau with other artist celebrities and were welcome additions to Louis's group.

Louis admired Zorn's London tailored suit and last word in men's fashions. Zorn became an eminent portrait painter and etcher, and his friendship with Louis lasted out their lives.

In 1889 Louis was elected to exhibit a pastel of a girl in a window at the World's Fair. He returned to the Académie Julian to work on his inspirations from Scotland. When he asked Gallén to return with him the following summer for another study trip, Gallén suggested that Louis come to Finland with him instead. It was to be the beginning of a new life.

Chapter 6

THE WEDDING TRIP

By the time Louis met Eva in 1892 he was already well launched on his love affair with Finland. After his first trip he returned to Paris in the winters, to work at his art and continue fencing in foil, a sport he had learned at 16. He practiced at Spinnewyn's salle under the first Parisian master to introduce fencing in sword. Its elegance and grace were well suited to Louis' temperament and lithe figure, and led to a place on the Swedish Olympic team in 1912, when Sweden hosted the games.

In the summer of 1890 Louis painted his first Finnish portraits, both exhibited in Finland. On his return to Paris, Zorn introduced him to etching, and perhaps in thanks, but certainly in friendship, Louis served as a model for the foreground dancer in Zorn's painting, The Waltz. (Louis may have been chagrined when the artist took his place opposite the young singer, Miss Petrini, though he continued to pose in a less prominent position as the partner of Emma Zorn, the artist's wife. Zorn sold the painting to Vanderbilt in New York.)

Finland continued to beckon. The long magical summer nights, hunting and fishing in primeval lakes and forests, steam baths in the sauna with clouds of vapor swirling around naked bodies, dances at farms to the music of the concertina, inspired his artist's eye and conspired to tie him to a life in Finland. He learned Finnish, a language with no connection to Scandinavian or other western tongues. He gave up his Parisian studio, sold his meager possessions and moved to Finland. The meeting with Eva and their marriage in 1893 sealed the commitment.

Eva's own ideas about an artist couple's life included rosy dreams of living in Paris and Rome, perhaps in Stockholm and London from time to time. She had never considered taking a trip to the remote wilderness of her own country. Louis talked her into seeing the landscape he had fallen in love with earlier. His special fascination was with Karelia, a region then divided between Russia and Finland, where people still lived in the ancient ways of their fathers, inventing rune songs in the tradition of the ancient Finnish epic Kalevala, as old as Beowulf. The verses had been passed down orally from generation to generation. In the mid-19th century, a young Finnish medical doctor, Elias Lönnrot, had written them down, transcribing them to a modern idiom.[14] Louis had joined the artist Axel Gallén and his bride for their unusual honeymoon in Karelia, and in 1892, he and his sculptor friend Emil Wikström spent almost two months exploring Russian Karelia. Louis and his artist friends were determined to open this Finnish culture to western eyes, and to illustrate a new edition of the epic with their own interpretations. Eva was to keep a journal while Louis sketched, both of them determined to help preserve a culture unchanged for six hundred years. Their own honeymoon in Karelia was the result.

Neither Eva nor Louis cared for conventional living. On July 19, 1893, leaving their wedding guests behind, they stowed their gun, fishing tackle, backpacks, blankets, painting gear and notebooks, and boarded the train in Helsinki for the first leg of their journey. Shouting their farewells over the engine's noise, they were bombarded with rice and flowers and a pair of shiny new galoshes. Louis, in a fit of Italian temper, hurled them back the same way, furious that these dreary objects should be part of their adventure. Upon arrival at Imatra, they stayed in a comfortable hotel as long as they could afford it. Their next hotel, in Kuopio, was a simple little place with thinner mattresses ("just as comfortable as those in the luxury hotel!") in the heart of Finland. There Eva made the shocking discovery that her Swedish was no longer understood. She was embarrassed that her Swedish husband had to be her interpreter in this, her own country.

From Kuopio they went to the tiny community of Iisalmi by steamer. That was the start of their real voyage of discovery. From there they traveled by two-wheeled cart some 54 miles to Kajaani, a trip taking two days on lumpy roads, through woods, uphill and down. Their baggage was stuffed as well as possible into the tiny cart, and caused amazement. Except for the gun and fishing gear, no one had ever seen such things before. Where had they come from? How long had they been together? What did their fathers do and how old were they? "What's your job?" asked a young cart driver in the most poverty stricken hostelry Eva and Louis had seen. "If I say I'm an artist, you probably don't know what that is," was the answer, but the boy was not dumbfounded. "I know what that is. There was one called Michael Angelo in Athens."[15]

Sympathizing with the hard lot of the emaciated horse that pulled their cart, they often got off and walked. In the light late evening of the northern night they arrived at their first little wilderness lodging. There was no key to their room, which held only the bare necessities: two wooden beds, one shaky table, a little black painted washstand, the usual pitcher and one basin with the remnants of a cake of soap. Despite a suspicion that the noisy travelers next door might pay them a call, they fell asleep. Not even curses and quarrels seeping in through the thin walls or the hard wooden pallets under them could keep them awake.

Arriving in Kajaani, they rattled in through the "city gate," a wicket painted red, past the town square and into the courtyard of the hostelry. Eva began to understand Louis's fascination with her country, so much of it unknown to her. The spires of a beautiful wooden church and bell tower pierced the sky, and near them the foaming, sparkling waterfalls made melodies at night. There were the ruins of the old fortress Kajaneborg, dynamited in an earlier war, a bleak reminder of their historic Russian foe to the east.

Louis painted his first watercolor, of the ruins and little bridge over the river beyond the falls. The result pleased him, unlike other efforts which seemed to him only a disappointing "grey ash." Their shoes were torn and frayed from their week's hunt for inspirations and subjects to paint. Food was a steady diet of salmon swimming in a sea of oil.

The wilderness Eva and Louis were exploring was an artist's and writer's dream. Nothing had changed in the Karelian wild: its peoples, costumes and inbred courtesies were unchanged since medieval times. The Christian religion was a thin coating over the old gods and magic cults. Eva and Louis recorded this culture, writing and drawing for the book they planned. Louis's boyhood dreams of American cowboys had been metamorphosed to this land, where he hunted and shot the rapids with the sturdy sons of the country. They welcomed him as one of their own.

The two now dreamed of living the life of an artist couple, free of prevailing tastes, fashions and petty conventions, and free to pursue their art, perhaps in the seclusion of the wilderness. This wife was not going to be a conventional housewife.

Eva described the postwoman. She was dressed like a peasant in a black skirt with jacket, a kerchief tied under her chin. She was armed with a revolver, its holster strapped above her waist. With one hand she carried an umbrella, with the other she supported the heavy black leather mailbag, fastened to a long leather strap over her shoulder. She was unafraid of bears, wolves, darkness, snow and cold, the forests and sandy plains, the heather-grown fields. She carried her burden nearly twenty miles. She was at work "early and late, summer and winter, defying all weather,"[16] another example of women at work in Finland.

The bear hunter, too, earned a place in Eva's journal. He molded his own bullets, but never took with him more than one bullet when going out to track bear with gun and spear. He respected his adversary, and considered it a combat between equals. It must be a worthy battle: the bear with his weapons of claws, teeth, power and motion, having the same chance to kill as man, armed with one bullet for his gun, and his spear.[17]

In Kajaani they watched the tar boats which ran from summer until late autumn. The experienced helmsmen, steering the long slender boats loaded with tar barrels, came from the east, near the border of Russia. They followed the rivers and lakes through the locks at the Koivu rapids and Ämmä falls. Split-second decisions had to be made on steering into the sluice channel, without being smashed against rocks. The dangerous voyage at last ended in Oulu on the northwest coast.

By now the two honeymooners were tired of all the salmon they had eaten, morning and night. They wanted more excitement and a release from the conventions of making polite conversation at meals.

They leased a nearby cottage from the rapids helmsman, whose duties included piloting boats over the falls.

The little grey cabin facing the calm waters, just beyond the foaming falls, became their first "home." Two straw mattresses on the floor were a sofa in daytime, and one table, a chair that was whole and one that was not, made up the furniture. Their clothes hung from nails on the wall. The kitchen was shared with their hosts but their own needs were simple: tea, cocoa, bread, eggs, milk and yogurt. They picked berries in the woods and took fish from the falls. Sometimes they went with their host on his boat, and Louis took the oar as helmsman to feel the thrill of racing over the cascades. This was the life they had dreamed of! But now it was time to turn east, into Russian Karelia.

Once again they packed their gun, fishing tackle, bedding and warm clothes for a trip by steamer to Sotkamo. The trip offered a landscape quite different from that of southern Finland. At the horizon beyond water and woods they could see the blue contours of the Vuokatti mountains. The steamer was hot, crowded with churchgoers, the men dressed in red blouses and fur boots, each one with his puukko, the Finnish hunting knife, hanging by its belt strap. The women were in jackets and skirts of varying colors, green, blue or brown woven wool, kerchiefs on their heads, psalm books carried in a handkerchief. Eva envied the men their pirogues, small pies of rye dough with a layer of cornmeal and another thick layer of home-churned butter swabbed on by puukko.

The next morning at an inn in Sotkamo they could find only a primitive two-wheel cart with no springs. There was room for no more than two to sit, so how would the driver solve this? Eva and Louis sat down, and then without warning the driver catapulted into Eva's lap. In good time he settled for a small footstool at her feet. At the hostelry in Kuhmo, their last contact with the outside world, they hired a room to rest up for the next day's long boat trip. The good weather was gone now, and rain in heavy drops poured down their backs and up their sleeves. Their goal was a croft not far from the Russian border.

At last they reached the Matokangas croft where Renne, Louis's guide on his former trips, had already spied them. His farmhouse was even more primitive than Eva could have imagined, for he had a "smoke hole" in the roof. And the smoke spun in clouds, darkening the whole little house, making it almost impossible to see across the room. Gratefully, despite the discomfort, Eva and Louis stretched out in blankets on beds of dried rushes, their wet clothes drying in front of the fire. But waves of starving mosquitoes defeated them, and they had to appeal to their host out in the shed. He gave them his bed.

He explained to his guests that one of his little daughters, Lena, had been bewitched by the forest. "Since that day she knows more than we."[18] Renne told them how the girl had gone into the woods, disappearing for two days. He had found her standing transfixed, as though chained to a fir tree. The pine did not release its power over her until Renne had read some prayers aloud. She had never talked about what she had seen during those days, and now sat silently in a corner speaking not a word to Eva.

At Renne's wilderness house Eva had her first taste of the Finnish sauna. In the smoky hut with its low ceiling and a heat fiercer than that of Hell itself, Eva put up with the steam bath and a good whipping with birch-leaf branches. As aromatic as the birch smell was, as cleansed and healthy as she felt, one visit was quite enough to last a lifetime.

They were ready to start, and Renne's older daughter Kaisu came along as a lookout and to help with the carrying. Only by walking or rowing could one reach Lentiira, very close to the Russian border. Renne led them in a balancing act over narrow paths, over swamps and woods, on small logs serving as bridges. When they reached a lodging, they were put to a test, being served coffee seasoned with salt. Eva struggled not to show her distaste for the brew. The atmosphere seemed heavy with silence and the grey, blackened interior. And certain forms of politeness had to be maintained: one must not be too eager to ask questions. The correct approach was to have long moments of silence between meaningless phrases, for that was what gave the host a feeling of confidence in his guest.

Eva sensed a change, even before crossing the border. The grey desolation of the western Finnish lodgings now turned into a new world. Here the Eastern Orthodox farms were welcoming; a feeling of color and joy was reflected in the women's costumes despite their poverty. Another long walk over swamps and through woods, and in a large forest clearing they crossed the border. Eva pinpointed this as being Akonlahti near the Kivijärvi Lake. (This may have been its name in 1893 but Kivijärvi in a modern atlas is far to the southwest. My best guess is that it was Luvozero, on the Russian side.)

They were heartily welcomed at the Tarassia homestead, and led to the guestroom. Renne, ever suspicious of Russian treachery, put his faith in Louis's revolver. Here Karelians lived with no western contact, their customs full of magic and superstition, their farms built in uncertain times when civil wars ravaged the country, and houses became the only shelter for their owners and cattle, all living under the same roof. But there was no strain in the easy hospitality, and Louis picked up where he left off at the homestead, which he had visited earlier with the Galléns. The homesteaders' courtesy and Finnish language suggested an old culture. The walls were scrubbed clean once a year in honor of Easter; window frames and parts of the big stove were painted red. Eva's eyes were dazzled by the women's brilliant colors, their hospitable brass samovar offering aromatic tea served in glasses and, as she writes, "seasoned with jolly talk, questions and jokes."[19] The meal was delicious fish pirogue and yogurt.

Eva wanted to hear a famous old rune singer, and made a trip to the village to pay him a call. With a bottomless collection of runes in his memory, he accompanied himself on a five-string kantele (a Finnish zither) and composed new songs about the happenings of the day. He said he knew the Kalevala from cover to cover. His notes were rich with feeling, but he sadly commented after singing that the rune-making would be forgotten, as well as the rituals for oath-swearing and the belief in the power of witchcraft. The young people of the day, he said, were callow and lived useless and empty lives, paying no heed to the wisdom of their elders.

The singer of runic verses catches words from blades of grass, from leaves, from heather. He hears them in the cold and rain, in the wind and waves and forest birds. Finnish nature itself gives the poetry its character; Christian and heathen symbols are part of the fabric. The Kalevala tells of the single scarlet lingonberry consumed by an innocent maiden that gives her a son who will be the new King of Karelia, a rival to the old hero and mighty magician, Wäinämöinen. Human suffering is reflected in the trees and leaves: the linden tree weeps, sighs are heard in the forest grove, the smallest herbs and heather blossoms drop their tears over the innocent maiden who has been seduced. The old hero's tears fall into the waters to form pearls. The Finnish lake-pike's jaw becomes the national instrument, the kantele, plucked by the old Kalevala hero Wäinämöinen to enchant the gods of air and lakes and river. Enraged to be displaced by a new King of Karelia, Wäinämöinen leaves in his boat and foretells that the people will call him back one day to give them a new magic device to bring good luck, the Sampo, which has disappeared beneath the waves, a new kantele, a new sun and moon. He leaves his own kantele and the runesongs to the Finnish people. These were the themes of Louis' and Gallén's paintings, a result of their earlier trip.

The Kalevala verses were thought to be an inheritance from the ancient Bjarmic people living in the coastal region around the White Sea and the largest of the Finnish and Russian lakes. The professor who transcribed and preserved the epic for Finland found modern traits still traceable to the ancient Bjarms, an inborn talent for trade, a cleverness at slipping around troublesome rules, and the poetic memory of ancient runic songs learned from their fathers, with occasional Swedish words in their speech. He found a swiftness in their body movements and in their ideas, a sort of communal inheritance from the proud and mighty Bjarmic people.

On one of his trips to Karelia before his wedding, Louis had returned to Russian Karelia with his old friend and fellow student from Paris days, the sculptor Emil Wikström. They recorded those places where the folk epic continued to live in song, and where "habits and customs . . . . were like those of the Kalevala and Pohjola tribes."[20] They sketched subjects and themes for future illustrations of the Kalevala in paintings and sculptures.

It was on this trip that Louis had gone with Wikström to visit a witch, to sketch her as she stirred her potions. They had understood her incantations because the purest Finnish language was spoken there, even in Russian Karelia. As they rowed across a lake they saw a hovel in the distance. The old woman approached them as they landed, rowing in from the opposite shore. Dressed in a dirty cotton shirt with a blue tunic and red belt, the pale, spare little woman wore a dark red scarf wound around the back of her head. She welcomed and invited them into her lair, looking like the fairy tale version of a troll's hut. Pine and birch stocks leaning against the gable made a shelter for the door and steps. The visitors noticed the mortar dug out of a pine trunk, the little bowl of birch bark and a pitcher, a washbasin also of birch bark hanging next to the door.

There was one room only, with a hole in the roof for the smoke, and two little glass windows to let in light. On one side of the door was the hand mill, on the other the stove with its hearth, and over that the hole for the bake oven. Two pots were hanging on large black hooks made of a knotted branch. An old bear spear leaning in the corner was used to open up the hole in the roof. In another corner the woman's clothes were laid out on planks, but her guests were not tempted to examine them further.

She boiled water for tea and soon the room was filled with smoke despite the opened hole. While they drank tea, sitting on the floor to escape the stinging in their eyes, the old woman lay on her pile of clothes complaining to herself about the hungry times. Between complaints she congratulated the guests' mothers for their handsome sons. Wikström wanted to catch some of her magic words, and they spent the night in an abandoned barn next to the hovel.

Rolled in blankets, they lay on hay and planks, helplessly covering their heads against the busy swarms of mosquitoes. In the morning they went back to the hovel, and Wikström read the rune songs he'd written on their trip, while the old woman sat on the floor slapping his knees with delight at every word she found funny. Dinner was a feast of birds and fish prepared by Louis and Wikström. The lavish meal was welcome to their hostess, weak from fasting for five days on bread, salt and water to celebrate a saint's day. She asked the visitors to let the Tsar know of her need. When the good bread had been eaten there would be only birch bark bread, the bark stripped from trees near the houses. They said goodbye to the old woman after giving her money, which she at first refused. Later she accepted it while kissing their boots. Alas, she had no incantations against hunger.

Eva had read Louis's notes of that trip, and now had some of her own to write. She went to visit the handsome homestead of a Karelian man of wealth. The high roof ridge and gutter beams were intricately carved, but the entrance door was low, as if to put one on notice that the Karelian home is not easily entered. Eva was the subject of much amusement and curiosity. She was invited to sit in the "women's corner" while the women took off her high-laced boots to dry, wondering at her feet, so untrained to walk barefoot. They touched her pale cheeks, so white, so smooth, compared to their weather-bitten and sunburned skin. They loudly disapproved of her worn but practical dress, and tried to tempt her with their wares. One by one she must examine the bright green silk apron, the shimmering violet silk tunic, the gold and pearl embroidered red cap of heavy silk brocade, all spread out for her inspection. Unfortunately, Eva's purse was as threadbare as her dress.

The women's place in this society was obvious. When Eva and Louis entered the homestead, the old patriarch with his flowing white beard rose to greet them. Eva felt like an insignificant wanderer into King Solomon's court. "What are your wishes, strangers?" the old man asked. Hearing that they came from afar, from Finland, he ordered his women in a commanding voice to put before their guests the best that the household could offer. All of them scurried to do his bidding. Women were completely dependent on their men; their place was at home. They were as much the property of the farm as the animals they tended, to be utilized as the man willed. But this homestead was unusual. The eldest son also had a shop in St. Petersburg and his wife therefore had special stature, the envy of other women. She was a 17-year-old with slanting eyes and high cheekbones, her movements as soft as a kitten's. Her dress, a scarlet tunic and brilliant blue apron of the finest silk, and a headdress embroidered with pearls and gold thread, were proof of her position as wife to the oldest son. She had to be satisfied that her rustling silk skirts made the other women jealous, for her world was narrow and would not change. Trips to St. Petersburg were no part of her lot, and she must spend many months in loneliness until her husband returned to give her expensive gifts.

Eva was intrigued by the greeting that was customary between women: they bowed their heads gracefully, and stretching out their right arms, touched the other's left shoulder lightly. Nursing the baby in the Karelian way was another custom that surely went back to ancient times. The mother bent tenderly over the infant, lying in a basket suspended from a hook in the ceiling. Eva remarked on the dignity of the mother, her red tunic falling "in rich folds around the young figure."[21]

They left their hosts on a Sunday to cross the lake. Everyone was in holiday garb, in tunics of red, blue, green, and yellow, their hair hidden under headdresses of heavy embroidered silk. The men dressed like Russian peasants, shirts gathered by a belt over the trousers, and wearing high boots. The trip was long, even with experienced rowers. They reached the hostelry at dark and the place seemed sound asleep. But moments later they were welcomed in, the samovar had appeared, coffee cake was ready and in the guest room (the "kornitsa") the bed had been prepared. Renne, ever suspicious of Russians, slept outside their door, fully dressed.

They were on their way to see the little church of Miinua, and traveled by boat again, snaking between islands and fir-covered peninsulas, finally having to continue on foot with back packs. The little red painted church went back, it was said, to the heathen times of eight centuries before. The cemetery's graves were weathered and overgrown by roots and stubs within a growth of huge pines, but some were marked by enameled bronze plaques of great beauty. Inside the church they caught a whiff of incense in the moldy darkness. Only a little light was admitted from two small barred windows, just enough to throw light on the altar with its old dark icons and light blue wall paper. There was a suggestion of a heathen and Christian mixture in the offerings of colorful rags and bits of ribbon hanging from hooks and nails in front of images on the altar. Were these gods or saints?

Louis renewed friendships at a homestead in the neighboring village, where they were treated to bread, butter and yogurt as well as gossip and questions. Bears had been seen recently, but Eva was calm since Louis was armed with revolver and rifle. She was secretly disappointed when no bear turned up on their wet walk to the Finnish border. Now they were on their way back, ready to cross half of Finland from east to west. Louis wrung his hands to think what his palette and canvas would forfeit. He regretted even the hazards to his art of the wilderness—an easel knocked over by a brazen wind; the canvas, wet with a new landscape, suddenly muddy and torn; a new cloud formation and rain squalls making a mockery of the composition. There was so much to record!

Despite the precaution of hiring a pilot for the first dangerous cataracts, the boat scraped bottom in shallow water. Renne saved them from an unwelcome bath, by jumping to a stone in the madly spinning eddy and freeing the boat. Louis shot and missed a duck, but fish baked in coals at their lair on a point of land gave them the energy to haul their boat a kilometer overland. It was easy for Eva to sympathize heartily with the men as she walked along unencumbered.

Back in the forest at Renne's croft they made preparations for their return to Kajaani. It took three days for Renne to roll his forty barrels of tar down to the tar boat on the beach. Eva and Louis would ride with him, for he must go westward on the waterways to earn his bread for the winter. He was a man of few words and no emotion that he cared to show. When Eva remarked that last night's frost might have destroyed the corn, he said only "yes, it may be frozen". He gave no time to looking. Without a harvest they would starve, but what good would it do to look and worry? Eva heard him singing as he put out his nets, in the slow rhythm of rising and falling oars. Here was the tempo of the Kalevala, "which goes well with the rhythm of walking or rowing."[22] She knew he was trying to calm his mind before leaving his little girls and wife alone in the forest. He would carry the pine tar westward to the coast, unloading the barrels in Oulu.

Eva breathed the pungent smell as the barrels were lined up two by two with enough room for the helmsman aft and the rower forward. They made a temporary deck of boards over the barrels amidships. Here they would sit for the long trip to Kuhmo, and it was indeed a long trip. Even with pillows and blankets one couldn't pretend that wooden slats were comfortable.

The long boat glided like an eel between rocks and points of land, deep in the water sometimes, but often scraping bottom and dancing on shallow water. Eva could foresee danger in Renne's face, as he stood at the helm with tense attention, making instant decisions, pitting himself and his precious load against the forces of nature. Near a dangerous waterfall the men, anxious about their heavily laden boat and passengers, decided to roll some of the barrels overland "to give us the same chance as the barrels." Eva, reaching a place below the falls on foot saw the boat "dangerously close to rocks and cliffs, rushing past with the dark sternpost sticking up through a white spinning cloud of scum."[23] That night, drenched and exhausted, they reached Kuhmo. Eva was surprised at some unusual hospitality, never to be forgotten. In a merchant's house where Renne could be certain of attention for the wealth of his tar load, they were welcomed by the sleepy owner, a candle-stub in his hand. Eva and Louis were offered his bed, the bedclothes warm and molded in the shape of his body.

Early the next morning, without devoting time to hunting or fishing, they piled into the boat again and Louis took Renne's place at the helm. There was another farm for another night. This time they were offered the farmer boys' bed without sheets, with a black sheepskin for a blanket. Eva resisted this temptation, and despite the late night hour they were welcomed by a farmer on a hill over the beach. The little room with clean sheets and crocheted lace on the down cover was a luxury, and the next morning they set off with coffee and home-baked bread under their belts.

Kajaani was the end of their travels, and by now feeling like real tar carriers, they easily steered their little boat into the locks at Koivukoski. Here they would leave Renne. Eva writes: "While we two youngsters have each other to greet the long day of life with happy expectations, Renne returns, silent and resigned, to the loneliness and darkness of the wilderness winter. The farewell is sealed without words, with a strong handshake and a staunch look in the eye."[24]

There is no record of how long the trip had lasted. Four weeks from their start on July 19th would have taken them to the beginning of cold and wet autumn weather, probably making further travels in primitive conditions too rugged even for those two pioneers. In 1945, Eva's journal became a formal account, illustrated by Louis's drawings, now on copper plates.

Eva Mannerheim Sparre at
the time of her marriage

Chapter 7

A TURNING POINT FOR GUSTAF

In the late 19th Century, one of the approved ways of dealing with a youngster who could not or would not behave himself was to send him off to military school. The Finnish Cadet Corps was an old and honored institution in Hamina, known as Fredrikshamn by the Swedish-speaking population. It was near the border with Russia, a day's horseback ride west of Viipuri.

Our story now returns to the Mannerheims, to Gustaf, who had been the family bugbear, restless and wild, disgraced by his expulsion from the Böök School in Helsinki at age 12 for breaking windows. (That same year his father had to sell an estate neighboring Villnäs, following the forced sale of a house in Turku and of his wife's inherited manor.) The family, as we saw in an earlier chapter, was living through traumatic times of financial loss, and this, even more than Gustaf's behavior, determined his education. His mother's family approved of sending him away to school, to prepare for the Cadet Corps where he would have an education at no cost.

Gustaf was seldom without reminders that he was now a poor boy. His Uncle Albert wrote "Don't forget that you must earn your own bread early in life." From his Grandmother Eva he heard that "poor boys who have had to struggle for their living often become men who are the most outstanding and well informed in their community." Aunts and uncles cheered Gustaf on when he was accepted as a cadet in 1882, and his grandmother Eva wrote that she couldn't wait to see "my little cadet in full uniform."[25]

Not everyone agreed that a military school was a good thing for Gustaf. His father, for one, did not hesitate to voice his sarcastic opinion of the military. He wrote to Gustaf from America, where he had observed the one hundredth celebration of the victory at Yorktown. "Some regiments are made up entirely of the rich, who have equipped themselves with dazzling uniforms . . . the troops march in martial order to the music, and a Negro walks behind each division carrying a basket with refreshments in one hand, and in the other half a dozen glasses. That's practical and sensible and worth recommending to the Finnish Cadet Corps."[26] He evidently could not resist this sardonic comment, though others could have found him wanting in tact. Why should he, his many creditors might have asked, offer his views on Gustaf's schooling, since he had left his wife and children without support or a roof over their heads, and made a life for himself in Paris? He could, apparently, also afford to travel to the U.S.

The die was cast. In the fall of 1880, Gustaf had taken his entrance examinations for the Cadet Corps and failed to get into the right class. His family had to accept an extra year of education for him. Gustaf traveled to the school by horse and carriage, advice from both parents echoing in his ears. His mother wanted him to read good literature, but no easy novels. She suggested Walter Scott and Jules Verne. His father, concerned about his temperamental nature, counseled him to be "kind, honest and straightforward"[27] and did not approve of his owning a revolver. His Uncle Christian wrote to his Uncle Albert, "He needs the strict discipline one hopes can be found in a proper school."[28] Everyone in the family was giving the same advice.

From the first Gustaf himself felt imprisoned and homesick in Hamina. He promised to send Sophie a map of his "mole hole"[29] to give her an idea of how bleak it was. Two months later, in January of 1881 the boy came home to help carry his mother's coffin to her early grave. He was thirteen.

His routine at the Cadet Corps emphasized his loneliness. He had not made new friends yet, and those who were near him sometimes found him distant and surly. In his barracks room, shared by seven cadets, he was wakened each morning at 5:45 a.m. by a drum roll echoing through the corridors. By six o'clock, any cadet still sleeping found his two thin blankets yanked off. A large copper cistern held cold water drawn for the morning ablutions. Morning prayer followed, and a fifteen minute walk outside no matter what the weather. His studies began at seven, and at eight a breakfast of milk and hard biscuits was doled out. From nine until noon and in the afternoon until dinner at five, classes were held in tactics, history of war, political science, Swedish, Finnish, Russian, and mathematics. After dinner there was no time for relaxation. All students were required to study and prepare for the classes of the next day. At nine there was a short pause for biscuits and at 9:15 p.m. the tattoo sounded to end the day.

It was hard to know what he detested most. Perhaps it was the lack of privacy, his close quarters at night, the stale air, the seven snoring boys with no space to themselves. Perhaps it was the distance from family and friends. He missed roaming and riding through his beloved forest, over beach and field. Were the fruit trees blooming now? Which dogs were whelping? Above all, was his horse well and being exercised? He surely missed the conversations at dinner with brothers and sisters, and particularly with his father and his uncles, on topics far from the narrow cadet world. He detested the loathsome salt herring and potatoes for dinner every afternoon at five, far indeed from the dinner cuisine at Villnäs under his Grandmother Eva's supervision, and Aunt Mimmi's fine tea in the afternoons. Once, the cadets had a treat. After the solemn funeral rites for a teacher who had killed himself, each cadet was given a mug of coffee and a piece of cake.

Gustaf hated his studies. Sports he loved, but even the riding was constrained, dreary endless hours of parade drills for the Tsar on his special feast days, every muscle taut, every movement stylized. Of course there were no gallops in open fields, racing with Johan or Sophie or Carl. Life was dull beyond belief, he wrote Sophie, his favorite subjects of music and literature barely touched. He disliked the military exercises and classes in weaponry. History was the closest to an interest, but the teachers were old duffers and their punishments extreme.

On his way home for a holiday in March, Gustaf's relief at escape exploded like a hidden bomb. He described the trip to Sophie: "My roommate and I left Fredrikshamn at 4:30 in the afternoon by horse and a drunken driver, we started to sing and continued through the night, we changed horses, I took the reins, we drove at breakneck speed. Again we changed horses. We got a jolly driver, the sleigh overturned, we raced with girls from the female school, we drove in one stretch to Lovisa . . . . [We had] new horses, we drove at full gallop and capsized, we arrived in Turku, we looked like waterfront bums."[30]

Gustaf rebelled almost from the beginning. He played silly pranks. Although he could have been first in his class had he tried—indeed, he actually succeeded the following year—he broke so many rules that he was not allowed to stick his nose outside the door for two semesters, according to his own words.[31] He was constantly being punished: for laughing in dancing class, for mumbling in classes whose teachers were old and boring, for laughing out loud when a teacher scolded him, for using bad language in class. This last earned him two days in the school's prison cell. There he made little bullets of his dinner bread, threw them on the floor and crawled on all fours to see if he could find them in the dark. That was one way of passing the slow hours. A greater crime was that he cheated on a written exam to help a classmate, and he cheated again by using another cadet's paper as his own. His incarceration in the Corps felt like a lifetime sentence in a dark and joyless prison, a mole's tunnel leading nowhere. He loathed the confining classes which bored him to tears. He even jumped out of a back window in an attempt to escape, but was caught. "I can breathe a sigh of relief now that three weeks have gone by," he wrote Sophie, "three weeks sooner until my escape from this nest."[32]

In his 17th year, in 1884, Gustaf was heartbroken. Constance Hisinger had just announced her engagement to one of his cousins. She had been his ideal, his dancing and tennis partner, his companion on long horseback rides in the country and sails in his boat, for long talks about things no one else would ever hear from him.

Only Sophie was privy to his heart, and to her he might have spoken about his love. He was often a guest in Constance's home, just as he eagerly visited other friends in neighboring manors, flirting, dancing, playing parts in theatricals. He had found out her plans one day when he was washing his white military gloves, an ordinary day, an ordinary occupation to mark the blow to his heart. When

Sophie told him, he had briefly shown bitterness. Then his mother's "English" upbringing of coldwater baths, hard mattresses and stoic forbearance to improve character, stood him in good stead. His hand must not tremble. He hid his feelings and complimented Constance for her good taste in a husband and his cousin for winning Constance. But thinking of these things again and again he wrote to Sophie, "Here it's just as dull as always, one annoyance after another. I look forward to the moment when I can turn my back on Finland forever and travel far away, God knows where to, but at least I'll be my own master."[33]

He dreamed of a transfer. The Pages' Corps in St. Petersburg was drawn from the bluest blood in the Russian empire and Europe, a world where he might hope that promotions and opportunities were not hindered by severe punishments for small infractions. There, in the Russian Corps, he could show what he was made of: that he had the heart and soul of a soldier. And from there, as he knew and wrote his benefactor, his mother's kindly brother Albert, he could be appointed to one of the top Russian regiments and be on his way in the world. Never again would he have to beg money from his kind Uncle Albert, or feel the shame of charity! Relatives in St. Petersburg with influence at the Tsar's court had already written to encourage him. The transfer orders would surely come, and day after anxious day he waited for a letter. He could be ready to leave in a matter of days. Gustaf wrote despairingly to Sophie: "I'm worried about my transfer, because if I fail this time, God knows what I'll do. I think I'll go to sea, because I can't exist here any more."[34] But no transfer letters came.

He had already written his father that he needed money, but there was no help from that quarter. His father regretted that he could not help Gustaf with a single coin. He was a scholarship student for that very reason. Aunts and uncles were all worried about Gustaf's handling of money, and considered him reckless. His misdeeds hardly seem catastrophic to a modern eye, for early in his cadet years it was his yearning for sweets that led him into overspending. The puritanical family elders on his mother's side invoked the image of his father and his financial catastrophe when Gustaf borrowed, not for the first time, a sum exceeding his pocket money.

When he expressed his dream of leaving the Cadet Corps, he was warned to remember that there were no scholarships to be had at the St. Petersburg Pages' Corps. Uncle Albert advised him to forget it, and gave all sorts of avuncular advice to help him form a good character, something he wasn't at all sure Gustaf was developing. His uncles in Finland and Stockholm felt that the society of rich young men in St. Petersburg would give him bad habits, financially and morally. They had to agree that the only safe plan was for Gustaf to stay in the Finnish Cadet Corps.

In Gustaf's last year, 1885-1886, a new commanding general of the Cadet Corps was appointed. He was an experienced officer both on the staff and in active command of troops. General Enckell was spare and strict, a man not given to smiling and certainly not to joking. The general had promised Gustaf a good recommendation if he improved his scholarship ranking. But the Russian school must seek him out officially. The general's word on Gustaf's behavior was summed up as "good", and that was not good enough, as the general must surely have known.

By November of his 18th year, Gustaf wrote his Uncle Albert "Everything I try fails. I thought I could transfer to the Pages' Corps, but now that's shot. I neither can nor want to be a good fellow and accept my fate."[35]

The only news he could have had at this bleak time were letters from home telling him that his little sister Annicka was ill and pining for Finland in her Russian boarding school, she, too, a free spirit, cooped up like a bird even more than he. Sophie and Calle and Eva, he knew, were writing to her. He too wrote an encouraging note inside Carl's letter to Annicka in an undated letter, probably late December, 1884, while he was still hoping to be in Petersburg with the Corps. "I hope the new year will bring my transfer to the Pages' Corps. That will be useful and enjoyable for me and you."[36] But in 1886, the news from her school was discouraging. Why had she been sent into this cruel exile? Now that she was so sick, why was she not rescued? Would they really see their little poet again? Such questions must have troubled him.

There was a threat of war between England and Russia in 1885-1886, and that made for some excitement. Gustaf's brothers and sisters used it as a spur on him: in a war, honors and promotions would come. But he looked with a cool eye on their attempts to cheer him. War-time vacancies in the officer ranks wouldn't help, he said, because there were endless replacements from the always freshly stocked Russian officer corps. He was condemned to the Finnish Cadet Corps. It would be a life of routine boredom, a provincial life in a tiny country where at best, as he bitterly thought to himself, he might become a postmaster. The boy was obviously going through a period of depression.

The crimes and punishments grew more frequent. He was repeatedly guilty of "lack of discipline" and "shameless lack of discipline," as the records read. Gustaf and two classmates were punished for absence without leave: they had taken off at dusk. He was defying authority and fate, and doing anything at all to change his life. It was as if he wanted by design to end his chances for a career in the Finnish army.[37]

In fact, that is what he did. Collecting straw from the stables, a daring friend and classmate made him a dummy the size of a man. He pushed and tied and shaped it, pulling a uniform coat over its form, stuffing stiff straw arms into the sleeves, slipping the dummy between the sheets at bedtime. By that time Gustaf was on his way to the nearest suburb. But now the story grows murky. Did he really go to an Inn . . . and from there to a place in the country where he knew a pretty girl? Did he hire himself a horse and cart to get there and spend the night in her arms? That is one version. In another he spent the night at the house of a district court clerk, an eminently respectable fellow well known to his family. Gustaf remembered into his old age the man's pate, as polished as an egg, his fine bushy beard and above all the songs he sang in his rich bass voice to entertain his young visitor. Legend suggests, though his memoirs do not, that Gustaf was inspired to drink many toasts, far too many to return to the Corps. A bed was improvised, a glass of milk placed on a bedside table. It was all very homelike. Was there a sharp knock on the door the next morning, just as dawn was breaking? If his temples were still pounding from drink, it would have been a gong from Hell. The Sergeant-Major of the Cadet Corps had come to wake the sleeping miscreant and take him back to the academy's prison cell, far too familiar already. The Captain on duty had discovered the substitute in his bed.

Otto, the friend who had made the dummy, was remanded to a cell for two days and forbidden home leave during Easter. But Gustaf's orders read that he was expelled and must leave that very day. He was not permitted a hearing. Gustaf made a brave show in front of his comrades. They laughed with him and slapped him on the back when he told them: "I'm going to Petersburg to enter the Cavalry Officer School, and then I'll become an officer in the Chevalier Guards."[38] And so he left. He would have been graduated in a few short weeks.

The boy's uncle Albert, informing his sister Hanna in Stockholm of Annicka's death at Smolny, mentions Gustaf's catastrophe in the same letter. "I should like to think," he writes, "that he understands he won't succeed if he doesn't settle down to be diligent. It's very sad that he should leave the Corps now that he's beginning to do well. He was first in the class and had been given high praise for his conduct."[39]

In a long life of successes and defeats, Gustaf never forgot the raw humiliation of this experience. His chances for a military career in Finland came to an end. With such a blemish on his name and record, what Russian regiment would accept him? It was, in an ironic twist of destiny, a major turning point in his life. It forced a change which would lead to an unimaginable career in the Russian military. It shaped the history of Finland.

Chapter 8

GUSTAF BEGINS LIFE IN RUSSIA

After the Cadet Corps fiasco and the almost simultaneous news of his youngest sister Annicka's death, Gustaf had to write Sophie that he had no money to travel to the funeral, nor any black clothes. "It was a heavy blow that struck us," he wrote, "when we, who have only one another to love and trust, lost our youngest sister."[40] A trip of three days would also cost him dearly in time, as he was still preparing for examinations to one or another of the Russian military establishments.

Now Gustaf had to put his thoughts in order for his future, something that loomed inexorably ahead without any of the usual youthful feeling of excitement and hope. There were several possibilities: a Finnish education for university entrance and a civil career; a Russian school with a university entrance as a prelude to a career in the Empire; or a Russian military career as a volunteer in a unit, with eventual entrance to a military institution and an officer's training.

His uncle now thought of sending him to a relative who ran a factory for ceramics in Charkov. This cousin, Baron Edvard Bergenheim, was well connected.

On his way to Charkov in the summer of 1886, Gustaf and an older cousin, Junne von Julin, were traveling companions and had many all-night discussions about possible careers. Russia needed engineers, and this possibility was weighed. The Russian marine cadet school was considered, but both this institution and the Russian army cadet corps would be barred by Gustaf's record at the Finnish corps. That disaster seemed a formidable barrier to his preferred prospects.

At the Bergenheims he began to think seriously about the Nikolayevskoye Cavalry School in St. Petersburg, an old fantasy of his. He could work hard and be ready to take his examination for the cavalry school in the fall of 1887. This indeed is how the matter was eventually resolved.

When he arrived in Charkov, Baron Bergenheim was pleased to find a splendid young man, well brought up, with a good mind, quite a surprise after the stories he had heard of Gustaf's heedless and giddy behavior. Edvard Bergenheim felt that Gustaf had been blessed with good fortune to be separated from the Corps, of which he was himself an alumnus.

Good-natured Uncle Albert had made an investment in this trip to Charkov, and Gustaf was careful to give an accounting of his expenses, including his trips to take lessons in Russian. He wrote his uncle that but for the enormous distances and tropical heat he would have walked. He reported that he had needed less money than expected.

Once home in Finland again, Gustaf prepared to take his exams for the university. His collection of family worriers was surprised by his conscientious studying. Uncle Albert was called upon again, sometimes to supply a partial wardrobe. A pair of trousers was needed and even a coat and vest as brother Carl's old ones were showing signs of exhaustion. Gustaf concentrated on learning Finnish (a language he would not fully master until later), and also trigonometry and physics. A bout of typhus felled him for some weeks; he was tended by Sophie and convalesced with the von Julins. By the spring of 1887 he won admission to the university with words of praise. His future education in Russia now need no longer depend on questionable references to shameful behavior from the Finnish Cadet Corps.

Not surprisingly, the happy news was of some concern for his family, especially Uncle Albert who paid the bills. But it was his Finnish-born Godmother who would become an important ally. Alfhild, Baroness Scalon de Coligny, had married into a leading Russian family and she believed in Gustaf. Her husband was an influential cabinet minister. Her sister, Baroness Aminoff, married to a lieutenant general, was also a godmother whose husband had held regimental commands. Gustaf was a favorite of both, and they were a presence at the Russian Court. A vacancy was found and he was admitted to the Nikolayevskoye Cavalry School, after successfully taking the examinations at the end of August, 1887.

When his appointment was official, Gustaf wrote his brothers and sisters. He left them his worldly goods: his riding crop to Johan and his books to Carl. His old worn shoes he would keep for himself. On that very afternoon of September 15, 1887, he would for the first time in his life wear a Russian uniform. He signed himself "Gustaf the Apostate", an ironic bow to hereditary family feelings about their dangerous neighbor he was now to serve. But at his farewell dinner with Finnish classmates, Gustaf solemnly spoke of never forgetting his country.

He swore the oath of loyalty to the Tsar required for the Nikolayevskoye Cavalry School in October, 1887, signing his name Baron Carl Gustaf Emil Mannerheim of Finland. He wasted no time, but became the first in his squadron to win his spurs. Long ago as a boy hiding from the grownups in his attic lair at Villnäs, he had dreamed of becoming a knight. The epic war poetry from Napoleonic times that all the young Mannerheims had learned by heart reverberated in his head. The beginning of this new life must have seemed a partial fulfillment of his old fancies.

There were languages to learn, Russian, German and French; as well as Russian literature, the natural sciences, the study of horses and military studies. Athletics included fencing, gymnastics, and, of course, riding instruction. Riding in the ring, or manège, was emphasized with the kind of acrobatics the Cossacks boasted of.[41]

In a letter to Sophie of January 20, 1888 Gustaf wrote: "Thanks to Aunt Hanna's shirts and wool socks I've been in fine fettle. Without these I don't know how I'd have managed the cold we've had. Our life is as dull and changeless as ever. Last week three French army representatives visited, who admired our discipline, riding etc."[42]

His second year in the school went well, but for an illness which forced a leave of absence in Finland at Fiskars. In May 1889, the young man finished second in the class of young noblemen, rather unexpected for one who had learned Russian only recently. The language lessons had been helped by Gustaf's visit to his Godmother, the Baroness Alfhild, at her country estate Lukianovka in the summer of 1887. When Uncle Albert had expressed his usual concern about wasting time in frivolous fun Gustaf assured him that he was learning Russian very well indeed, thanks to some beautiful young Russian ladies also visiting his Godmother. He had also taken formal lessons from a Russian army captain, though his accent never lost its Finnish intonation.

One incident of July, 1889 involved tipsy behavior and rude remarks to the duty officer. Mannerheim never forgot it. He earned arrest and incarceration in a sour room with an icon, yellow walls and furniture nailed to the floor. His rank was lowered, but restored a month later with the notation that as camp guard he had thwarted theft of military property.[43] The demotion, as he knew, could have put a stop to his career. Drinking was impossible to avoid; it was an important and convivial affair among officers. Ten glasses of champagne were considered obligatory, but Mannerheim forever learned to do his drinking in such a way that he stayed sober.

A few days after Mannerheim's reinstatement, Alexander III congratulated the young noblemen on their promotions. The order was tucked in under the vest, and each young man was saluted and complimented by officers he met in the city. Mannerheim was invited to celebrate at the Scalons.

Gustaf was posted as cornet, lowest ranking officer in the cavalry, and the one carrying the colors. He was now attached to the 15th Alexandrisky Dragoon Regiment stationed in a town in Russian Poland, Kalisz, on the border of Germany. He reported for duty October 1, 1889. It was not, as he cautiously wrote his Uncle Albert, a sophisticated assignment. The officers had little respect for their chief, their wives were simple and poorly educated, and there was no social companionship. When the daily duties were done, all repaired to the town bars. Gustaf noticed the anti-Semitism typical of a Polish town. It was his first brush with this prejudice, one that has been and is, foreign to Finland.

The cavalry maneuvers on chill November days, the Russian neglect of the territory, the daily scandals and arrests at headquarters, were offset by the work entrusted to Gustaf, of shaping up the rough Russian peasant recruits. Adding to his experience were forced marches, maneuvers with other regiments, the orders from a "wild" Cossack general. He was assigned from his regiment as orderly to the larger imperial maneuvers. This would give him experience of active service with armed Russian units in the field and observations on how they operated in this terrain, all valuable to his future in the Russo-Japanese war and World War I.

His Aunt Hanna in Stockholm, Uncle Albert at home in Finland, the Bergenheims in Charkov were all well aware of Gustaf's ambition to join the Chevalier Guards, but his Godmother was the one who could help him most. She moved in court circles, aware of the hurdles that met a young man in search of a place in the Chevalier Guards. Ideally he should have an aristocratic name, be wealthy and have excellent connections at Court. His upbringing should have been impeccable, his past behavior thoroughly scanned and his family tree scrupulously examined.

Baroness Alfhild talked to her friend, lady-in-waiting to the Empress, about her godson's ambition. As she hoped, her words were forwarded to the Tsar himself. The Tsarina's recommendations, as honorary chief of the regiment, were attended to. In October, 1890, the order was signed to move the cornet Baron Mannerheim from Kalisz to St. Petersburg to take his entrance exam to "Her Majesty Empress Maria Feodorovna's regiment."

The Guards officers' most important duties were their attendance on the Tsar and his family for state occasions. Gustaf jokingly wrote home that he had noticed a serious shortage of tall officers in his new regiment, and perhaps he might stand a chance of being chosen an Honor Guard. His sister Sophie had remarked on his size, too. "He's a giant, though his width doesn't match his height," she had written her Aunt Hanna in Stockholm.[44]

When he wasn't busy steeplechasing, Gustaf cut a wide swath in St. Petersburg. He had sent a photo home of himself in his new uniform: tight elkskin trousers, a scarlet vest with the grand silver star of Andrew emblazoned on back and front, lacquered black boots reaching well over the knees, and a helmet crowned with the Tsar's silver double eagle, somewhat sarcastically nicknamed "the Dove" by the young officers. Two stout men helped "shake" the new recruit into his dampened trousers, powdered soap sprinkled inside, pulled onto bare skin. They fit exactly but caused suffering as they dried for 24 hours, after which the newly uniformed man received a two-day leave. For a Chevalier Guardist, seven different uniforms were required.[45]

Gustaf was making easy progress in the glittering St. Petersburg society which had opened its doors to the young officer candidates of his cavalry school. The Empress had herself given the officers tickets to the ballet and theatres, where they were escorts for young noblewomen attending their last years of school. Gustaf had been to a ball at Smolny Institut the year after his sister Annicka's death there. He was well on his way to learning the ways of elegance in the incredible splendor of the last Russian Tsars.

One thing in particular troubled Gustaf's family, especially Uncle Albert, his brothers Carl and Johan, his sister Sophie and their father Count Carl Robert Mannerheim. They were uneasy that this quick-witted Gustaf of theirs might become "Russified," too Russian in his thoughts. That sometimes happened to young Finns who saw their future in the Great Russian Empire, with all its wealth and fascinating opportunities. This distressed them more than Gustaf's need of money, though that was also an anxiety. Somebody had wangled money for his uniforms from a special purse of the Tsar's, but still he needed more. He was expected to live the expensive life of a Chevalier Guardist, to show off Russian might and the richness of its many-colored cultures. Gustaf was not the only Finn in this crack regiment, but he was a poor boy competing with the most ancient and honored titles in the whole of the Empire. His family fretted particularly because he was now so successful in knowing exactly what to do, and in his new regiment would be under the influence of the sons of powerful families—not necessarily the most admirable or virtuous of young men. Who could resist all that glitter? Careful and frugal Uncle Albert, always helping him with cash and advice, was ill at ease.

Gustaf's brother Carl wrote a scolding letter to him, saying that Gustaf had expressed some political views that were entirely foreign. In fact, he had found Gustaf snobbish for the first time in his life, and Carl marked that as unpleasant. But their father tried to mend everything by making a joke of his sons' differences. He had, he said, one Swedish son, (August, still in school in Sweden), one Finn, (Carl), one Dane, (Johan, taking agriculture courses in Denmark) and one Russian, (Gustaf). And so the differences were mended if not entirely explained, and never marred the brothers' affection for one another, though it was tested often.

Gustaf seemed to know precisely what he must do. He must learn the arts and weapons of the soldier, the skills of the diplomat, the courtier's easy grace, and these could all be learned at the center of Russian power. Did he have a foretaste of the future? One must assume rather that he was consciously following an honorable path, as other Finns had done, serving the Russian Tsar, the Grand Duke of Finland, and carving out a career for himself. He could hardly forget his own family's role in Finnish diplomacy, his great-grandfather's strategy in securing Finland's ancient rights, negotiating with the Tsar himself. That Russian connection had been a vital part of the family chronicle for nearly a century. His service under Russian arms was therefore a natural step to take.

Some time during her first year home in Finland in 1891, his sister Eva offered her inheritance from their maternal grandmother Louise von Julin to help Gustaf meet his great expenses. Although Gustaf's absent father had become bankrupt, the von Julins' own considerable assets were untouched. Eva's generosity was by no means unique among the brothers and sisters, who throughout their lives all helped one another. Gustaf was grateful for her help, and accepted it as a loan to be paid back.

In more recent times, Mannerheim's problems with anti-Semitism arose when Finland was forced to be allied with Germany in the early 1940s, fighting a common foe. Finland's very existence had been threatened; the Russians had bombed Helsinki in 1939, and despite the peace agreement of 1940, the Russians attacked Finland the day the Nazis invaded Russia in 1941.

As Commander-in-Chief of Finnish forces, Mannerheim was an ally of Hitler (after the Winter War of 1939-40, and during the Continuation War of 1941-44). He refused to allow persecution of Finnish Jews. Stig Jägerskiöld, in his seventh of an eight-volume biography, writes:

> "It is clear that Mannerheim at an early stage had come to a sharply negative opinion of Hitler. Mannerheim's strong feeling for law, tolerance and understanding led to his repugnance for the German dictatorship. The politics of violence, manifested in Germany from 1933, and later in 1938 in Austria, the anti-Semitism and tyranny of opinion revolted him . . . . [His] distance from Nazism was strongly apparent in the Jewish question. With his humanitarian point of view, Mannerheim was a stranger to anti-Semitism.

He reacted strongly against the discrimination of Jews. This was observed. When the National Socialist politics against the Jewish citizens radically sharpened in 1942, Finland ran the risk of being placed under the same German demands as the Norwegian Quislings had agreed to: the domestic Jews would be handed over to Germany and the concentration camps. One could expect such demands during the trip Himmler planned to take to Finland in 1942 . . . Mannerheim declared then, that he as Commander in Chief never would agree to similar proceedings against any soldier in his army, or against any relative of such a man. Only over his dead body would something like this happen. This was brought to Himmler's attention . . . . On Mannerheim's orders, [infantry general] Talvela is said to have tried to influence Himmler about the Jewish Finns. Probably this conversation is one of the reasons for Himmler's successive actions against Talvela, which only with difficulty could be stopped."[46]

Jägerskiöld abridged and translated a one-volume English edition of his work. In it he continues the story of Mannerheim's reaction to Hitler's policy: "[Mannerheim] successfully opposed all German attempts to carry out Hitler's racial policy with its persecution of the Jews . . . . German demands for the hand over [sic] of Jewish refugees had been handled in similar fashion."

Wuorinen, in his *Finland and World War II*, writes: "Finally, it must be stated that the position of those Jews who were Finnish citizens did not suffer the slightest change during the war, nor did the Germans make any demands in this respect because they knew in advance that they would have been firmly refused . . . In the fall of 1942, an attempt was made, apparently by some subordinate officials, to expel Jewish refugees who had arrived since the spring of 1938. Before the effort was brought into the open—it aroused a storm of protest when it became known—eight refugees had been expelled from the country. The laborite, V. Tanner, was among those who raised their voices on behalf of the Jews and saw to it that no further deportations occurred."[47]

Gustaf Mannerheim, Chevalier Guardist

Chapter 9

A RUSSIAN MARRIAGE

Many of Mannerheim's Russian officer colleagues regarded military service as a way of passing the time before assuming roles at family estates, or in the diplomatic or civil service. But Gustaf Mannerheim was a hardworking professional cavalryman. It was his responsibility to train young soldiers with one year of service, and take guard duty in the Winter Palace. Later, even one of his enemies referred to the young soldiers' review as "brilliantly handled," citing a complimentary note in regimental orders.[48]

Gustaf's first meeting with Anastasia Arapova, who would become his bride, was at "La Balle Rose," in February 1891. The ladies were dressed in ball gowns of rose, with shoes and gloves to match, all embroidered in different patterns of black. There Gustaf was introduced to Anastasia by her cousin. Only three days later Anastasia's uncle, Maj. Gen. Konstantin Arapov, a member of the Tsars' suite, invited the cornet to a family ball; a series of balls followed in the winter, and one in March at the Winter Palace. This was not for the regiment's enjoyment, they were reminded, but a fulfillment of duty: there was to be no standing around in groups, and the rule of one waltz only per young lady was strictly enforced.

Gustaf's godmother Alfhild was ready, as always, to put her influence to work for her godson. It is said that she arranged his marriage. Anastasia was a girl with an old noble name, considered a good match because of her elegant relatives and even more because of her rich purse. Anastasia's father, a general, had also served in the Chevalier Guards. After his death, her mother was married to a Polish prince for the last few years of her life. Anastasia was related by marriage to military and diplomatic families of Russian importance; her sister was married to a Baltic Count, also a Chevalier Guardist.

Gustaf had been living on Crown property, in three rooms and a hallway with quarters for his servant and groom, a stable for eight horses and a coach house. It cost him a month's pay. But the first and most important purchase was his horse, of a specific size and color brown. Gustaf was proud that his horse was one of the best in the regiment, bought in Breslau to avoid the steep prices of Petersburg. Before long he had sold it for twice as much, and bought from his friend Pjotr Arapov a brown gelding named Mery-Boy. It was at this time that his 21-year old sister Eva gave her hard pressed brother her own share of their grandmother's estate.

Gustaf's godmother made a call, according to convention, on her acquaintance Madame Maria Zvegintsova, the maternal aunt of a rich and marriageable girl. Their conversation led to Anastasia and Gustaf. The two ladies came to an understanding, and revealed their thoughts to Anastasia. The young woman had remarked, in answer to the question of how she regarded him, "Who wouldn't want the elegant Baron Gustaf? His name is on everyone's tongue."[49]

No one had ever called Anastasia, or Nata as her family called her, beautiful, but she was said to have a graceful figure, though a trifle thickset. She was rather tall, with a round face and blue, protruding eyes. Exactly when Gustaf was informed about the conversations between his Godmother and Madame Zvegintsova no one knows. At parties, Anastasia had the habit of pointing Gustaf out to her friends as her secret fiancé. Gustaf found himself invited to see her dance in a performance at the palace of Countess Kleinmichel, a glittering society hostess.[50] Anastasia's aunt overlooked no opportunities. She made sure her niece saw Gustaf at his best in horsemanship competitions. He took part in stag hunts, and, riding his best horse, won first prize in the race of March 11, jumping the 14 difficult hurdles.

Gustaf went to Moscow to propose in December, 1891. His regimental chief, Prince Kara-Georgevitch, gave his consent to the marriage. Anastasia satisfied the requirements of the regiment's marriage code, with her rich relatives and large dowry; their engagement was announced on March 19, 1892. In April, Gustaf became a member of the Imperial racing assembly in Tsarskoje Selo, which gave him entry to all competitions.

No one in the Mannerheim family was happy to hear that Gustaf was engaged to a Russian, but they all tried to put their disappointment aside. Sophie met her and reported that she was merry and musical, and a lover of sports. She thought it interesting that Anastasia's great-aunt had married the Finnish Minister Secretary of State, Count Armfelt, thus giving her a Finnish tie. Eva and Sophie tried to see the best in a young woman they found hard to know, but they liked her breezy way and her love of sports. Nevertheless, Gustaf's sisters felt they were losing a brother rather than gaining a sister, and his brothers were not taken with the idea of his Russian marriage, no matter how conveniently rich the girl was.

The wedding, in May of 1892, was a small one. Gustaf's brother Carl and father were there for the Russian ceremony in the regimental church, and the Lutheran rites in the home of the bride's maternal aunt. Gustaf promised to raise their children in the orthodox faith, but refused to be converted himself. When the couple boarded the train for their honeymoon at Anastasia's estate Uspenskoje, near Moscow, they looked happy, and Gustaf wrote Sophie a cheerful letter after the wedding. He felt the religious question would not be complicated now, and that his bride was not "too Russian" as he had feared earlier.[51]

At Court balls, after Gustaf's introduction to the Empress, she made a point of speaking to Gustaf and Anastasia, whose family had served in the regiment. She remembered, too, Gustaf's father, and his grandfather's work as an entomologist.

After their honeymoon, Gustaf brought Anastasia home to Finland and Sweden. His relatives liked her well enough and Aunt Hanna agreed that she looked European, not Russian, which was a compliment.

The young couple visited Grandmama Eva at Villnäs. The old lady wrote a very frank letter to her son-in-law, Adolf Nordenskiöld,[52] who had long been close to her grandson. To say the least, she was not enthusiastic about his bride. She wrote that her son, Carl Robert, "looks pleased with his ugly daughter-in-law. She will certainly need gold plating to be considered beautiful."[53] Gustaf had arrived in lordly style, she wrote, by rented steamer direct to Villnäs, and departed in the same way. Grandmama's tone was mocking.

The fact that Anastasia was a rich girl may have been the driving force behind Baroness Scalon de Coligny's search for a suitable bride for Gustaf, but probably also had a good deal to do with Gustaf's agreement to marry her. It is obvious that he enjoyed her wealth in the early part of their short marriage. But he was motivated also by a strong personal sense of obligation, given the social expectations of the day. That same sense later impelled him to maintain contact with her long after she had chosen to leave him, long after she had lost her fortune.

Professor Leonid Vlasov, with access to Russian archival material, writes that Mannerheim had a period of "genuine family happiness" in the first apartment he and Anastasia occupied. It was a light and airy home with a large staff to look after the twelve rooms, three stables and four carriage houses.[54] Gustaf was at first enchanted with his young wife, their palatial estate and his new ability to buy fine horses thanks to his wife's dowry. The young Guardsman won praise for outdistancing Petersburg's best riders, for his elegance and cool head. The newspapers reported that he made "games of jumping the hurdles."[55] His favorite horse Lilli had "flown" over the water jump, the only one to clear the hurdles.

Nata's and Gustaf's daughters, Anastasia (Stasie) and Sophie, were born in 1893 and 1895. It was an era when upper-class parents spent little time with their children, leaving their upbringing to governesses. The young Mannerheims shared the same pleasures in social life and music, although Nata often went astray in the hat shops and stores with luxury items. Both of them were fascinated by Charles Fabergé's wares, particularly his silver miniatures. Gustaf continued his regimental life and was promoted to lieutenant, his new gold braid handed over by the officers with a glass of champagne.

Nata and Gustaf moved into new quarters. At Christmas they attended a festive religious celebration, and had a party in their gaily decorated apartment that lasted until six in the morning. There are records of balls and weddings, theaters, receptions, dances, blinis at the Zvegintsovs, races and prizes won by Gustaf. The Mannerheims took their daughter Stasie on a trip to Biarritz in 1894, and on their return moved to a large new house with a stable for four horses. In 1895, Gustaf competed at the Michael manège on his Irish horse Trick, winning second prize. Two weeks later, Trick again won a prize, and horse and owner were admired by Countess Betsy Sjuvalova. He was invited home to see Betsy's album with its drawings of the finest Russian steeds.

Alexander III died in 1894, mourned and loved by most of Gustaf's countrymen. He had been faithful to his sworn oath of letting Finland keep her own laws and institutions and her Lutheran faith, although some slavophile tendencies were alarming. His son, the new Tsar Nicholas II, was less well known. The Finns kept up their watch, suspicious that the new regime in St. Petersburg had designs on changing the old Grand Duchy of Finland with its autonomous Finnish laws, into a Russian province.

The coronation of Nicholas II had been planned meticulously. Stately Honor Guards were needed. These were always drawn from the Chevalier Guards officers, whose duties were to attend the Tsar and be on hand for every event of the coronation week. It was the final spectacle of the Russian Empire's glory and broad reach through the world. The Imperial Russian vastness stretched from the Grand Duchy of Finland and the Arctic tundra in the north, south along the central European borders and Turkey, east across the frontiers of Iran, Afghanistan, China and Mongolia to the port of Vladivostok on the Sea of Japan, and northeast to the Bering Strait. The Guards' moment of glory had arrived.

Gustaf was the sum of style and tradition. His upbringing at Villnäs under his grandmother's sharp eye and the strong influence in his mother's family of the "English gentleman ideal," were the background of his success in Russian military life and society. His attendance at Russian balls and ceremonies, his presence at Court and knowledge of languages, even his steeplechasing, had begun to give Gustaf the aura of command.

Four days before the coronation, the Guards had been moved to Moscow, to be in attendance as the Tsar and his wife were to make their formal progress to the Kremlin. Fifty thousand troops formed on both sides along the five-mile long procession route, a wall of Guards regiments, Grenadiers, Cossacks, soldiers from all the corners of the Empire. The Tsarina and her mother-in-law, the Dowager Empress, rode in gold and jewel-bedecked carriages drawn by eight roans, and the Tsar himself was astride one. Priests in their golden robes stood outside the churches swinging their censers before the holiest icons. At the entrance to the Kremlin, the most exalted priests of the Russian Church waited to bless the Tsar and his wife on a platform dressed in royal purple. Inside the Kremlin were the groups sent to represent the Empire's many parts. Gustaf remembered that his maternal grandmother's father had been a delegate for Finland at the Tsar's grandfather's coronation.

The coronation day of May 26, 1896, dawned in glorious weather. Early in the morning the Dowager Empress, wearing her diamond crown, had walked from the palace to the Cathedral under an ostrich-feathered canopy, surrounded by officers from the Chevalier Guards. Chevalier troops massed around one side of the palace courtyard, and at 9 a.m. the long coronation procession began. Chevalier Guardsmen led, followed by pages, nobles, officials, heads of Cossack tribes, and delegates from all the Empire's peoples. The royal insignia were carried: crowns, spires, swords. Gustaf, one of the Honor Guards, marched just in front of the canopy on the Tsar's left hand; his partner, Andrej von Knorring on the right. The Tsar and Tsarina walked under the baldachin borne by 20 generals; grand dukes with their wives followed, then foreign royalties, ending with ladies-in-waiting in court dress, a division of the Chevalier Guards, the generals and aides-de-camp. The many voices of the bells pealed out in darkly sonorous to silvery tones as the procession passed across the great Kremlin Square and into the Uspensky Church for the crowning.

An old friend of the family in Finland wrote home to describe the scene with the kind of humor Grandmama Eva enjoyed: "It was pitiful to see the poor ancient generals who had to hold up the Imperial canopy, tottering this way and that with their burden. I was afraid some of the old boys would have strokes. Their backs were hunched and they were sweating and miserable in their fur caps . . . Gustaf walked in front of the canopy with saber drawn . . ."

In the autumn of that year, Nicholas made a point of speaking to Mannerheim, thanking him for his part in the coronation day. This was the poised and courteous Tsar whom Gustaf remembered, and whose portrait he always kept in a place of honor.

But on the home front, there were signs of trouble. Countess Sjuvalova invited Baron Mannerheim to attend her charity ball. Gossip had linked the two and it caused a storm at home. Anastasia had in small ways tried to please her husband. As long as they owned her castle Uspenskoje, near Moscow, a Swedish flag flew from the rooftop mast, and the servants were dressed in blue and gold livery, the Swedish colors. (In Russia, Swedes were considered "more refined" than Finns, who often came to Russia as servants and were thought of as stupid and boorish.)

They soon faced financial difficulties as well. Uspenskoje with its forty-four rooms and marble staircase, its park and woodlands and magnificent stables had to be sold in 1894. In an effort to run another of Anastasia's three estates, Appricken, in Kurland, as a business enterprise, Gustaf started a dairy and fish hatchery, but they were not successful. The third estate, Aleksandrovka in Voronez, suffered poor harvests and negligent tenant farmers. In 1895 a stock market crash left Gustaf unable to make the planned reforms there. He continued to try to make the estate a commercial success. In 1898 Gustaf was still interested in horse breeding. He bought five fillies, four of them broodmares, for Anastasia as the basis of a trotter stud farm. He dreamed of buying Villnäs but his Aunt Mimmi refused even to let him rent it. He and Johan corresponded about buying jointly one or another of the Finnish manors, but that dream was not to be. Eventually all Anastasia's estates were sold.

In 1897 Gustaf was ordered from his Chevalier Guards duties and seconded as assistant Director of the Imperial Stables in St. Petersburg, though still kept on the rolls of the Guards. This was not a ceremonial or empty post, but one of importance and of interest to Gustaf. He was responsible for the purchase, training, care and harnessing of the Tsar's horses, and finding four-in-hands for the Dowager Empress. Appointments for the post were courtiers and cavalry officers: the Director had himself been commander of the Chevalier Guards. Gustaf's knowledgeable brother Johan went with him for horse purchases of his own, the two traveling to England, Germany, Austria-Hungary, France and Belgium. On one of these trips Gustaf fell with his horse and broke his leg; during a visit to the imperial stables in Berlin, a horse kicked and smashed his knee. By good fortune, the damage was not permanent and his career as an active cavalry officer did not come to an end.

His new assignment entitled him to an elegant house in St. Petersburg and apartments in some of the imperial castles, and despite the difficulties on their estates his wife's money gave him the means to keep up an appropriate lifestyle. But at home the marriage was fraying. Nata's jealous attacks and teary storms led Gustaf to spend longer hours at work. Professor Vlasov's research reveals lists of street addresses where guards officers visited in the evenings; Gustaf was a regular visitor at Countess Sjuvalova's house at Fontanka 21, and Bolshoi Prospect 102, where he called on a beautiful young actress, Vera Sjuvalova.[56]

But the problems were not only his attraction to ladies. He was something of a martinet at home, with a sense of order to the point of pettiness. In everyday life his tongue could be sarcastic, a sometimes cruel family trait difficult for an outsider to deal with. His younger daughter, Sophie, remembered that everyone had been afraid of her father except the horses and dogs. Years after the collapse of his marriage, Gustaf wrote his sister Sophie about his wife's disorganized habits, so at variance with his own, her seemingly incurable laziness and a deliberate contrariness. She was jealous of the women who were attracted to Gustaf. Her own behavior with men drew criticism. One of Gustaf's biographers has suggested she was trying to make her husband jealous.[57]

Nata avoided duties at home and spent her evenings with a friend, Princess Sjachovskaja, and other ladies. One of them was chairman of various Red Cross divisions. The ladies formed a "Women's Council" to advise Anastasia on a strategy. They decided that she should take a course in nursing at the St. George Hospital, without telling her husband. The Dowager Empress issued a summons to send medicines for Russian troops in China, where the Boxer Rebellion had spread. In June, 1900, hospitals in Petersburg and other cities in the empire were sending the first contingent of doctors and nurses to China. A Red Cross group was even then being readied to leave for the Russian Far East.

At the end of her course, Anastasia secured money and an order to leave for the Russian Far East with a Red Cross delegation. She arranged to have her daughters stay with her maternal aunt, and after a religious service at the St. George Hospital departed in late August. She served in military hospitals in Chita, Harbin and Tsitsihar.

Meanwhile, Gustaf had been on a committee to register horses in Novo Aleksandrovsk. On his return to Petersburg, his new orderly gave him the first news of Nata's departure. The shaken husband called on Maria Zvegintsova, Nata's aunt, who did not hesitate to be very frank. He began to watch for news from China, looking for his wife's name in the news reports.

He did have a letter from his wife, posted from Singapore. He wrote Eva in December, 1900, of his relief at hearing from the Red Cross that Nata had been sent to Khabarovsk, a city of some consequence as it was the Governor General's residence, with rail service to Vladivostok. In the same letter he mentions that Countess Sjuvalova "whom I met the other day, asked me to find out from Louis about her latest order—a cupboard and something else."[58] Louis Sparre was designing and building furniture for this important lady.

In September Anastasia returned with a medal "in memory of the China expedition 1900-1901," and the pain of a broken leg. She and Gustaf divided the house in half. They barely spoke. Nevertheless, in a letter to Eva dated December 22, 1901, Gustaf writes admiringly. "If anyone had told me one and a half years ago that [Nata] was capable of doing what she's done, I wouldn't have believed it . . . . serving and cheering sick soldiers." He writes of his daughters, and wonders how "they will be raised to become uncomplicated and sturdy women."[59]

Gustaf's father came for an unexpected visit, to discover what he could; his son said not a word about his marriage. In 1902, Nata left again, this time for good, taking their little girls with her. One was nine, the other seven. Anastasia traveled to France, where she was to live the rest of her life.

Gustaf stayed at his post in the Imperial Stables until he was appointed Commander of the Model Squadron in 1903. "Thanks for your congratulations," he wrote Johan in May. "Ordinarily I could hardly have wished for more interesting work, but after the last 12 months of upsets, I don't know what I want."[60]

During the Russo-Japanese War, Anastasia kept in touch with Gustaf's father in order to have news of him. The spouses corresponded only about financial matters, and the girls' upbringing. Their views were sharply different. Gustaf's daughters grew up in the Russian Orthodox faith, and their education had to be left in Anastasia's hands. With the failure of his marriage, Gustaf had no resources to improve what he considered a poor choice of schools for the girls, or to make a home for them. His military career was an obstacle; he frequently had to be away. Repeatedly he tried to have them in Finland in the care of his sister Sophie. He even removed them against Anastasia's wishes from their strict Catholic school. He would have liked a sporty outdoor life for them, and an avoidance of the society atmosphere in St. Petersburg.

Eva, writing from Cannes in 1904, made an effort to communicate with Nata, and admired her little girls. Her heart ached for Gustaf, unable to be with or guide his daughters. Gustaf wrote Eva in April 1904, thanking her for her understanding. "Of course it hurt me deeply to have affirmation of what I long since have thought. As you can understand, it makes matters doubly worse to be completely helpless. I can do nothing." About his children he wrote, "To try to influence their upbringing would, knowing Nata, only make her more strict and pursue a course diametrically opposed to my advice. On principle, I have let them know me as little as possible . . . to prevent their being torn."[61]

Gustaf and Anastasia were legally divorced in Finland in 1919. In 1936, shortly before her death, he went to Paris to see her. Their world had been shattered in wars and revolutions, but now in this last meeting their own wounds were healed. He revealed his sense of loss and wasted years in a letter to Eva, moved at the strangeness of their discovering one another after so many years.[62] The meeting was both penance and absolution.

Gustaf made his decision to seek active service as an officer in the Tsar's army, to fight on the Russian front in the Far East war. He had given his personal oath to this still absolute monarch, considered, as his forebears had been, the personification of Russia. Gustaf turned to his career to fulfill his energy and intelligence, finding in it a purpose and a help in stifling the pain of his failed marriage. He could not know the future, but he had been liberated, unwittingly, to prepare for his eventual role in his country's emergence from Russian rule. His unhappy marriage deprived him of personal happiness; its ending freed him for a national calling.

The predatory hunt for a husband by Anastasia's family, ambition on Gustaf's part, perhaps even greed, played their parts in the drama; there was apparently no affection to cement the couple in any lasting way. The failure was a tragedy for both, but it can be seen as an important link in Gustaf's development as a national figure.

In Finland, the months and years that followed the coronation were anxious ones. The Russian Governor General of Finland, appointed by Nicholas in 1899, was hated and distrusted. The time would come, in the next century, when a Finn would assassinate him. That time was drawing near.

Gustaf at Czar Nicholas' Coronation
(to the left of the Tsar)

Chapter 10

ART AND DOMESTICITY, 1893-95

Eva Mannerheim Sparre, having returned from her wedding trip, continued teaching classes at the Ateneum. She instructed some students privately, and executed commissions in leather work. She needed, as always, to have an independent income. This was a lifelong desire she could fulfill with her art work and later her writing.

No matter how meager their finances, the Sparres always seemed to be able to afford household help. This speaks volumes on how little servants were paid in those days. Eva's girl-of-all-work during this period was Fanny, who had the additional merit of being a culinary expert, her delicious "pommes de neige" a favorite of their friends. Fanny was undemanding, and in accordance with the custom of the times lived in the kitchen. The bed was her only private nook. Her cooking helped make the Sparre home central to the pleasure of their friends, and freed Eva to be an artist.

Louis had put some of his work into the autumn exhibit of 1893 in Helsinki, and sold one piece, but another painting was roundly criticized, even mocked. He doubted himself, and longed to flee to the wilderness and search his artistic soul.

Seeking the solitude of a farm in Sotkamo, the Sparres made a winter sleigh trip to northern Finland in February of 1894. Starting out in Kuopio with the help of their artist friend Juhani Aho's brother, who had ordered the sleigh and driver for them, they traveled with books and painting equipment. Louis, his mustache and heavy eyebrows etched in ice, kept warm in a black fur with its collar standing well over his ears, and Eva was wrapped in grey lamb, stretched out in comfort beside him. Their feet, tucked into felt boots, were warm under heavy fur covers. They visited their artist friend Pekka Halonen's parents in their wilderness home, where his mother played songs on her kantele.

They stayed at a primitive old inn, with a smoke hole in the roof and blackened timbers. There the people on the place slept on benches along the wall, while the children lived on the floor. The sleigh horse was also led into the tiny building for the night to keep warm.

In Kajana they found room in an inn they had visited the summer before. There, in a forest of stacked skis and lively traders buying and selling horses, furs, fish and all manner of wares, the Sparres bought food and skis for camping. Then it was on to the final destination, a large peasant farm on the road to Kuhmoniemi. It was a harum-scarum trip in melting snow. They raced with inebriated traders who cursed and shouted, trying to pass them, the drunkards driving headlong into drifts along the road.

For the remaining winter weeks Eva and Louis were installed in their little two-room guest cottage. Eva lit the stove early in the mornings and made breakfast of hot cocoa, biscuits and butter. A small army of women marched in to make beds, stow wood for the tiled stove, gossip and sweep. Eva's and Louis's skis were outside, waiting to take them over the snow fields toward the Vuokatti mountains. Louis found a favorite theme for his painting "Christmas Night" in the big room of the main house. The atmosphere was just what he wanted: smoke-stained beams competing with pale gas lamplight in a corner, the rest plunged in darkness. His models for Mary were Eva or his hosts' daughters. They posed, taking turns in the cottage by the light of a gas lamp, two peasants in Lapp boots kneeling at Mary's feet. Later, Eva helped him make a frame for this painting, in "old Karelian" style, its gilding rubbed off against a red background.

The long, cold, slow spring of 1894 brought Louis out of a heavy depression. Eva, never inclined to talk about her feelings, nevertheless relieved her anxiety by writing her brother Calle. In a letter of May 31, 1894, she writes, "Now I'm going to take you into my confidence and ask you to promise silence." All during the autumn Louis had not been himself, tiring quickly, spending days in bed, unable to do anything but fret. During the winter he had often felt so sick and dispirited that he could hardly lift a finger, and his work suffered. Their wallets were empty as a result. She had never spoken of these things and tried to calm her fears by writing.[63]

Eva might not have had any realistic sense, before this, of Louis's volatile temperament. Their daughter-in-law, Anna, wrote me about her memories of Louis and his depressions. He could sit with his head in his hands during a whole dinner, and say not a word. Worse still, he could, as in a trance, talk with invisible persons, play-acting a whole scene. Anna discussed her observations with Eva, who said she had lived through such moments during her entire marriage, with the hopeless sense of not being able to reach Louis.

In her May, 1894, letter to Calle, Eva hoped he might come to visit them, but warned that he should be prepared for a cuisine of meatballs and nights on a hard mattress. Both Sparres felt the weight of their isolation, and their food supplies shrank—there was even a scarcity of raisins in the sweet soup. By June they had returned to Kajana, renting a portion of a girls' school for the summer. Louis pursued peasant themes, a tar-burning scene with clouds of smoke, young birches in flames and tar running in a gilded stream through wooden pipes into barrels. Louis slept during the day, to paint the magic of the midsummer night sun, while Eva chose to sleep out on a hillside on a bed of woods flowers.

Their departure for town was by tar boat down the rapids to Oulu, and by train to Helsinki on wooden seats in a third class overnight carriage.

In Helsinki they prepared for the autumn art exhibit of 1894. Louis was hailed by his artist comrades. Gallén too had been out in the wilderness, and had written that he had almost finished a portrait of Sibelius. There was much talk of symbolism, a concept that Gallén had adopted, but that Louis did not enjoy. Louis' eight paintings were approved by the jury. He drew a suggestion for dining room furniture "in the Finnish style." This was bought by the Friends of Finnish Handwork, a foretaste of what soon would come.

Louis and his fellow artists, Sibelius, Halonen and others, regularly met in the evenings, discussing everything in their postprandial wisdom under the evening lamp at the Hotel Kämp in Helsinki—magic, symbolism, the Rosicrucians and, as the painter Albert Edelfelt longingly wrote them from his exile in Denmark, "alcohol-tinted philosophy." At home in their darkened studio Pekka Halonen always brought his kantele and played the ancient melodies of the Finnish wilderness in the romantic atmosphere. The exciting evening meetings apparently were strictly a masculine affair. Louis needed no stimulants, but, according to Eva, his awakened bachelor feelings appreciated "the happiness of marriage with certain definite reservations."[64] Those reservations surely were shared by Eva, but she hinted at no problems. Her faintly negative, barely noticeable remark was the only one of its kind she wrote in her book.

Louis' father Ambjörn, always popular with Eva's family, came to spend Christmas with the Sparres. A month later, on January 30, in the new year of 1895, Eva's and Louis's first son was born. In her memoirs Eva gives little warning of this birth. One has the impression that Victorian women were treated like porcelain during their pregnancies, but Eva had slept outside, ridden a tar boat down the rapids, and taken a hard wooden train seat back to town. The birth of her son was welcomed with delight, but there was little sentimentality and the reader is not prepared for the event. The boy was a wonder of beauty, and his name easily settled: Pehr for his great-grandfather, Gustaf for his mother's brother, Ambjörn for his father's father. Eva quickly returned to the important matters of Louis' art exhibits in Helsinki and Stockholm. He now appeared for the first time as a portrait painter.

Axel Gallén wrote his congratulations on the birth of the Sparres' son from "unartistic" Berlin where he was painting, he said, a boring portrait of the redingote-dressed Baron von Bodenhausen, the driving force behind a new art magazine.

In April 1895, Louis exhibited paintings at the Turku spring show. This was his first opportunity to be judged in Finland as a portrait painter. His work was prominently displayed, and at a dinner for the opening the speech to participating artists included warm words to him. The show resulted in two commissions, portraits of a colonel and his wife. This was more than welcome for the meager family purse. "It's like a dream!" Louis shouted, "our loan is paid off." Louis's portrait of his father was, he thought, responsible for his success. But he was disappointed that the most "Finnish" of his paintings, the tar-burning scene and "Christmas Night" were not in the public's taste. Public taste, he said sarcastically, preferred pictures of kittens and Indian dancers.

In Helsinki, in the 1895 autumn art show, many of the best known Finnish artists were represented, including Halonen, Edelfelt and the last canvas of the Sparre's good friend Gunnar Berndtson, an artist who died suddenly in his prime. Louis' portrait of Ambjörn Sparre was hung in a place of honor.

Gallén had buried himself in the wilderness, building and doing heavy work to dull the anguish of grieving over the death of his little girl. He was not represented in the exhibit. He sent Louis a print from a woodcarving called "Death's Flower," a child on the edge of a woodland lake, black and shaped like a heart, death keeping watch among the pines. Nevertheless, despite his depression, Gallén encouraged his old friend and congratulated him on his progress, telling him that admirers at the art show had been reminded of Velazquez.

Louis had been recognized in Finland but he had not neglected his Swedish ties. He had, while still living in Paris in 1889, shown work with the Swedish art society in the World Exhibit that year, and in 1890 at an art salon in Stockholm. In the spring of 1895 Louis took part in the Swedish Art Society's show in Stockholm. In Finland he sold a painting in Turku and gained a new portrait commission. He won a new and demanding Finnish competition for an altar painting for the church in Vasa. The Sparres depended heavily on that to keep them afloat in the coming months. For all the success, the family income was far from secure.

Eva had dreamed of changing their life, moving to cosmopolitan Copenhagen, both of them renting a studio and working there for the winter. But now that Louis had won the competition they had to stay home. For all her wishes to test unknown waters and her strong sense of adventure, Eva always deferred to her husband's needs without devaluing her own career.

Eva did not give up her art. This was in contrast to many well known women artists of the time. Some felt marriage and art were incompatible, and therefore remained single; others gave up their art as the price they paid for personal happiness. The example of Carl Larsson, famous for painting idyllic scenes of family life and household activities, was a case in point. His wife Karin had to give up her painting, bore seven children and helped create the domestic scenes that became Larsson's trademark. (She later satisfied her creative talents by becoming a designer of textiles and furniture.)

Since the 1880s, a number of Finnish women artists, unable to find encouragement at home, fled to Paris to further their art. In the 1850's and 60's, Düsseldorf had been their Mecca. A few went to St. Petersburg. Sometimes they found marriage partners in a more supportive atmosphere. Some stayed home in Finland and taught drawing. If they married, their careers as artists often ended. In Finland there were no life classes; it was considered that nudes were not a fit subject for women to paint or sculpt, and models were expensive. The lack of nude models drew less serious students. Women artists were seen as practicing a hobby, or as being amateurs at best. Those who were able to study at private academies ran into barriers as soon as they approached art as professionals. One woman artist remembered bitterly the role consigned to women in her adolescence: they were gossips, appendages to their men, uninterested and unfit for matters of intellect. They might learn to decorate china or teach drawing, but that was all.

Although Eva does not devote much space in her memoirs to fellow artists, she mentions some of them briefly and a few repeatedly. Eva's natural reticence makes it difficult to know exactly how she saw herself or what she thought of her colleagues, those women who either stood in their husbands' shadows, disappearing as artists, or refused to become invisible and continued to paint, sculpt, design and show their work. Often, of course, their continuation as artists after marriage depended on the emotional support of their husbands. She took no part in Victorian judgmental attitudes about marriages, her own or others. She had her own problems which she faced quietly, and never showed any inclination to introduce her views, whatever they were, to friends or children. [65]

Eva was lucky to have her husband's admiration. Louis had no such denigrating view of women artists; but the underlying diffidence of many women artists may explain Eva's silence about her work decades later, in talking with me. Eva and Louis achieved an artistic partnership and equality that were highly unusual.

A new and important source of art critique abroad opened to them through Axel Gallén. He had written Charles Holme, editor of the periodical The Studio in England, offering his services as an art correspondent. The offer was accepted. In January of 1896, Holme's periodical introduced Finnish art for the first time, showing among the few selected works Louis's portrait of his father. A wonderful year had begun.

Jean Sibelius
when Louis and Eva knew him

Chapter 11

1896, A PIVOTAL YEAR FOR EVA AND LOUIS

Portraiture took up most of Louis's time and brought in the dependable part of his income. By the spring of 1896, he had three substantial orders to fill. But he also threw himself into etching, at first in his free time. In the process, he inspired new creative paths in his friends Axel Gallén and Albert Edelfelt.

Etching was not an art that had been practiced in Finland. Edelfelt had been initiated in technical experiments only by the Swedish artist Anders Zorn in Paris in 1890. In the 1890's still other artists followed Louis's example and took up etching. Among them were two young women artists, Ellen Thesleff and Hilda Flodin, who in time added to the luster of Finnish graphic art. (Hilda Flodin was a sculptress as well, a student of Rodin in Paris, and his lover.) The artists planned to open an etching school, but when this proved impractical each one continued to study separately. Eva Sparre called Ellen Thesleff a rising star, her themes intensified by simplicity and blurry greys.

It was just at this time that Eva was working on the Imperial Address cover for the coronation of Tsar Nicholas II and Tsarina Alexandra. Marketta Tamminen, Director of the Museum in Porvoo/Borgå, has written about the history of this address, offered to the imperial couple by the Four Estates of Finland (the nobility, clergy, bourgeoisie and peasants). She speculates that they may have wished to stress their "not being Slavic" by this particular gift, as the usual offering was a plate with bread and salt. The parchment itself was painted by Albert Edelfelt. Mrs. Tamminen has described it from notes in her archives: "[It was] a water color depicting the new emperor and empress in a gallery with the statues of their predecessors," and the painting depicted "a Finnish lake scenery in the background." In the foreground "a large number of people [were paying] homage to the imperial couple."

The Imperial Court painter, Edelfelt, painted the Tsar. Louis's contribution was to work out the design for Eva's leather work. He was advised by Edelfelt on the nature of the composition. It was to be done "in the English taste," using stylized flowers. Thus Eva and her husband together designed and executed the leather work. Mrs. Tamminen's letter continues: "The gold ornaments in different colors of gold, from pale yellow to deep orange, were made by the goldsmith Hjalmar Fagerroos. The bookbinding, including the gilding, was done by Mr. Ahlström from Borgå, then working in the workshop of the Frenchman Rau in Petersburg. The silk lining was painted by Beda Stjernschantz, the iris motif was English and a favorite of the Empress and thus the tasteful work was all executed by Finnish hands."

The letter goes on, "The Address, though superbly designed and executed, did not meet with success. In fact it caused a lot of difficulties. The official Finnish delegation representing the Four Estates was not allowed to present it. They were told by the Russians that a deviation from the old honored tradition of bread and salt was extremely improper and was liable to grave misinterpretations. An enameled silver plate with the Russian and Finnish coats-of-arms was hastily procured, and bread and salt were presented by the delegation to their Majesties. The Address was, however, given to the Emperor a week later in a private ceremony by the Minister Secretary of State."[66] It is interesting that Mrs. Tamminen's colleague, the curator of the Kremlin Museum, reported that the binding for the Coronation Address was displayed in December, 1993, "in an exhibition called 'The World of Fabergé'," which also traveled to Australia.[67]

In April of 1896, Eva and Louis made a journey to Paris via Hamburg and Holland. Six-month old Pehr was left with Eva's Aunt Hanna in Stockholm and his nurse. In packing for the trip, Eva reflected guiltily that her huge grey trunk represented no bohemian concept of simplicity—hardly comparable with the single birchbark backpack carried on her trip to Italy by Venny Soldan-Brofelt, wife of the author Juhani Aho.

This was Eva's only mention of Venny, who at 14 had left her hated school to become an art student. She was a bohemian who loved the Parisian life without chaperones and worked in a damp studio in Montparnasse, always outspoken, idealistic, uninterested in luxurious living as long as there was someone who needed bread. Eva's mention suggests an admiration for a contemporary woman artist who shared some of her own characteristics: Eva herself had achieved independence early, was unconventional, outspoken, and idealistic. They shared experiences and friends: Venny and her husband had visited the border country of Karelia one year before the Sparres' wedding trip there. Venny and Juhani were neighbors of the Sparres' artist friends, Sibelius and Halonen. Eva, like Venny, spoke Swedish as her first language, but Venny took her Finnish lessons more seriously and became fluent. Both women were designers of textiles and admirers of John Ruskin's views of handwork's artistry, and the deadening effect of industrialization.

Venny was able to carry on her art while maintaining her role as wife. So, too, was Eva. But Venny's husband must have tried the limits of her tolerance: he fell in love with his wife's sister, who bore him a child. Venny refused to let anything disrupt their marriage, and it continued with less warmth, but still as a kind of partnership. Venny may have recognized that she was stiff and matter-of-fact, and seldom expressed the tenderness that Juhani may have needed. This could have been a portrait of the cool Eva and her susceptible Louis. (There is evidence in a letter from one of her own daughters-in-law that Eva, too, had to deal with infidelity, though no time or person is named.) Venny felt that her own role as mother and even as wife increased her artistic sensitivity. But Eva, while loving her boys, expressed no views that they were assets to her art.

Juhani openly expressed his gratitude for Venny's shy and delicate sensibility, her uncomplaining silence, her support and honest criticism. Here, too, Venny's support is reminiscent of Eva's for Louis. As Venny expressed it, the woman is flexible, while the man "rules with inborn lack of consideration, and pushes aside the complications that every day life, such as marriage, often cause him."[68]

Juhani was mentioned by Eva in several connections, once attending, with other leading artists, an important opening of Louis's gallery at the Porvoo/Borgå Museum in 1902.

Paris, home to many a Finnish artist, was the city of Louis's early childhood and young manhood, when he had been a student in the Académie Julian. Now on the visit of 1896 he was able to borrow his absent friend Albert Edelfelt's studio in order to draw preliminary sketches of the altar painting commissioned in Finland.

Louis's father made his Paris apartment at 16 Place de la Madeleine available to the young pair. To Eva's joy, Louis decided he could afford to enhance her wardrobe. Ever since her childhood Eva had adored clothes, and now she might have remembered her first new dress as an eight-year-old, with its broad sash and parasol to match. She was adorned by her husband in a straw hat with flowers and silk tulle, a new blouse in pinstripes of rose, black and white, and "with small steps and a Parisian's grip on the long skirt, I was no longer set apart from the great city's international scene. There was little risk of being taken for one of the high-bosomed, sumptuous females sauntering on the Boulevard, whose wasp waists, cherry lips, white-painted cheeks and other sinful signs were still unknown in our uncosmetic northern countries."[69]

Eva and Louis did not see much of Louis's father Ambjörn, who was usually away on trips trying to get approval for his newest invention. At this time he was in London. They were comfortable and quite independent in his charming apartment with Louis XVI furniture, paintings and a water color of Louis's grandfather's bridge, designed by the old engineer in Italy. The apartment and Count Ambjörn were looked after by the faithful Marie, whose daily delicious meals saved the young Sparres money and energy.

They enjoyed an orgy of museum visiting and had some old friends to amuse them. Their future sister-in-law Aina was studying voice and knew the Finnish diva, Aino Ackté, at the Paris Opera. They met young Parisian painters and Swedish-born artists including Louis's intimate friend Anders Zorn, who took Eva under his arm and introduced her to the can-can at the Moulin Rouge. Guided by Louis, Eva saw all the small, interesting cafés and restaurants, the "right" ones for true Parisians. Inspired by his still boyish love of adventure and Indians, he took her to the theatre and showed her Jules Verne's Le Tour du Monde en 80 Jours.

It was on this trip that Eva met the Finnish artist Ville Vallgren, an old sculptor friend of Louis, now living in Paris with his Swedish-born wife Antoinette Råström. She was a book artist, a few years older than Eva. The Vallgrens had a flair for creating a harmonious home where artists gathered, attracted by Ville's culinary talents and the joyous bohemian atmosphere. Eva was well aware of Antoinette's talents, "earning laurels" for her work in bas relief leather designs for books. Despite the Vallgrens' poverty, there was always fun to be had in their household. They worked and played with the Scandinavian art colony—Carl Larsson and his wife Karin, August Strindberg and his wife, the actress Siri von Essen, and the journalist Spada, who was along for dinner when the Sparres came. Ville was an amateur chef, and had met his future bride at a party where he was in charge of mixing a sauterne punch flavored with orange and brandy. Evidently it was a heady mixture, for the two instantly fell in love. When he asked Antoinette for her first dinner with him, he was careful to explain that everything—oysters, lobsters, champagne, fruit and cake—was on credit so there would be no illusions about his finances. They were married on credit in Paris in 1882. But nothing prevented the fun they always had and shared with their artist friends—masquerades, tableaux, costume dinners, singing quartets in summer meetings in the country and winters in Paris. Ville's and Antoinette's first home was a single room made to look like four with walls of cardboard. Antoinette had worked on Larsson's illustrations with a woman artist friend, who engraved wood slabs for Gustave Doré's Bible. It may have been to the Vallgren's new home, a rented house with garden and studio, that the Sparres went for dinner on their trip to Paris. Ville, unlike many men of his era, did not demand work of his wife. They were a partnership, supportive of each other, admiring each other's work. In this they were like Louis and Eva.

A Frenchman who was a leading pottery maker, another who was an art critic of renown, responsible for much of the El Greco cult: all these and the Vallgrens gave Eva and Louis new insights into each of their specialties.

At the Galeries Art Nouveau, in an international exhibit of modern book art, Eva and Louis were able to represent Finland with some examples of their own work. The exhibit was later described in an October, 1896 article of The Studio. This recognized their contribution to Finnish art. The author of an important work on book art, Octave Uzanne, had seen Eva's books in the show and in 1898 asked to reproduce her Imperial Address. This was the first mention of her work in foreign professional book literature. The photographs of her book covers in the Studio and other publications opened orders to her in London, Paris and Leipzig as well as in Finland.

Their visit to England was a turning point which would soon begin a long interruption of Louis's painting. They visited Liberty's in London. (Louis would later become their agent in Finland.) They were invited to lunch with Charles Holme and his wife. The Holmes lived at the Red House in Bexleyheath, Kent, a short distance southeast of central London, where William Morris had lived in the 1860's. In 1861 Morris, the preeminent handcraft pioneer, book designer and publisher, poet, translator and writer (to name but a few of his passionate pursuits) had started a decorating firm to reinvent medieval decorative arts. His aim was to banish the deadening effect of factory-made objects—a capitulation of art to practicality. For his Red House he had created stained glass, furniture, tapestries and fabrics; he designed type and bindings for his own Kelmscott Press. Morris's ideas found an echo in Louis's dreams. Louis wanted to be the precursor, in Finland, of a return to beautifully crafted furniture, even educating popular taste to demand beauty in the simplest utilitarian furnishings.

Holme was editor and founder of The Studio. Both Eva and Louis were beguiled by the tiled Red House, its medieval atmosphere and leaded windows, the frescoes by Burne-Jones, its Pre-Raphaelite history. Before leaving, they cut their names with a diamond into the windowpane of a door, already signed in the same way by William Morris himself, Burne-Jones, and Dante Gabriel Rosetti. The latter's affair with Morris's wife, Jane, inspired paintings of this woman who became the model of the Pre-Raphaelite beauty. Holme was himself interested in the rebirth of artistic handcraft products, the making of ordinary household and other tools judged by artistic standards of elegance, made with an artist's eye for harmonious proportions and design.

Eva went home to Finland via Antwerp and Amsterdam, where Louis studied the old masters and copied a Pietà by Van Dyck. Then he went back to Paris to work on the burgeoning sketches for his altar piece.

Among the artists Eva and Louis had met in Paris was a young Jewish painter, André Davids. What a period piece he must have been, as Eva describes him! "Consciously precious, dressed in black with a broad 1830-period cravat, delicate pale features, red beard and hair, he stood . . . leaning against the open fireplace" in the pose of a romantic poet.[70] Davids served as a model for Louis's head of Christ and later for the whole figure. One of Louis's models for the Magdalen figure was a young woman from Antwerp: young, luscious and red-haired, her skin color lustrous as a pearl. Another model was Davids' gloriously redhaired sister.

After Eva departed for Finland, Louis entertained himself by bicycling in the Bois, and moved from his father's apartment at the Place de la Madeleine to Edelfelt's studio, where everything, including the lighting by gasoline lamps, was arranged conveniently. He needed solitude to replenish his ideas and work on his sketches. But he missed his family; life seemed not worth living without them. He fell into one of his severe depressions, that lifelong torment which alternated with high exuberance and his explosive temperament. Now he needed to come home.

He weighed anchor with a huge palette and new tubes of oils. He carried with him the results of two months work: sketches and studies in pencil and oil, good photographs and a sense of accomplishment in having found Davids to be the ideal model for his Christ.

Louis came home to have two portraits selected for the fall exhibit in Helsinki. Now Eva found that she was not the only teacher in the family, for Louis had taken on some young artists for watercolor sessions. One of the future masters of architecture, Eliel Saarinen, was a pupil. The enterprise was a boon, helping counteract Louis's self-critical feelings about the results of his work and the future he was planning as a founder, with his close friends, of a handcraft company. Eva's brother Carl was enthusiastic about his ideas for the little factory, and wanted to lend his support. He agreed with the basic plan that there would be no profit motive.

In the new year of 1897, Carl became one of the directors of the new company, to be called Iris.

Eva's Leatherwork: Two Covers for formal Addresses to King
and Queen of Denmark and Tsar and Tsarina of Russia

Chapter 12

SOPHIE'S RETURN TO FINLAND AND HER MARRIAGE

Sophie Mannerheim came back to Villnäs in September, 1885 from her position as governess in Stockholm, one of the occupations a girl of good family could consider. She needed a change from the uninspiring twelve-hour days that had given her little feeling of satisfaction. "I could not have endured another year there," she wrote her brother Carl. During those years in Sweden she had lived with her mother's sister Hanna while finishing her schooling, and her aunt had taken a course in emergency care, what to do in case of accident or disaster. The conversation was ghastly, Sophie wrote, exclusively about "erupting arteries, fractured bones, half-scorched people . . . . I would certainly not do as a doctor."[71] She had no idea that this would be a foretaste of her eventual career as a pioneer in nursing.

It was to a changed and gloomy household that she came home. A northern autumn is seldom a cheerful time, when the long light days give way to the blackness of long nights, and short days of rain or snow, and pale sun. She longed for gusts of wind to clear the air of the "narrow ideas and prejudices" she found around her.

Sophie's grandmother, old Countess Eva Mannerheim, was still a beauty, with her pink complexion, dark blue eyes and face framed by the starched white muslin cap and its billowing ribbons. The old lady missed her school-bound grandchildren, Eva and August in Stockholm, Annicka in Russia, Gustaf misbehaving in his cadet corps, Johan at Sällvik with his other grandmother, and Carl studying law in Helsinki. To Carl she wrote, describing herself with her usual sharp humor as "toothless, gouty, forgetful, rickety, boring and shabby."[72] Until Sophie's arrival she had only her daughter Mimmi and her granddaughter Jeanne for company, Mimmi dutiful but dull, and Jeanne, lazy and spoiled. Sophie must long since have discovered that her cousin and she had nothing in common except age and family ties. Jeanne had shown no inclination to turn to any work, and it was hard to know what interested her.

Sophie was restless in the silent household that Villnäs had become, and before many days had gone by she set to work translating articles from French newspapers. One of them she described in a letter to Calle: "It was a political treatise, very boring, with sentences as long as rubber bands."[73] He helped get them published in Helsingfors Dagbladet, Helsinki's daily paper.

The spring of 1886 marked disasters for two young Mannerheims. The first was Gustaf's expulsion from the Cadet Corps, which called forth a characteristically tart comment from their grandmother Eva. She wrote Carl that Gustaf's behavior "before and after the Cadet Corps is well known; he could have been forgiven, if only he had continued to earn good marks." She asked, "What in God's name can a young man accomplish, without protection and with no money?"[74]

Added to this was the tragic death of the youngest Mannerheim sister, Annicka. At her funeral, Sophie was briefly back in her role as surrogate mother to the grieving younger brothers and sister.

These events must have added to Sophie's wish to move to Helsinki from her isolated post in the country. There she was promised a job at a bank in the near future and found temporary work in the statistics department of the Customs office. She wrote Calle that she was continuing her school tutoring, something she had been doing since her return to Finland.

Sophie's friends remembered her from this time as clear-eyed and realistic, elegant in her bearing, quick to laugh, impulsive and sensitive. Her voice was soft yet distinctive, its melodious pitch one that she would keep all her life. She could be quick to anger, but had no patience for hurtful or tactless expressions, and was not reluctant to voice her opinions. Her friend and biographer Berta Edelfelt said she made an "English" impression, her skin like "white roseleaves," her profile charming.

Sophie's biographer Tyyni Tuulio writes that bank positions in the 1880s were favored by girls of all backgrounds. This is a commentary on how modern and unpretentious most of Finnish society was in its view of women and careers. Sons and daughters of noble families were not content to play their days and nights away on inherited wealth. The bank job was Sophie's for six happy years. She made friends in all the stages of her life, from all levels of society and age groups.

Sophie left the bank at the end of 1893 to join her father as an office girl in his successful new business "Systema," manufacturing office equipment. He had come back to Finland from Paris with his new wife and small daughter Marguerite. Sophie was happy to see him more. She adored her father, even catching criticism from her mother's family for so swiftly forgiving him his desertion of Hélène and their seven children.

In the early 1890s, a distant relative needed a traveling companion. She was Aurore Karamsin, an honored guest at Eva's and Louis's wedding in 1893, the legendary grande dame of Finnish society. Madame Karamsin's "Villa Hagasund," near Helsinki, was like a small royal court. The ancient beauty from the days of Tsar Nicholas I was pleased to serve her guests tea in the garden or park; her horses and carriages were at their disposal. In her St. Petersburg life, "Tante Aurore" had made a habit of singling out one or another of the young girls at home in Finland to visit her and have the exciting experience of being presented at the Russian Court. In 1894, it was Sophie's turn to meet her in Paris. Tante Aurore's courier met her at the station, but Sophie wrote to Carl that going out alone was not encouraged. This, for a girl who had found her way to Paris from Finland, seemed ridiculous, but Paris was abloom in May and nothing else mattered. She bought herself a new hat and coat and observed that the Parisian women on the streets were "old, awful, with eye makeup, cheeks rouged and hair dyed red."

The trip brought the old lady and the young woman close together, and it was only natural that Sophie should be one of the few daily visitors admitted to the 88-year-old lady's sickroom a few years later.

One other visitor among those few permitted to see the old lady in her illness at the Villa Hagasund was her great-nephew, Hjalmar Linder. Hjalmar was a friend of Gustaf's, known as a witty and popular partygoer, an industrialist and later a rich landowner. Sophie was 32 years old, beyond the usual age for marrying, and she may have dismissed the whole idea of sharing her life with someone. However that may be, she did fall in love, to her family's surprise.

Hjalmar and Sophie must have taken pleasure in each other's company. They had known each other since childhood, and now had ample time to become companions, with the park, gardens and drawing rooms to talk in undisturbed. One of Hjalmar Linder's companions has written that he had a streak of sensitivity which he did everything to cover up. This may have been obvious to the finely attuned Sophie during their anxious days of attending the old lady. Hjalmar's Russian mother, Countess Marie Mussin-Pusjkin, had written an anonymous novel championing women's liberation, and was said to have urged Tsar Alexander II, in private, to give women the freedom to choose their religion. Hjalmar seemed to have inherited these liberal tendencies, so attractive to Sophie. His mother had died young, as Sophie's mother had. This may also have affected Sophie, who had taken her own mother's place at an early age.[75]

Ever a decisive woman, Sophie made up her mind quickly, for Madame Karamsin fell ill in the spring of 1896 and the two young people announced their engagement in May. The news, says Sophie's biographer, hit the family "like a bomb."[76] It had never occurred to anyone that Sophie would marry someone so unlike herself. Having been free and happy earning her own bread in her unassuming jobs, she was perhaps unconventional in her indifference to the social class of her friends. Now she was following the conventional path of marrying a man of her own class. She had been independent for a considerable time; with strangers she was said to be cool and distant. Hjalmar was a charmer. He was not yet a rich landowner, but certainly a man of his time—forceful and not someone who would allow a wife the leader's role. But Sophie was smitten. The germs of incompatibility between them, and Sophie's strong sense of independence, had not yet developed. Perhaps her brothers and sisters knew her better than she knew herself. The surprise of family and friends at her choice of husband foreshadowed her short and unhappy marriage.

When Sophie agreed to marry Hjalmar Linder he had not yet acquired his uncle's money. But by the time of their honeymoon, Baron Fridolf Linder had died suddenly and deeded Hjalmar his twenty-eight room Laxpojo Manor.

They were married on July 11, 1896. Two days later, Sophie wrote to Calle, whose apartment she had shared when working in Helsinki, "You can't imagine how hard it was to say goodbye. But it's the world's way, to marry and leave one's family." She described the lazy life they were leading, and Hjalmar's need of rest, strained as he was by problems. "We've driven with the new horses, very handsome, and the little cart Hjalmar bought in Copenhagen. The wing that's been prepared for us is attractive, and we'll feel at home here until the main house is ready."[77]

Sophie's sister Eva has said that Sophie married Hjalmar "under entirely different assumptions than those she had made initially. On his uncle's death, Hjalmar also inherited his great fortune. Thereupon his earlier work as a lawyer in Tampere came to an end."[78] The bride and groom took a conventional trip to Paris and Italy. Sophie responded to the sunshine and fragrance of the Italian landscape, driving away what she felt was the grey existence of her everyday life. She was reborn.

Her two-year marriage was to be a troubled one. She remained devoted to Hjalmar, but his behavior toward her was erratic and demeaning. Sophie's health suffered, and eventually the marriage broke up.

It seems a plausible supposition that Sophie, like many women deciding to marry, consciously or unconsciously had been looking for her father's traits in her future husband. Hjalmar's witty conversation must have been one of many attractions for Sophie. His interest in a growing collection of paintings was another. These were certainly among Carl Robert Mannerheim's qualities and amusements. Linder has been called one of Finland's few "Renaissance men", a known lover of art, a consummate gourmet who imported his food from Petersburg, not finding Finnish foodstuffs sufficiently exotic.[79] Sophie's father was a culinary expert also, an admirer and student of Escoffier's art, and, to the consternation of some hostesses, not hesitant to tell them when their dinners failed to meet high standards. Carl Robert was an art lover like Hjalmar; his close friends were artists. He was known, the historian Jägerskiöld writes, for "meaningful collections of art work and antiques,"[80] all lost later in his bankruptcy. Hjalmar was said to be a ruthless businessman who practiced the risk-taking of a gambler.[81] Indeed, Hjalmar Linder was a gambler, like Sophie's father, and at the end of his life he, too, lost his fortune.[82] It is possible that if the gambling trait showed up during their brief time together, Sophie might have had more than a frisson of anxiety, in remembering her father's financial disaster, caused partly by gambling debts.

Linder argued for political reform. He was a liberal for his time, personally interested in his workers. When he inherited his uncle's manor, his new responsibilities included thousands of retainers and tenants. He was concerned for their welfare and good housing.[83] At meetings he argued specifically for social reforms for farm laborers.[84] When Sophie's father started a successful business after his bankruptcy, he, too, was a considerate and thoughtful employer, a liberal in his political thinking. With her own interest in liberal political movements, Sophie and Hjalmar Linder must have found that a common ground, perhaps before their marriage.

Her close friends, visiting Sophie as the new mistress of Laxpojo, had much to admire. There were servants for every kind of activity. Each was an expert, and each was under the command of a higher authority, though not of Sophie's. It was like the Villnäs of her childhood, and in this sense she must have felt at home. But Sophie's husband made all the decisions and controlled the smallest detail of their life. He literally poured jewelry and lace on his wife, adding old silver to the many antiques of his beautifully appointed manor. He was the first man to own a car in Finland. It seems unlikely that Sophie, a mature woman with an experience of independence, would have accepted his domination without chafing. Hjalmar was the type of "grand seigneur" well known in tsarist Russia, with careless extravagance and limitless hospitality.

By November, 1897, there were already strains in the marriage. Sophie wrote her brother that it was best to write in Hjalmar's absence, because he would have guessed she was continuing "to open my heart to you, which he made me confess I'd done." In fact, he made her confess "that I'd talked to you, which I did without details, and then I heard that I could have been worse off, with a drunken devil or an unfaithful one." Perhaps "he'd like me better if he could be with others." He had no idea what she was complaining of. His business affairs were no concern of hers. "Other men may behave as they wish with their wives," he had commented, and Sophie had to promise to let him do as he wished, and ask no questions. Best of all, Sophie wrote, would be if she could become indifferent, "for it's sad and pitiful to care for one who does not value my affection, but I am so stupid that I can't stop hoping he'll come back to me. It might be better to know it is impossible."[85]

Her friends sensed tedium and restlessness in Sophie. It was clear to anyone who knew her that she longed to use her mind and energy. One of those closest to her said Sophie felt merely like one of the many luxurious objects in the house. Only one old gardener needed Sophie's direction and served her devotedly. They shared the work of creating the garden, the only domain that was her own.

By the winter of 1898, Sophie spent time in the care of a leading doctor in Enköping, Sweden. It is thought that she had a nervous breakdown. Her health in any case was not robust. She continued her letters to Carl. "I wonder if Hjalmar's trip will be limited to hunting in Russia. Any change in our relationship I no longer believe in, and I can't hope for it either. If we could be in each other's presence without tormenting each other, not caring what the other is doing, it might be bearable. I try to think as little as possible about Hjalmar—if only I could be indifferent and not tremble like a silly goose at the thought that he might possibly be displeased. Instead I should be calm and cold-blooded, and myself once again." He had declared that he certainly did not intend to write or receive letters, but "there was a slight hope that he would regret the harshness he showed me the last days at home and let me have a letter, no matter how short. Naturally I was mistaken, but when your letter came without news of him, I became depressed and imagined that he had asked you not to give any information about him so I'd stop thinking about him, which is what he wants. I imagined a whole lot of stupid things and wrote everything to you, feeling very lonely and unhappy. Next time I feel unhappy and want to write, I'll leave the letter until the next day, when I surely will not send it." She went on to write about her new life in the sanatorium, with a light and airy room, good food and friendly people. "It felt a little odd to be able to talk without feeling that I was saying idiotic things, but my self-confidence is returning. The doctor believes that I need distraction. I've made a friend, a head gardener, whom I'm surely going to like. The Doctor has ordered me to help with the gardening work every day, and I love it (but don't tell anyone). That doctor is a wise man."

Sophie had promised not to write about Hjalmar again, but soon again she needed this release. "Don't worry," she wrote Calle, "that I'll cut short the cure or get homesick for Laxpojo." She was "almost mechanically" not thinking of anything upsetting. Carl could tell Hjalmar about their correspondence. Hjalmar had told her he would not write or receive letters from her. But now his dictate that she should not have letters was probably a matter of indifference to him. Perhaps he could understand that it might be hard for her to be cordoned off from all news of home. She had to ask Calle to remind her husband that she needed money; it was a painful aspect of her dependency.

In March, Sophie thanks Carl for news of Hjalmar. Evidently there might be a correspondence. "I'm curious to read what he may write. As for me, I feel almost shy and embarrassed to start corresponding after such a long silence." Hjalmar's sister Emily was with him. "I'm afraid she might counter my written orders to the head gardener, if she doesn't like them."

Hjalmar did write, a letter full of admonitions "not to hurry my trip home" and that being with people was a waste of time. It was his only letter. "I feel so mean and bitter," Sophie wrote. "I expect nothing of the future, and for Hjalmar it would be best if I never returned. He might have been happy with another, but with me he never will be, no matter how hard I try and even succeed in controlling myself. We're simply too different." Sophie was overcome with her own inability to keep her feelings from Carl and his wife. "You'll have to forgive me for whispering in your ear. It helps a bit. I'm a great egoist and have not become any better here." She asked that her letter be burned.

A letter to her father at the same time reveals none of her thoughts. She covered up by telling him about a pretentious couple, of whom she drew wicked caricatures, and a "fool" who showed her mute adoration at a safe distance. The other patients were half crazy or close to madness. "Perhaps I've become that way, too. Who knows where it will end in this kind of air laden with nervous anxiety." Sophie writes about an antique Louis XVI table she had bought which would "fit magnificently into the big salon at Laxpojo." She had found it in a kitchen, where it was used as a table for dirty dishes, and bought it for nothing. She was still planning her return to Laxpojo.

The doctor had told her, she wrote Carl, that she should not return now, but stay at the sanatorium. Her goal should be to spend the end of the summer at a mountain resort in Norway. The doctor had seen tears in her eyes at this thought and told her, "if you can't do it with good courage, nothing will help." Sophie knew, she wrote, that if she stayed away so long, Hjalmar would stop thinking of her as "something that belongs to Laxpojo. He would forget that I exist." She thought he had already done so, and that "it would be a disturbing to his habits if I came back. But," she wrote, "since he accomplished the great deed of writing me once, I haven't heard." She had written him a happy letter. "One must play at comedy, but I had to weigh each word, because he never understands me when I am myself," and so her writing had become labored and dull. She asked Carl to burn the letter.

A month later Sophie wrote that nothing could change the affection she had for Hjalmar. "I think I now understand Hjalmar much better, and all that has been since we married. I now see it in quite another light. If I'd understood him as I do now, all would have been quite different. One thing remains, my affection for him. He's the one I care for and nothing can change this. My hopes are that all might be well after this time of trial. If he needs me now when he's changing servants, I'd happily give up all wisdom and come home." But a week later, she had heard nothing. "I'm outside, and there I can stay."

She left the sanatorium in May, with warnings from the doctor to return after her visit to Norway. Again, she needed money from her husband.

Her trip to Norway in June was captivating. "Snow-covered mountains, ice green lakes and foaming waterfalls," a "magic power" she remembered from former times. She wrote from Holmenkollen in Norway, with a view over the city and fjord. "I had hoped a little that Hjalmar would come here. Has anyone heard?"

Sophie returned to Finland after her summer in Norway. A friend saw her in Helsinki, doing the usual Christmas shopping. She had a long list of servants to take care of, she said, and was packing and sending the presents out to Laxpojo in good time. About her marriage she was silent. A friend asked if she planned to return soon to her estate. She was given a short answer: "Never more."

Her brother Johan had become ill at his job as manager of Jokkis estate, and Sophie went there to care for him during the winter. "I long for Johan to get well and that Hjalmar will decide what he'll give me to leave." She was still a dependent woman. "I feel so thoroughly unhappy, my life so failed, which makes me bitter and unjust even with those I love," she wrote, apologizing for her anger. By January she had reached a new decision, a "solution," as she wrote Calle. She would get a divorce, "which could be obtained quickly."

Johan's illness had given her an undreamed of opportunity. She would go to London and study nursing at one of the famous teaching hospitals. Writing at the end of her time with Johan, she observed, "I'm beginning to long to get on and start to work. It would be all right for a nurse who had finished her training to follow a single patient, but it would drain the life out of me. It's much more tiring to deal with one than many." Mixed with the new excitement was her indecision about her things at Laxpojo. Should she claim them? Could Eva or Carl's wife Aina arrange this?

There is no suggestion, in any of Sophie's frank letters to Carl, that she ever discovered the reason for Hjalmar's cold anger, his taunts, his disgust. She blamed herself. She did write, at the end of her stay in Enköping, that she understood him better, "and all that has been since we married; I now see it in quite another light." What did she mean? Sophie's niece, Elsie Uggla, believed Hjalmar was a homosexual, and wrote this to me as though it were common knowledge.[86]

The brief marriage, and Sophie's reason for ending it in divorce, may never have been explained to her family. For a woman of such determination, a divorce was a most surprising turn of events, and a most unusual one in those days. For all her frankness with Carl, she may have wanted to protect Hjalmar. Silence would have been her way of dealing with a taboo subject. Sophie, in any case, made the crucial decision to leave her marriage, to lose all, home and security, in order to recover the creative life she needed. The divorce was granted Sophie on April 20, 1899, at a special session of the court at the Vendelä Inn.

After their divorce, Sophie and Hjalmar met accidentally on the ferry crossing from Finland to Sweden. They chose to sit together for meals, and quite clearly had a very good time. Toward the end of his life, Hjalmar Linder willed half his money to abandoned children, with the hope that Baroness Sophie Mannerheim would administer the fund. However, his entire fortune had been gambled away by the time of his death. Sophie was said to have attended the burial and tossed a bunch of pink roses into his grave.[87]

In 1992, Sophie Mannerheim and her distant cousin Aurore Karamsin were honored by Finnish postage stamps. Mme. Karamsin had founded the deaconess's institute in Helsinki in 1867, a year of famine. She appointed a remarkable woman of her time, Amanda Cajander, as head. This woman, forerunner of modern Finnish nurses, was the wife of a doctor and had become interested in nursing. She educated herself at the deaconess's institute in St. Petersburg. Tyyni Tuulio wrote of Amanda, "She was the first educated woman in Finland who chose nursing as her calling. The new institution pursued many sorts of philanthropic activities, but during the epidemic of the famine year, care of the sick became of necessity the principal preoccupation. The care offered by the deaconess's institution was definitely superior to other contemporary nursing care. In this institution deaconesses began to be educated as a goal [as] most of the doctors did not yet understand the need of educated nurses."[88]

Chapter 13

IRIS AND PORVOO, 1896-1900

Eva and Louis Sparre's visit to Charles Holme's Red House in Kent in 1896 inspired Louis to dream of being a pioneer in Finland, promoting a new approach to the design and materials of home furnishings. Fifty years earlier, William Morris had owned the Red House. He and John Ruskin and other writers, poets and painters had formed the so-called Pre-Raphaelite brotherhood. In their articles, poetry and paintings, in the furnishings and fabrics of Morris's house, in the typography and printed borders of his Kelmscott Press books, the Pre-Raphaelites influenced a new trend. Its simplicity harked back to medieval designs and the careful handwork of the old craft guilds, a revolt against the tasteless mass production of household goods and furniture in newly industrialized England.

The English periodical The Studio, an arts and crafts magazine founded in 1893 and edited by Holme, was another source broadcasting the same message to continental Europe. Its publisher, Charles Holme, owned the Red House when Eva and Louis visited him there in 1896, and Louis wrote an article on Finnish art for his journal the same year. Louis began to develop his ideas of designs in the "new style," the so-called art nouveau, which he hoped would lead to a renewal of the handcraft and furniture industry in Finland.

It was after this visit that Louis began to think about the actual production of furniture. He saw it as a possible cultural contribution to his adopted country and a source of dependable income.

Louis talked endlessly with his friends, Gallén especially, about his ideas, particularly about the founding of a furniture factory. His aim was nothing less than educating the general public to demand good taste and practicality in household furnishings. He would be the furniture factory's director, combining his artist's eye for the products with a businessman's responsibilities. In the latter he had no experience.

It was Louis's brother-in-law, Carl Mannerheim, who had practical ideas of how to finance the venture. He had been able to bring in a modest capital base, launching the new company through his connections and standing as a director of the Northern Bank of Helsinki. He approved of the basic idea of creating furniture, textiles, pottery, even the most utilitarian home furnishings, according to principles of "simplicity and functionality in combination with good artistic taste." The crassness of commercial profit would not enter into the guidelines.[89] Carl's wife Aina suggested naming the factory the Iris Company.

Toward the end of 1896 Louis had taken a long ski trip to visit his old friend Gallén in the isolated wilderness of Ruovesi. He traveled through the woods at night without signposts or fresh tracks to guide him, a happy woodsman in control of his skis and perhaps of his future. Louis craved the companionship of his old artist friend, the very man who had changed his life and brought him to Finland. He announced his arrival with two blasts from his revolver, an old signal. Seconds later his friend embraced him and the two spent long nights etching and discussing Louis's new plans. Later, Gallén, smoking the long peace pipe his guest had given him, wrote him of his own conviction that Louis's presence in Finland was a happy chance for that small country.

The Sparres spent the Christmas of 1896 with their in-laws, Sophie and Hjalmar Linder, at their luxurious Laxpojo manor. Eva and Louis were waiting for their own new house two kilometers from Porvoo, bought at a bargain. The villa with garden and two acres of land was near the Iris Company in Porvoo and not far from Helsinki. While marking time they stayed at Sällvik, Eva's grandmother's manor. There Louis continued with his portraits, a life-size charcoal drawing of his little boy Pehr and an oil of himself in a black fur hat. Louis was also struggling with an altar painting that had been commissioned in 1895, sketched and worked on earlier in Paris.

The great event of the summer of 1897 was an invitation to the Art and Industry Exhibit in Stockholm. Louis stayed away despite warnings from his painter friend Zorn that it was dangerous not to appear officially as a Swedish artist, for he would lose invaluable connections with his own country. But Louis wanted to give his full attention to his new venture. In addition to the domestic furniture industry he planned, Louis dreamed of buying exclusive textiles, home furnishings and artistic knick-knacks from international sources. He stayed behind also to oversee the move to the new house, and was not happy to have to deal with the contents of the pantry. As he wrote Eva accusingly, "Till the last second I've had to slave with those jam pots!"[90] The spring rains dripping on the metal rim outside the window felt like Chinese torture, and the solitude and general chaos of moving were a prison sentence, especially when Eva was having fun in Stockholm.

She was having the time of her life. For one thing, she adored her new outfit from Paris. The dark blue and green dress with its finely pleated ruffle of iridescent blue-green taffeta happened to be the color of the "Painter Prince" Eugen's latest twilight paintings on show. And Prince Eugen, brother of the Crown Prince of Sweden, was to be the host at the outing to the Royal Castle of Gripsholm. Eva took the chartered steamer to the castle, riding out with all the artists from Stockholm in the day's long summer sun.

It was not often that Eva felt sure of herself, but at dinner outside in the castle gardens the Prince sent for her. She found herself seated next to him, and observed that His Highness kept gazing at the neighboring tables where the merriment was louder and gayer than at his own. "What a shame he has to be a Prince!" she wrote home to Louis.[91] Years later the "Painter Prince" would be their neighbor and friend in Stockholm.

Eva did not realize what an attractive and interesting young woman she was. With the other artists, she was invited by the King himself to the Royal Castle in Stockholm. The King made his rounds among the guests and stopped in front of Eva. Who was she? When she answered that her maiden name was Mannerheim, His Majesty remembered that her Aunts Mimmi and Anna Mannerheim had danced at the castle in the 1850s and 60s.

In June Eva and Louis met briefly in Stockholm and looked at the art nouveau furniture there, which did not impress them. Louis traveled on alone to discover more about business methods and industrial arts in other countries. An advance payment on the altar painting financed the trip. In Copenhagen Louis was impressed with the pleasant working conditions for artists at the Royal Porcelain factory: flowers, live birds and fish were used as models, and a beautiful landscape outside the windows pleased the eye. At Liberty's in London he discussed ideas for modern furniture, though he felt it would take time before Liberty curtains would hang in Finnish windows, or their velvets cover Finnish sofas.

At the Brussels Exhibition Louis's eye was caught by some unusual clay pots. This gave new impetus to his thoughts of adding ceramics production to the furniture factory of the Iris Works.

Louis also met Alfred William Finch, a former student of Louis's favorite painter, Whistler. He forthwith hired Finch to organize and be artistic director of the pottery factory. Finch was to have a significant influence, laying the groundwork for Finnish ceramics. The pottery artist was the first instructor in ceramics at the Central Art School, now the University of Industrial Design in Helsinki, and spent the rest of his life in Finland.

In July 1897 the carpenters were busy with the new factory, and the Sparres moved from Helsinki into their new house. Their slender purse was helped by another partial payment in advance for the altar painting. Eva and Louis were faced with more than the expected annoyances of carpenter repairs and mattresses on the floor. Their little boy had a high fever and a diagnosis of diphtheria.

By October Louis's altar painting had been accepted for the fall art show opening, but exciting as that was he found himself already troubled by problems at the fledgling Iris Company. One seeming success was a paradox: the furniture deliveries had begun but there were so many orders that new ones had to be postponed. A new order for five rooms in a private house was seen as the beginning of the Finnish market conquest. But decisions to pursue commercial enlargement and tendencies to look for profits were beginning to push away earlier ideals. A new piece of property next to the old was bought for a larger factory complex, completed in 1898.

Louis was discovering that in splintering his interests he was putting his position as an artist in jeopardy. His fascination with too many things at once had been a lifetime problem. His friend Zorn expressed it all: "The worst thing is that everything is so damned much fun!"[92] Louis had been left off a jury selection by artists. The factory in Porvoo was expanding as well as the shop in Helsinki. Louis's own jobs were staggering: he was designing furniture, overseeing the office and carpentry shop, the pottery factory, and the shop in Helsinki; at the same time he had to keep the books and correspondence. His altar painting had been delivered to the Cathedral chapter in Vasa. But now there was no time for painting. The stockholders' decision to enlarge Iris showed a clear drift toward commercializing the enterprise. Only this could break Louis's determination to instruct and introduce high standards of art into everyday life. Finch's pottery was attracting notice in Germany and England though the products were selling at a loss. It was time, Louis felt, to separate art and business, find a business manager and keep the artistic development as his domain. He was frittering away energy and time in business matters that lay beyond his competence.

Despite his all-consuming work Louis never entirely stopped painting. Eva was quietly relieved every time he grasped the palette and brushes. She knew painting was and would always be his first love. He had neglected it too long, and in 1898 returned to his artistic source in a new commission—a large portrait in Turku of the Cathedral's archbishop. As he wrote in thinking of this time, "It is too bad one must age in order to understand oneself, one's resources and the way to use them."[93]

Gallén and Pekka Halonen congratulated their artist comrades Louis and Eva on the birth of their second son Clas in June 1898. The event slipped in without disturbing Eva's work for long, or causing much more than a casual mention in her book. She evidently had no thought of leaving or lessening her work. The family purse depended also on her income as teacher and book artist.

She was busy with her decorative drawing, filling an order for a book collector in England, and making a pair of trousers for her son Pehr, whose clothes were in rags. It was not easy to combine her roles of mother and artist. She was relieved that Louis had hired a new office manager to leave him free, but silently worried that the new business enterprise was still taking away all painting time. And she worried about the fact that Louis, such a fervent adopted son of Finland, was in fact a stranger, a foreigner. Was he really being accepted by artists other than his good friends? Was something destructive growing underneath the pleasant exterior? Was he too excited and happy to notice? At this point he was only concerned about the growing mercantile greed.

Eva's worries multiplied. Louis's many-sided interests were a danger to his painting, but a necessity for his own life, she knew. His enthusiasm and boyish zest, part of his charm, could so easily be misunderstood by her countrymen. His trusting and open ways, his eagerly expressed views might not be appreciated, but instead seen as tactless or even directly wounding.

Louis's frequent absences on travels, his trips between the factory and Helsinki left Eva alone, though she was busy with drawings and orders. But it gave her an opportunity to visit Sophie at Laxpojo in the summer of 1898 and make a trip to Villnäs with her. The two sisters needed to see each other and have real talks, uninhibited by any other company. Neither of them could easily reveal problems; they had been trained too well to silence in their childhood. Sophie took her time to tell Eva that she could no longer keep her marriage together and that she longed for work. Perhaps Eva talked about the problems of being married to a man whose temperament—depression alternating with wild exuberance—was so different from her own. When his mood was down, he retreated into himself, enveloped in a cloak of black self-loathing that snuffed out every creative impulse in his painting. Eva learned to dread the warning signs and called his black moods "psychic," but tried to distract and encourage him. Years later she told me that she felt helpless, unable to understand how he could so totally give in to his emotions. He sometimes embarrassed her with his sudden tears, moved by music or a passing thought. But the sun eventually came out again, and with it the other side of his nature, the ebullience and mordant wit that made him a sparkling companion, on fire to paint. Eva's upbringing had trained her to show nothing, to endure silently, though it is possible she hid a passionate nature under her cool control. Her dry, ironic humor helped her over many rough passages. What she and Louis shared was, in the end, far more important than what separated them, but the differences were sometimes a painful discovery early in their marriage.

The directors of the little company overruled Louis's judgment that their Helsinki shop should not be enlarged or made more pretentious. In 1899 a new showroom was opened. Now toys, fabrics and luxury items would be sold. Louis worried, and in between made linoleum cuts. (One of Finch would be used for an imprint by the Finnish Post Office in 1991, together with stamps of Iris pottery and one of Finch's seascapes.) It was as if Louis's dream had turned into a monster. But he went abroad for purchases, accompanied by his assistant draughtsman.

Eva went on one of his trips. From Berlin, in June, 1899, she wrote of seeing the type of glass panes they planned to make in Porvoo, perhaps the decorative leaded glass forming part of the furniture, in cupboards and writing desks.[94] She mentioned that Finch had had splendid success in Munich, with his faience pieces and tiled stoves. Munich was a center of culture, showing 19th century German paintings. The Chancellor at this time was a Hohenlohe-Schillingsfürst, perhaps the Prince Regent Eva refers to, who had bought Finch's crocks and tiled stoves.

Louis took on responsibilities to prepare an "Iris Room" for the Finnish Pavilion at the 1900 Paris World's Fair. Gallén promised to stand behind it so long as he could have the freedom to follow his own ideas, a wide-ranging variety for furniture, textiles, lamps, even door handles and candlesticks. This eased Louis's anxiety and gave him hope that showing off its wares would help the Iris Company survive.

While Gallén was breaking out of his isolation in the wilderness to work on the Iris Room in Paris, signs continued in Finland of Russian violations of their political compact. It was a period of intense political strain. A new period of "Russification" had begun, encroaching on Finland's rights: making Russian the language of the land and the principal subject in the curriculum; filling civil service positions with Russians; abolishing an independent Finnish post office, tolls and monetary system; merging Finland's army into that of Russia. There were those who favored the "politics of compliance" with the Russians, seen as traitors by defenders of Finland's historic autonomy. It was a foretaste of things to come.

At the Iris Company, debts were beginning to rise because the enlarged shop was not selling as expected. Louis's own income was highly uncertain. Even in her retrospective writing, Eva does not dwell on the pain of having to sell their house and rent an apartment in Porvoo. She writes merely that "noticeable sacrifices" were in order. So tight were the time and the budget that Louis dared not go to Paris for the Fair. There Gallén was painting his frescoes for the Finnish Pavilion which had been designed by young Finnish architects, among them Saarinen. This was a turning point for Gallén, whose recent pilgrimage to Italy and Giotto's frescoes had resulted in his fascination with this art form. He felt that his way of living apart in his wilderness at home was imbedded in the Finnish character, but now he needed to shake off his isolation to be refreshed by the company of friends and artists.

In spite of the uncertain times Eva and Louis went to St. Petersburg to probe the market. The date is not clear from Eva's memoirs. She mentions March, and it must have been in 1900. Iris could not depend on the World's Fair alone. They visited Eva's brother Gustaf and his wife Anastasia. Eva admired her sister-in-law's chic clothes and the hats that were worn to lunch in a worldly metropolis. In Finland, head and ears were snugly covered with fur caps of uncertain style, and woolen scarves tied around the ears. Eva had nothing appropriate to wear but was happy to borrow a red velvet hat from a chic friend, even though it had nothing to do with the rest of her clothes. At least the top of her head was warm and fashionable as they drove through St. Petersburg with its icy March winds in an open sleigh. They paid a call on their old relative Tante Aurore Karamsin, and enjoyed late theatre parties "in the Russian fashion" after the performances. Princes and dukes, countesses and bowing gentlemen from all corners of the Empire were part of the entertainment. One young prince, Eva writes, "was said to have fled Caucasia with a stolen diamond cut into the calf of his leg!"[95]

The luxury mesmerized Eva—servants standing on each step at the entrance of a marble palace, with van Dycks and Rembrandts in its gallery; a private theatre; the embroidered silk curtains and soft, heavy oriental rugs under their feet. Louis was pleased that the trip resulted in orders. However, by now their house had been sold and from that there was no retreat.

At Iris there were new and disturbing signals. Suddenly new stockholders appeared. Louis's ideas of letting the shop include non-exclusive wares and be managed by someone else were not approved by other shareholders. The Swedish architect Louis had hired as assistant draughtsman and sales manager had been making intrigues. In a book on Louis's furniture the culminating betrayal is described. There was a general meeting of the company on May 17, 1900. "False information had been spread that Sparre was interested in quitting . . . At a stormy meeting in Helsinki, Sparre succeeded in refuting all the groundless accusations made against him and managed to get his adversary dismissed."[96] However, Louis had seen the writing on the wall.

Perhaps there was a feeling in the family that one could not permit the external events of Russian transgressions and political turmoil to interrupt the rhythm of ordinary life, for that would be an admission of defeat. Eva took her little boys to see her childhood home, Villnäs, and all of them spent a magic summer in their cottage, picking berries and mushrooms, swimming and rowing. August, who had come home to Finland in 1898, married his childhood sweetheart Elsie Nordenfelt and Eva picked out a house for them in Porvoo. There were words of praise for the Iris Room and Gallén in Paris. Louis had won a reputation as a pioneer in modern industrial art design. But at home he blamed himself for not understanding in time that Iris had started down a path that could result only in the defeat of his own plans. The emphasis on profit, the enlarged factory, had blown away what he had hoped to do.

Louis could not blame himself for neglecting his workers at Iris. He had liked them and knew some as friends. He saw to it that discussions and lectures were held in their clubroom, with its fireplace, games, and newspapers. As much as he wanted to bring art into daily life, he hoped also to improve the quality of the workers' free time. It was part of his ideal of a world where everyone had common goals and shared interests.

At a time when a ten-hour day was normal he made sure the workers took one afternoon off a week, to have time for pleasure or an interest. There was a small library in their club room. Louis understood that if the products were to be effective in raising taste, the craftsmen should have a strong sense of what they were making and why. The revolution in designing even humble objects with attention to color and form, combining beauty and utility, should begin with the craftsmen's understanding of the work they were doing. There would be no class differences in the appreciation of beauty: it was not to be seen as an élite interest. Louis's ideals of social betterment and creating harmonious household furnishings for everyday life, were to be parts of a whole.

The reasons behind the collapse of Iris included the recession in Finland, the disagreements within the company, and decisions made behind Louis's back, such as the enlarging of the factory and abandonment of Louis's wish to run the company without mercantile profit or mass production. Doing the work of secretaries and bookkeepers himself, Louis had undertaken too many business responsibilities in which he had no experience. In November of 1900 he resigned his position but stayed on until the year's end. In January 1901 only his membership on the company's board remained. "With Sparre's departure as designer-in-chief, the demand for Iris furniture declined accordingly."[97]

The Iris Company survived only a few more years, from 1897-1900, before collapsing into bankruptcy after Louis had left. But he set his stamp on applied arts and furniture design in Finland, in single pieces and in furniture with a combination of functions. Porvoo Museum has documented the history of his company, located individual pieces of furniture and owners, discovered original fabrics, some still being produced on the same looms. Louis's vision survives.

There was no stinting of excellence in materials. Finnish birch of several kinds, oak, ash, sycamore, beech, walnut, satinwood and mahogany were among the many species used. The design was often the grain itself, polished and/or stained. Textiles for upholstery were largely imported from Liberty's in London—velvet, silk, wool, linen—sometimes elegantly embroidered with linen yarn using motifs of poppies, irises and even the common dandelion.

Eva herself embossed leather, in Porvoo motifs, for furniture inlays, while Louis designed hinge mounts of wrought iron and inlays of bone, pewter and brass. Medieval arts on view in Morris's Red House had influenced the production of tiles and leaded glasswork. Swirling plumes in carvings and inlays of a mosaic wreath with ribbons or Greek key design were for elegant furniture. But even in utilitarian pieces marble and colored inlays were applied, using poppy and water lily motifs. Whether utilitarian or luxurious, furniture and fixtures were designed with the same attention to the quality of materials and workmanship. Much was built in, as at Morris's Red House, and often it was made for multiple uses, as in a settee with bookshelves. The styles were modified Swedish 18th Century, Empire or Biedermeier, but the authors of Louis's furniture book have declared that he "did not copy anything directly, but rather that he always adapted or redesigned various types of furniture and the accompanying details."[98]

Although nearly overwhelmed by his responsibilities at the Iris Company, Louis, true to his custom, had indulged in another fascination. In 1898 his passion for preserving the old part of the town of Porvoo nearly took over his life. He fell in love with the whole community in his twilight walks along the crooked streets and quarters around the medieval cathedral. It was in danger of being overrun by developers, with their straight-edged rulers and dividers, already making known their plans to march through this part of the town without regard for history or structure. He felt there was no time to lose. An Imperial decree in 1833 had been intended to demolish buildings, flatten hills, straighten roads. Luckily, it was not carried out, because of lack of funds. But the ordinance was still valid. The modern part of town, built after 1833, had been revamped following the Tsar's command, with broad straight streets and houses built according to plan. Now, when Louis stepped in, new prosperity endangered the Old Town once again. The town fathers wanted to copy and apply to the oldest quarter of town the straight streets of Porvoo's newer quarter standing below the Cathedral hill and rebuilt in the 1830s. But Louis argued that the ancient core and soul of Porvoo must be left in its beautifully untouched state.

With his usual imagination and energy Louis found old town maps from the 17th and 18th Centuries, showing the roads and lanes following graceful natural contours. If the modernization plan was carried out, the old houses around the cathedral on the hilltop were doomed to be destroyed by heartless symmetry. How could he reach the people of Porvoo, how could he give them the passion to preserve their town?

Louis went forward with advertisements, posters and notices in county newspapers, for a meeting in the school auditorium. He had planned a lecture.

"All these evocative little streets and alleys clambering between and around the fragile life of the town's two focal points, the cathedral and the Town Hall, will be swept away and replaced by unartistic and pedantic regularity . . . The old part of town with its uneven terrain, picturesque buildings, surprising perspectives . . . can, in the future . . . make Porvoo into one of the country's and the Northern countries' most beautiful and notable towns."[99] His lecture in April 1898 received serious attention at the time, and was later published. Although it took ten years before the authorities in Porvoo would approve the reservation, Louis won the day. In a 1991 book on Finnish artist couples, a chapter about the Sparres gives Louis much of the credit for the preservation of Porvoo's "Old Town" section.

In 1991, the Director of the Porvoo Museum wrote: "The efforts of Louis Sparre have become almost a slogan in this town: 'The Empire Town is today exactly as old as the Old Town was when Louis Sparre began crusading for it!'"[100]

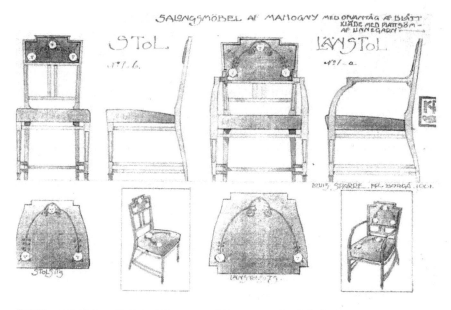

Drawing-room chairs with blue cloth covers and linen-yarn satin-stitch. Louis Sparre 1901. Ornamo/Museum of Applied Arts.

Louis Sparre's chairs

Chapter 14

TURN OF THE CENTURY POLITICS AND

A COSSACK CHARGE

Some words are needed here to explain Finland's political situation at the turn of the century, and about the neo-romantic interest in Finnish historical and artistic roots. It was a time of self-discovery, of consciousness by Finns that they had a separate history, apart from their rulers, first Swedes, then Russians. As education became more universal and the Finnish language achieved more official prominence, the interest in Finland's unique history spread from the educated classes to the general public.

The scholar J.V. Snellman, writing in the 1840s, stressed the importance of a national culture as well as the Finnish language, and wrote articles appealing to the educated classes. He also reached Finnish-speaking readers through a newspaper for farmers.

J.L. Runeberg (1804-77), a journalist and poet, also found his audience among the Swedish-speaking educated classes and the Finnish-speaking population. His most famous book of poems, the Tales of Ensign Ståhl, aroused national pride with its heroic verses about the Finnish war of 1808-1809, the last war under Swedish rule. The first collection was published in 1848. In 1858, Carl Robert

Mannerheim, Eva's father, had a hand in bringing to public attention for the first time some significant unpublished Runeberg verses. He read "Den Femte Juli" (The Fifth of July) at a celebration for the surviving veterans of the 1808 war. As the historian Jägerskiöld notes, these particular verses have exhorted the Finns in their hours of trial, even in modern times, much as Francis Scott Key inspired Americans with his lyrics, first circulated as a handbill in 1814.

Journalists were important shapers of public opinion as early as the 1770s, in both languages of Swedish and Finnish. Although Runeberg earned the title of national poet, he also served as journalist, as did the historical novelist Zacharias Topelius (1818-98). These two, Snellman and others had played leading roles in the political development of Finland, despite the imposition of censorship during several periods in the 18th and 19th Centuries. The press did not become fully free until 1918.

One powerful cultural discovery had made its way to the masses. In 1835-6 the recently founded Finnish Literature Society had published the fruits of a young medical doctor and student of folk poetry, Elias Lönnrot, who wrote his doctoral thesis on the "magic medicine of the Finns . . . its folk tradition with its incantations and remedies."[101] From his travels by foot, boat and horse cart, he had collected a mass of poetry dictated and sung for him by the still active rune singers of eastern Finland and the White Sea region, in Karelia. He brought the dialect of his work closer to modern usage, to make it accessible to all, and followed the ancient verse form himself in composing new lines. The Kalevala was immediately recognized as a treasure by the educated classes. Runeberg himself compared it to the Homeric epics. The Finns were now seen to have a history of their own, a culture uniquely theirs. The poetry was translated into Swedish, French and German; Longfellow was inspired by it to study American Indian culture, and wrote his Song of Hiawatha in 1855. However, not until the end of the 19th Century did ordinary people in Finland find the Kalevala fascinating as an historical and cultural base.

The complication of two separate languages in Finland divided parties and confused the issue of autonomy. Speakers of Finnish and Swedish tended to be separated along class lines, but the population speaking Finnish as a birthright overwhelmed in their numbers the far smaller groups of Swedish-speaking Finns along the coast and western portions of the country. The "Svecomans" or Swedish-speaking party suspected the "Fennomans," the Finnish-speakers, of valuing their western laws less than the promotion of new laws to strengthen the official place of the Finnish language. The opening of a school for Finnish speaking students was the beginning of a broader educational system in the 1850s, although it was not until the 1880s that Finnish-language secondary schools began to have an effect on the peasants' interest in learning. In 1889 there were as many students in Finnish-language secondary schools as in the Swedish ones. The historian Yrjö-Koskinen addressed the House of Nobles in Finnish in 1894. At the University, lectures had been given in Finnish for some time by many professors.[102] Under threat of Russian domination, nationalistic feelings were heightened, and under the pressure of being "Russified" the disparate language parties of Finland united. Anything was better than the imposition of Russian as an obligatory language. Once Finland became a sovereign nation, the constitution of 1919 proclaimed both Finnish and Swedish national languages. In 1923 instruction in all faculties of the university in Helsinki was given in both languages by law.

This rediscovery of Finnish cultural roots coincided with a golden period of Finnish art. Sibelius composed his tone poems, including "Finlandia," based on folkloric tales and folk music. Alexis Kivi promoted Finnish-language theatre. Gallén painted themes from the Kalevala with his friend and fellow-artist Louis Sparre. The Finnish poet Eino Leino used meter and motifs from the Kalevala. Eva's and Louis's wedding trip to Karelia was itself part of the nationalistic movement, to preserve in word, paintings and engravings the costumes and customs, the wooden churches, the smoke-hole huts, all still part of daily life in Finland's and Russia's fragile Karelian wilderness.

Economically, too, the country was opening up. No longer was Russia the sole important trading partner, for timber began to be exported to the west. The ports could be kept open by new icebreakers in 1890. "Humble cottagers" began to move from country to town, drawn by industrialization. There were the beginnings of workers' organizations. Heretofore, workers had been excluded from any position of influence or representation in the Estates. The workers' groups had been content, in the early 1890s, to ask for universal voting rights. There was no issue yet of strife between management and labor, and the workers' organizations did not want their banners in red, the color that represented Marxists and radical socialists in other countries. Finnish workers were advised by members of the educated class, but by 1899 they had separated from "bourgeois" leadership and founded a political party.

After Finland was given up by Sweden and annexed by Russia in 1809, in the Napoleonic wars, the Russian Emperor Alexander I had sworn to uphold Finnish autonomy. It was Carl Erik Mannerheim, great-grandfather of Eva and her brothers and sisters, who had traveled to St. Petersburg in 1808 with his delegation of representatives, to argue his country's case successfully before the Tsar. Finland remained a Grand Duchy under Russian rule, but with autonomous laws; Finnish legislation was not administered by Russian ministers. Finnish matters were decided personally by the Tsar, who was crowned Finland's Grand Duke in Porvoo's cathedral, promising to rule Finland's people with justice and leniency.[103] Each succeeding Tsar had sworn the same oath, guaranteeing Finland's laws upheld by Finnish courts; freedom of religion for the Lutheran Church and education free from interference. (Tsar Nicholas II, the last Tsar, was the first of his line to break his oath to the Finns.) Finnish local administration was not affected by the 1809 Russian domination . . . The Senate, half representing the Finnish nobility, the remaining half representing the three other Estates, dealt with matters of law and administrative affairs.

The two languages, Finnish and Swedish, were protected; that is, Russian had not yet been enforced as the official language. Civil servants were Finns; coinage, post office and tolls or customs, remained in Finnish hands. The Tsar accepted the establishment of Finnish military units.[104] The office of Minister Secretary of State, the Finnish representative to the Russian Crown, had a history of serving Finland's interests successfully The Russian Governor General had been seen, until Nicholas II's time, as working harmoniously with the Finnish Senate.

This situation had generally obtained until 1890. But Alexander III, the father of Nicholas II, was influenced by a slavophile philosophy looking toward absolute rule, suspicious of Finland's freedoms and western leanings. It was feared in Finland that the Russians would seek to impose punitive and limiting measures on Finnish trade with Russia. By 1890, the Finnish Post Office was transferred to the

Russian ministry of the Interior, by direction of a Russian government committee. To the consternation of most Finns, the majority of the Senate, fearful of offending the Tsar, did not refuse recognition of the new postal transfer. Word of the anger caused by this "reform" (in actual fact, a fundamental breach of the constitutional law) reached the Tsar. His professed willingness to guard Finland's status was, according to one historian, "the first of several worthless imperial declarations."[105]

In 1891, in Helsinki, Sophie Mannerheim reported to her brother Johan in Denmark that there were heated conversations about who did or did not accept invitations to the Governor General's ball. She herself could not imagine how one "could make oneself go to him, eat his food, drink his wine and show him a friendly face . . . one finds oneself in a permanent state of rage from morning 'til night."[106]

In 1894 the new emperor Nicholas II swore to uphold Finland's rights. Finland's national militia had been established by the Tsar's act of 1878. Finnish soldiers were protected from serving under Russian flags on foreign soil, except in times of extreme danger to the Tsar's throne. The officer corps was Finnish. But in January 1899, in his speech from the Throne, the new Governor General Bobrikov announced that Finnish military service would be under Russian protection. The Tsar issued regulations in his February Manifesto a month later confirming imperial rule over Finland, abrogating "antique laws." The Finnish army would be abolished and merged with Russia's. The Imperial Senate, closely linked to the Emperor and therefore more inclined to bend, voted 10 to 10 to publish the manifesto, from which moment it would become law. The Estates pronounced the February Manifesto invalid.[107]

In the passive resistance that followed, shop windows were dressed in black and white, and a period of official mourning was considered. People dared no longer speak, they whispered. An Address from the people of Finland was a swift answer to the Governor General's speech. Among the half million signatories were bank directors, doctors, lawyers, farmers, those living in Finland's wilderness country, and university students. The Address humbly asked that the delegation presenting it be allowed to meet with the Tsar. His answer was this: "Make it known to the members of the 500-man delegation that I of course will not receive them, although I nevertheless am not angry at them."[108] Grand Duke Vladimir had come for a visit to Helsinki in the summer of 1899, but when he went to church there were only a few priests present with the archbishop. There was no fanfare. The new century's dawning was looked upon with dark suspicion by all political parties.

In the summer of 1900 political storms were brewing around the Sparres. There was censorship, and newspapers were being closed down. Finnish patriots in Sweden had printed an underground paper, brought to Finland in a sailing yacht which flew the burgee of Helsinki's Nyland Yacht Club. The distribution was wily, preferably made in double-bottomed suitcases or concealed in inner pockets by respectable old ladies. In 1901 a new conscription law was imposed. The Finnish army was dissolved. Conscripts could be ordered to Russian detachments in Finland or St. Petersburg. Russian was decreed to be the language of Finnish non-commissioned officers. It was no less than a coup d'état. The Tsar, with that, lost the loyalty of his hitherto faithful Finnish subjects. Nicholas became known to Finns as "The Perjurer." Not only university students but the élite of Europe's scientists and "other famous persons appealed to the Russian emperor to respect Finland's position."[109]

The illegal conscription that followed in 1902 enraged Finns of all parties: the Constitutionalists, who demanded strict compliance with Finland's autonomy, and the Compliants, who reasoned that great powers would always be unyielding and some compromise was necessary. The latter argued that the Finnish language surpassed in importance the body of western laws as a national tool of survival. In fact, during the reign of Governor-General Bobrikov, the Compliants influenced the passing of an edict making the Finnish language the equal of Swedish in public affairs, but their triumph was lessened by a decree that Russian would be used at the higher administrative levels. As many as five-sixths of the university students refused to report for army duty. On the advice of those who would Russify Finland, Nicholas had already imposed a new system of Russian laws on Finland's western-based courts. Judges who would not uphold the new laws were dismissed. The Governor General gave himself the right to decide what should be taught in the schools, and precisely how it should be taught. In girls' schools Russian was to be the main subject in the curriculum, to make certain future Finnish mothers would speak Russian at home. If spies did not approve the teachers' words, schools were closed. Shops, bookstores, newspapers, businesses were closed on Russian whims.

The historian Jägerskiöld explains Gustaf Mannerheim's ability to maintain relations with his Finnish family while serving Russia during these tense times. How could he continue in loyal service to the Tsar, whose advisors were threatening one brother and falsely accusing another? He returned to Russia after a visit home, hoping that reasonable views would change the Tsar's tyranny in Finland. His friendships with liberal elements among the aristocracy—"liberal" in comparison with the absolutism of most—gave him a perspective not available to family members. Gustaf Mannerheim was aware that there was furious disagreement within Russia on the question of Finland. He saw no need to despair, and was even able to instruct his family on how to gain access to powerful Russians in or visiting Finland. He knew that some relatives of the Tsar did not favor the restrictive policies. One of them was the Tsar's mother, born a Danish princess; another the Grand Duke Vladimir, the Tsar's uncle. Indeed, there was a report that Count Carl Mannerheim (presumably Gustaf's father) had attended a restaurant in the company of the Grand Duke and his wife.

By 1902, Eva and Louis had long since settled into their apartment in the small town of Porvoo, which had an old history of survival as it had been on the direct route of every Russian land invasion. But now the Governor General, given dictatorial powers by the Tsar, had become a tyrant. Russian warships in the harbor were a threat to the existence of the city.

On what seemed a perfectly ordinary April day in 1902, Eva went in to Helsinki. Walking to the great square, she saw a huge crowd. She heard bits of conversation. The air was buzzing with words about a demonstration against the latest order of the Tsar. Finnish soldiers were being called up to Russian colors. Now fifteen thousand youths were prepared to strike despite threats of exile, deportation or service in a Russian penal corps. The conscription was unlawful, a threat far more terrible than the punitive actions to which Finns were already subjected.

Eva thought quickly. She could go to friends with an apartment overlooking the square. The nearer she came, the greater the crowds. She saw her brother Carl coming out of his bank, trying to persuade people to leave. More and more people blackened the square.

High on her perch in the borrowed apartment, Eva looked down. She had a broad view of the scene below. Like a gigantic stage, the whole square was visible under her window. A mass of bodies gradually filled it. She could see the side streets leading into the square, and knew with icy certainty what the next act would be.

Under her gaze, unseen by all the thousand actors massing in the square, was a troop of Cossacks on shaggy horses, advancing on the central square from a side street, deliberate, measured, menacing, their hoofbeats silenced by the snow.

As though in a trance she waited for the horror. It came. In a rush the Cossacks raised their arms, brandishing sabers and long whips, slashing into the screaming crowd, riding like madmen. Up on the sidewalks, around and out into the side street, into the neat front yards, wherever people were running, the Cossacks flailed whips, sliced sabers. She could see men and women running up the steps of the cathedral to seek sanctuary. She could clearly see blood on the snow, wounded civilians carried away. She saw a group of armed Russian soldiers advance, stop, assume firing positions. Afterwards she remembered her helpless, silent raging and the pitiful snowballs hurled by the protesters against the attackers.

In that charge, one young man was ambushed and whipped in the face. At that moment, he was said to have made an irrevocable vow. He would offer his life to assassinate the despotic Governor General.

As a result of the demonstration which Eva had seen, the Court in Turku indicted the Russian Governor General. This, in turn, led to the change of the official staff of the court. Now the Tsar was more eager to listen to Bobrikov, to take up dictatorial powers. These would doom Alexander to the assassin's bullet in 1904.

The Tsar's proclamation of exile for Carl came as no surprise to him. One year later, Johan followed him to Sweden. Of the surviving brothers and sisters, August, Eva and Sophie, who had come back from London, were left in Finland.

Chapter 15

CARL'S EXILE

Carl, her oldest brother, was Eva's favorite, always there to listen and help. He was a tactful man, though he spoke his mind when something seemed amiss. Neither snobbish attitudes nor saying something slick to appease Russian authority were to his liking.

Carl became head of the board of directors of the new company, Iris, in 1897, investing money and his business expertise. An "Iris Room" was created for the Finnish Pavilion of the Paris World's Fair in 1900, the choice of typical Iris furniture supervised by Gallén. Iris had collapsed after three years, but its wares are recognized today as the pioneers of modern industrial art design in Finland.

Carl had become a leader among the rebels, head of the so-called Kagal group advocating passive resistance (named for the organization of the Jews persecuted in Russia). The Governor General in Finland now had the power to exile those who did not follow Russian views. They were sent to Siberia or other remote places in the huge Empire.

By 1903 Carl had begun to make plans. He thought he might be seized and sent to Siberia, and that this could well happen at night, with a knock at the door. Rumors whispered that he was in danger. His brother Johan had been accused of being an "animal torturer." He, too, might be seized.

Carl's wife was to sing in public, in Helsinki's music hall. She was being watched by Russian spies. Her concert had just begun when the doors of the hall were flung open and Russian police, dressed in civilian clothes, burst in. They demanded that the audience leave. No one obeyed. Threats and words were shouted as the singer, not one to be frightened, calmly continued singing. Carl himself at last asked the audience to leave. There had been too many sudden arrests, too many silenced newspapers, and no laws to protect them. No one was safe, no house secure. There were unannounced house searches.

A proclamation from the Tsar exiled Carl and five others. They were all warned to leave within seven days, accused of "conspiracy against the State." Carl's sister Sophie and his wife Aina hid his important papers, and when police came to his house, Carl took pleasure in wasting their time while they read his ordinary mail.

Carl moved to the house of a friend to avoid a midnight arrest without witnesses. But at seven in the morning the house was surrounded by police in civilian clothes. They forced their way in, giving Carl the Tsar's orders to leave, and papers to sign promising not to attend meetings or give cause for demonstrations. He refused to sign, and was tailed by detectives.

On April 27th, the railroad station was strictly guarded by police, yet thousands of people had heard the news and pressed in to say goodbye. At a signal the train began to move. The mass of people followed it down the tracks, shouting hurrahs, weeping, singing the Finnish national anthem. A crowd of students from the university had come to sing their student song, as the train rolled away. Carl and Aina stood on the platform at the end of the last car, waving to the crowd. Louis and Eva had taken their oldest son to the station for a last glimpse. Johan and his wife Palla were there, too, watching the train pull away in hushed silence. In Turku, at the boat docks, Carl and Aina boarded the ferry taking them to Sweden, across the Åland Sea. The family could hear Aina singing the national anthem as the boat left, her voice carried to shore by the waves.[110]

On the day of Carl's forced departure, Sophie, August and Elsie took on the job of packing up his house and receiving bouquets to him from admirers. Sophie herself was writing anonymous articles against the repressive Russian government, but the work, she said, was becoming more and more difficult because spies were everywhere. Letters were now opened at the post office. She worried about Carl, with two children and a wife to support. He was without work, and at 40 rather old to be looking for the sort of leading banker's position which his experience merited. Aina wrote her sister-in-law Elsie from Stockholm, thanking her for the comfort she had been to them their last days at home. "It feels bitter to have left everything and everyone!" She was moved, she wrote, by a concert of Scandinavian music. "Heads were bared for Finland's song . . . the flag was lowered."[111]

Eva, traveling in Italy, had followed the Swedish press. She, too, worried about Carl, and what sort of work he might find. One familiar name after another was listed among the exiles. Eva later wrote that despite the help and friendship offered by individual Swedes for the homeless Finns, "the attitude toward them in official circles [was] often careful avoidance."[112]

Eva wrote Carl from Cannes, sadly noting how far from each other they would be: August in Africa, Carl perhaps moving to America, the Sparres unsure of their own future. "In Sweden," Eva wrote in February, 1904, "one will always feel like a foreigner."[113]

Carl decided to settle in Sweden. He told Johan of this decision, adding that he keenly disapproved of Gustaf's joining Russian arms to fight in the Russo-Japanese war.[114] It was not the first time he had been concerned about his brother's too-Russian stance; in a letter of 1890 he found Gustaf's views "as different as possible from our attitudes here at home . . . Your perceptions were those of a stranger; it upset me and came between us as a barrier."[115] Like his brothers and sisters, Carl was disturbed by Gustaf's marriage to a Russian lady. He attended the wedding in St. Petersburg as a duty, not a pleasure.

Keeping his distant brother August in South Africa informed about Finland, Carl wrote him from Stockholm in November, 1905. "Since the revolution of October 31, there hasn't been a single letter from Finland. The only news we have are two-day-old telegrams and dispatches from the news agency. Last Friday we were in terrific suspense, and as we've learned, the mood in Finland was ghastly. The Russian warships lay menacingly in the harbor, the cannons of Sveaborg [the harbor fortress] were said to be turned on the city, and Obolenski [the Governor General] had gone on board a Russian cruiser. At the same time, the city was in the grip of the workers, and these, in a state of rage, wanted nothing to do with the 'gentlemen'," as they called the upper crust. "I decided suddenly to go to Copenhagen to try to bring about an intervention to hasten government action, which alone will save the situation." [116]

In Copenhagen, Carl paid a visit to the Dowager Empress Maria Feodorovna, who lived at Amalienborg Castle in Denmark on visits home. Born the Danish Princess Dagmar, she had been the consort of Alexander III and mother of Nicholas II. She was well known by Finns for her support of their cause and her disapproval of Governor-General Bobrikov. Among others, Aurore Karamsin, Carl Mannerheim's elderly relative and once a favorite at the Imperial Court, appealed to the widowed Tsarina by a message forwarded to Tsar Nicholas.

When Carl called on "the widow of Amalienborg," he wrote, he found her "immediately ready to do her best, and I spent days with her people to find an effective measure. When I came back to the hotel I found the manifesto had been signed and everything restored!"[117] The Tsar's dictatorial decrees had been cancelled. Carl goes on: "Last Sunday I again had an audience with 'the widow' and we exchanged mutual congratulations."[118]

In the same letter, Carl expressed admiration for the workers' "masterful leadership and the unity which marked them all over the country. That order was maintained so admirably and with such restraint was thanks to the workers and students; these two united to form the national guard in Helsinki . . . Above all was the joy of having lived through these great events, restoring one's faith in the Finnish people."

Although Carl's exile was lifted in January, 1905, he decided to remain in Sweden, where he continued his work as director of the Stockholm-Öfvre Norrland Bank. Earlier, he had been offered a government position as Finance Minister in Finland, and when the exile ended, he was sought as a senator. Despite all flattering entreaties, Carl declined, citing his failing health—the result of a kidney operation—and the volatility of the Finnish political scene. In 1908 he became a Swedish subject. Two years later, he tasted the bitterness of bearing the blame for reverses suffered by his bank.[119]

Like the other Mannerheims, Carl hoped the Entente powers would win the First World War. His visit to England soon after hostilities began only strengthened his views. German brutality in Belgium appalled him; pro-German sympathies in Finland were as foreign to him as to his brothers and sisters. Carl died at 50; he did not survive to celebrate his brother Gustaf's command of the Finnish forces that achieved independence in 1918.

Chapter 16

JOHAN AND PALLA

Johan's life too was to take a decisive turn during these turbulent years in Finland. By 1904, he too had moved to Sweden, where he pursued his lifelong interest in animal husbandry and forestry.

In 1893, Johan corresponded with Gustaf in St. Petersburg. He was concerned, as always, with buying horses, especially ones which "carry neck and tail high." But something else was on his mind. He wanted to buy Villnäs with Gustaf and Carl. Aunt Mimmi could continue to live there with a garden, earning an income from their running the place as an agriculture school. Cousin Jeanne would also have a stake in it. But their Aunt Mimmi did not agree with their suggestions, and in the end Villnäs, to their great distress, was sold in 1903. This had an effect on all the Mannerheims. Johan bought a Swedish manor, Grensholm, to replace the old family home, and Gustaf, toward the end of his life, lived in a manor once owned by the family that had built Villnäs in the 17th Century. In Gustaf's words at Johan's funeral, "it was as if he had absorbed the marrow of his bones from that hard clay of our ancestral home." It was, for all of them, their vital center.

On being rebuffed, Johan could always comfort himself with thoughts of riding. "Perhaps we could ride in the Hungarian hunts" he wrote Gustaf from Paris.

In 1895, he took time to congratulate Gustaf on the birth of a daughter, but continued, "I hope to be of use to you in the Caucasus, Poland or elsewhere." From the agriculture school in Ruovesi, where he was a teacher, he wrote Gustaf that he was giving notice. He would spend the next several weeks finishing a travel book about his trip in 1893-94, which was published in Helsinki in 1896, and would then study livestock breeding abroad. At the end of 1895 he asked Gustaf to help him find a position as steward in Russia, on one of the great estates. As he wrote, he had high recommendations from schools in Denmark and Finland. But in his own country he felt no opportunities existed.

Then his correspondence began with Palaemona Treschow, his future wife. The first letter, March 17, 1901, was as formal as the times required; he addressed her as "mademoiselle." They had met as groom and bridesmaid at the family place of his brother August's wife Elsie, Höganäs, in southern Sweden. Johan asked, in this first letter, for her photo. "I hope, mademoiselle, that you will not ill perceive such a favor." He wrote carefully that if Palaemona visited Elsie at Höganäs again, Johan would attend the agricultural meeting nearby, instead of in Stockholm.

Six months later, his letter was addressed to "my own dearest Palla." Palla had expressed doubts about herself and their close friendship. But Johan replied, "whether radiant or not, happy or not, you are everything for me . . . You have confidence in me, and therefore I accept setbacks easily. [But] to get to know me through letters is not a good way. I have always been reserved, which you have learned from my 'not unpleasant silence'." He had never, he wrote, revealed his inmost thoughts in words, and found it even more difficult to do in letters. Now her bright and candid way of meeting him, made the experience easier. "I consider frankness and openness a condition for our happiness."

In October, 1901, Johan assures Palla that she can change the marriage ceremony any way she likes, "the main thing is that it won't be too long in coming." He goes on to say, "I have carefully considered things and have seen too much of an unhappy marriage not to be careful. My parents were not suited for each other. Nothing can induce me to experience the misery I was witness to as a child. I say this to convince you that even I have doubted and grappled before I became certain. But why talk of this? We suit each other as no one has ever done." Johan, always the silent observer, opened his heart to Palla about this childhood trauma.

From his estate manager's place at the enormous estate of Jokkis, he writes of following Palla through all of Finland and half of Russia, and was ready to continue through Sweden and the rest of Europe. "But you spared me the pleasure by saying 'yes.' As for the situation on the steamboat deck, you must give me the credit that I chose one place where you easily could have got rid of me."

Then, describing the change for Palla in moving from her "happy life with many people around" to a more desolate place, he writes that in Finnish terms it was a well populated area. He hoped she would take an interest in his work: "agriculture is the most many-sided and interesting of all occupations. One feels free and unencumbered, in contrast to the forced stress of official and military careers." He described his own work, in charge of "estate and forests and thereto belonging mills, brick works, peat bogs, etc." He wrote he had reached the conclusion that "Jokkis depends on me more than I on it. You think I'm full of myself, but that's not the case. I am full of faults."

Their engagement was known only to Elsie and Gustaf, but Johan suggested they let Sophie know. "Poor Sophie has had adversity in her life, married to an unpleasant man. Having divorced him, she is now a nurse in London."

From Jokkis, November 1, 1901, Johan gave Palla a review of his life, "before the happiest day of my life, when I met you. Anno 1868, born to Christian parents, I first saw the light of day, then was baptized and confirmed, and am free to marry. My father had two properties. We lived at one in the summers, Villnäs, a very old place. During winters we lived in Helsinki. My father was joint owner of certain industries and managing director of a large paper mill. An unsuccessful venture resulted in bankruptcy. Not long thereafter, my mother died, broken by anxiety and sorrows. My father remarried in Paris and lived there many years." He recounted how the children had been left without money, the girls' governess the boys' tutor had been dismissed, their childhood home sold, and all of them scattered and sent to live with relatives. Johan had been farmed out to his grandmother. As Johan writes, "We children were forced early to stand on our own feet. I was quite lazy in school, but plodded along, studying at the technical college in Helsinki for two years. I was rather practical and handy and mathematics was easy for me. But my eyes gave up on me, strained by a lot of drafting. I'd decided to stick to agriculture . . ."

Palla heard about his stubbornness, forcing his way through problems despite the lack of money. An uncle, an important personality in the agricultural world of Finland, said something that made a deep impression on Johan: "'Whatever you undertake, you must be the first.' I was always ashamed if some fellow-worker was about to get ahead of me, and did my best not to let my old uncle's thoughts fizzle out."

Johan described studying in Denmark three years, and coming back to the agricultural college in Finland. "The teachers requested a travel grant for me to study domestic animal breeding in Europe, particularly of horses. For a year I visited the finest stud farms in Europe, and wrote a report of my travels, published with many illustrations. My objective was to go into public service to try to get horse breeding on a new footing."

Johan went to southern Russia with Gustaf, with the thought of buying a large estate, but then was offered the place at Jokkis. "You know the rest," he wrote his fiancée.

In December, Johan wrote about the oppressed atmosphere in Russia. The regime was expecting troubles; "Seventeen cities in Russia are declared to be in a state of siege. There is only violence, and no justice."

His favorite sport, riding, was tempered by the winter cold. "I've never liked riding outside in winter. I think, Palla, when it's cold we'll practice inside." Palla wrote him of her own horsemanship, riding every day. "Here they ride at a wild pace, with no thought of schooling, but it's just my style. I like the horses to run as fast as they can."

By January 10, 1902, their engagement had been announced in the papers. He enclosed a clipping, "as I know it will please you."

They argued. "I insisted that your last letter smelled of perfume, and you denied it stubbornly. Brought to despair, I gave you a kiss and that helped, as you conceded the letter was perfumed."

He sent her a book by Gorky, "the original and brilliant Russian author, who suddenly is world-renowned. He depicts the inexplicable in human nature, all the good and evil which exist in those who have sunk to the lowest level, the power of passion to break down all barriers."

In February he bought a stallion which was "four years old and of the same color as the four-in-hand you saw in Petersburg." His favorite, Izmos, "trotted so high that he hardly touched the ground. I am a horse fool, in such good humor when a horse performs well." He was afraid Palla would "fall in love with him and forget me. He trots the high trot as though he had done nothing else."

In April Johan was beside himself. "I often want to kiss your letters, but the ridiculousness stops me. I have several times lost my head and done it, but would have been ashamed if anyone had seen me."

He reported on his sister Eva. "Louis and Eva left today. Louis promised to play tennis with you. They really are an artist couple, always cheerful and agreeable. They were both very interested in meeting you, and liked your merry portrait—it's comical how they always think alike."

He wrote about tension in Finland after the Cossack charge. It was a bloody punishment for peaceful civil demonstrations against the Tsar's illegal order of calling up Finns to Russian colors. "Another incident would not occur without bloodshed," Johan wrote. "Most are armed in Helsinki, and all revolvers sold out. A decree from on high has come out, prolonging the time for mobilization. The population is put to a harder test than ever. Plehve is now the mightiest man in Russia, but his is not a kindly disposition." Vyacheslav von Plehve, Russian Secretary of State for Finland, was the first Russian named as Finland's representative to the Tsar, and hated by the Finns. He was assassinated by Russian revolutionaries in Petersburg in 1904.

In May, 1902, Johan worried about a back injury Palla had suffered. Johan himself didn't believe in doctors, "but one can always listen to their opinion without having to follow their advice, or cram in their nasty medicines."

He had sent in a petition on freedom of speech to the Senate. "The petition may be rejected, and then one has to figure out another way." Palla was concerned about censorship, and customs duties levied on what she was sending to Finland in preparation for their new home. "There is no tariff on books, but they must be examined by the press ombudsman."

As for her wedding dress, he thought she had ordered one made in Copenhagen, "and now you're trying on another one in Stockholm. You'll have enough wedding dresses!" He ended his letter, "you are the most dearly loved friend of the heart, the only one in all the world." Writing of their wedding, Johan says that Sophie will serve as hostess. In two succeeding letters, Johan writes that their carriage has come from Petersburg, and that a new charming foal has been born.

At the end of May he philosophizes: "Perhaps it's a good thing we can't be together too much. It's too soul-shaking for us both, and it can also be so when we're parted. You make it possible for me to see beauty where I didn't, before; to see life as brighter and more lovely than it's been possible earlier. I can't take life lightly, for everything, happy or adverse, leaves indelible marks." Palla, impulsive, with her own brisk opinions and perceptions, was giving the serious, self-possessed Johan a new direction. "If I ever lost you," he wrote Palla, "I'd be an invalid, a maimed man."

Johan imagines the future. "If only I had you here! We could ride together these beautiful days." He was working his favorite stallion Izmos, "so he'll start to pace better when you get here. Even if he won't be the ne plus ultra as a jumper, he'll be able to clear ordinary hurdles satisfactorily." He continues, "I went to the stud farm and walked around several hours on foot. It's lovely to be outside after several days of sitting at the office. I'd never do as a civil servant, or want a job that keeps me inside."

Their wedding was approaching, and presents were piling up. Johan writes of their china. There were, among many other items, 120 plates, 12 large platters, 34 soup plates and 24 for dessert. "These 120 plates and the Flora Danica means we can have a lot of courses for dinner without having to do the dishes."

There were two more letters before their marriage in July. "In three weeks you'll be my little wife, Palla! I won't be alone any more, the one I love most will be at my side." He mentions that Louis Sparre was working on the bedroom furniture.

In his last letter, Johan writes, "How strange life is. I, always tormented by letter writing, have really made my fiancée's acquaintance through letters." He writes of plans for their house: "Now the material has come from Liberty's. We'll have a saddlemaker cover the chairs while we're away. The bedroom furniture is ready in Porvoo; it will be very attractive."

Explaining why his last letter had been so hasty, Johan writes, "I couldn't resist going sailing, so you just got some pitiful lines. The boat we sailed on is a fine cutter, known for racing in Finland and Sweden." His love of sailing and riding were part of his legacy to later generations in the family. Johan taught his nephew Pehr, my father, to ride as well as sail. The love of sailing is, of course, a Scandinavian trait, and Pehr Sparre took the sport to heights never imagined by his Finnish family. He came in first in his class in the Newport, Rhode Island-to-Stockholm race in 1955, in his ketch "Arabella."

Palla and Johan were married July 5, 1902, in Sweden, shortly after his last letter to her.

After Carl Mannerheim's exile, Johan's position as manager of the Jokkis estate was no longer secure. Cleared of charges that he was an "animal torturer," he had been defended by the lawyer who would become Finland's first Regent, Pehr Svinhufvud. The ugly atmosphere under Russian oppression of Finland—and the acute possibility of being jailed—made Sweden a more natural home for Johan, and it was also his wife's country. Johan followed Carl to Sweden. Like his brothers and sisters he had been trained to grasp the nettle, and find in it a new challenge and life. A letter from his brother Carl, written from St. Louis in March, 1904, reports his relief on hearing that Johan, his family and house pets had arrived in Sweden to begin a new life in freedom. Gustaf had sent Carl money for Johan, the proceeds of a horse he had recently sold. Eva, Carl said, had left some clothes with Aunt Hanna in Stockholm for Palla's little girls. They were as always taking care of each other, keeping in touch wherever they were.[120]

As a silent and shy little boy growing up at Villnäs, Johan had learned more from his country life with the dogs and horses he loved, than from the school bench or the company of men. His early years had foreshadowed his later education in agronomy, animal husbandry and forestry. With the help of his wife, Johan was able to buy a manor in Sweden early in the new century. There he bred Arabian horses and specialized in forestry, carrying on pioneer work in tree planting and modern dairy farming. Johan moved into the business world as well, and eventually became a major player in the Swedish wood pulp industry.

When I was a child, traveling in the summers from our home in America to Sweden and Norway, my mother and I always visited Johan's and Palla's Grensholm. It was, for a child, a fairy tale place: woods and a lake, myriad field and forest flowers, blueberries and wild strawberries to pick, and chanterelles, avoiding the scarlet mushrooms with white poisonous spots. There was a maypole to dress, and Midsummer Eve with singing and dancing the bright, sunlit night through, as late as the grownups would let me. I loved Aunt Palla, but Uncle Johan frightened me. He seemed silent and severe; in my childish eyes, even his grown children seemed wary. I knew nothing about his life as a forester or his horse breeding. I did know him as a splendid horseman, one I would like to have cantered with.

These letters to Palla show a side of him that he kept hidden from all but his wife. Shy man that he always was, did anyone but Palla discover his interest in literature, his insight into the Russian master Gorky? Perhaps only Palla and his brothers and sisters understood his vulnerable nature.

In 1937, three years after Johan's death and just before World War II and the invasion of Finland, I went riding on one of Johan's horses. I have enclosed the snapshot in memory of a private man known to few, and of my last visit to Grensholm.

Portrait of Johan Mannerheim
By Louis Sparre, 1916

Grensholm Manor

Baroness Palaemona
Mannerheim

Author on Uncle Johan's
horse at Grensholm

Chapter 17

Louis continued his furniture design after leaving Iris, boldly undertaking a new enterprise in Porvoo, called "Eva and Louis Sparre Design Studio." His former foreman and two carpenters who had left Iris became partners, and all Sparre-designed furniture was made at the small-scale carpentry shop they started in 1902. The studio itself was operated from Louis's and Eva's home. Louis continued to design furniture in Porvoo and Helsinki for Finnish and Russian clients until his move to Sweden in 1909. (When the Sparres moved to Stockholm, two of the partners continued to make furniture in Louis's style until 1914.)

Eva had already made her name known internationally as a book artist. There were reproductions of her work in publications in Sweden, England and France; her work was represented in St. Petersburg and Copenhagen, and there were orders to fill abroad and in her own country. One observer argues that it was Louis who was influenced by his wife in the art of decorative book covers, not, as their family often seemed to think, Eva who was the less important artist. "Within the [decorative bookbinding] field Eva was in her own territory and Louis her journeyman."[121] Her deference to Louis was undoubtedly a matter of upbringing and Victorian habits. The man came first. While Eva had neither false modesty about her art, nor felt the slightest inferiority about it, her custom was—at least in later years—to stand a figurative two paces behind her husband, to show and discuss his work rather than her own, and, literally, to be the mat maker for his water colors. There was no better mat maker! Her commissions were essential to their livelihood, now that Louis was at a crossroads and had to abandon his idealistic dream of revolutionizing Finnish taste through his factory products.

Eva and Louis opened their new studio on New Year's Day 1901, with a squirrel as logo. This was an old sign of luck for them. Eva had never liked the business end of the old enterprise, because it diverted Louis's energies from his creative gift. But although Louis himself would like to have concentrated on painting, he dared not depend entirely on such an uncertain source of income. Louis won first prize in the competition for furnishing the "Students' House" in Helsinki in 1901, and Eva was busy with ten copies of the Finnish national poet Runeberg's "Ensign Ståhl's Tales." Although Iris had failed, Louis might still, through his good designs, raise the taste level of craftsmen, where the real education had to begin.

Despite his worries and the newness of their design enterprise, Louis plunged into new enthusiasms. He was chairman of the Borgå (Porvoo) Museum Society[122] and now he could give it a measure of his attention and new ideas. He loved its location in the old, 18th Century Town Hall building—a real bit of cultural history for the town.

One of his plans was to promote art education for everyone. His idea was to organize a gallery within Porvoo Museum—a gallery within a gallery—with excellent reproductions of classical art, making the best of European works accessible to the general public. In November 1900 his plan was approved for Porvoo by the board of the Museum. From his own pocket Louis supplied black and white photo reproductions of masterpieces and miniature plaster sculptures of some great works. As nearly as one can date it from Eva's memoirs, the little gallery opened within the Museum early in 1902. In April, 1903, an architect from Helsinki gave the idea and its execution an enthusiastic review in Helsingfors Posten. Once again Louis was the champion of art for everyone. His small gallery would help erase the idea that art was an enjoyment belonging only to the leisured class.

Louis hoped that such a gallery might be copied in other Finnish towns and be available to school children and to those who could not afford travel.

In the new year of 1902 exciting orders came from Petersburg. Six rooms were to be furnished, designed and installed for the Art Academy's director, Count Ivan Tolstoy at his country estate near Viipuri (Vyborg). Gustaf Mannerheim's good friend, the witty and influential Countess Betsy Sjuvalova, needed chairs for her formal dining room, and Grand Duke Vladimir's palace library was to be completely refurnished. These new Russian clients and their world would have been more exciting if political movements now unfolding had not cast threatening shadows.

Under the new laws imposed by Russia, Finnish army officers were dismissed; Russian troops marched in like an army of occupation to take over the barracks the officers had commanded and the houses they had lived in. As Swedish subjects Eva and Louis could not join the passive resistance organizations. With anxious hearts they followed the strike of fifteen thousand youths against the new military conscription law requiring service under Russian arms.

In the midst of these disturbing events, Eva's and Louis's new design studio was becoming too busy to be housed in their dining room. The studio was moved to new and larger quarters in the same building.

A trip that Louis made to Paris was far from encouraging. His father Ambjörn Sparre was still dreaming of future millions. As Louis wrote, "an endless number of zeros with some number at their head, represent the brilliant prospects, whereas only the zeros describe the present reality." The old man had dreamed the same golden dream for 55 years. For the moment he needed help to acquire international patents for an uncorking apparatus. But Louis could not stay in his apartment. "One can't walk through the rooms for all the mechanical gear that fills them. The dining room is full of machines. Papa's room also. We eat at a little table squeezed between all sorts of scaffolds and junk. What air and what dust!"[123]

One bit of excitement for Eva and Louis was to be invited by their old friends the von Etters at Haiko Manor near Porvoo to meet the visiting Grand Duchess Marie Pavlovna. Eva worried about not having the right clothes, but "a bit of powder on my nose, eyebrows moistened, a court curtsey and kissing of the hand were the only decorum I could produce. The Grand Duchess is radiantly charming and gracious, perhaps slightly surprised by Finnish society's controlled behavior during the sharply critical political situation in the country. She is the grateful spectator of a scene from Finnish society life, and on her nod—'Maintenant je ferme mon petit théâtre' ('now I'm closing my little theatre')—the curtain goes down on our departure in the evening . . . . The return trip to Porvoo takes place in distinguished company on a steamer placed at the Grand Duchess's disposal. Louis showed his carpentry and the furniture being built, all of which were approved."[124]

During the late summer of 1902 a new type of client had come to Louis from a surprising source. Louis had been invited to lunch on the flagship Suvaroff, lying at anchor in the Finnish archipelago, to discuss the furnishing of the commander's cabin. Months later he would revisit the commander in St Petersburg.

Needing as always to make money, Louis made a trip to Grand Duke Vladimir's palace in Petersburg with his foreman, some carpenters and three railroad cars full of furniture. Eva, recuperating from many months in a sanatorium after abdominal surgery, was regaled by daily letters from Petersburg, where Louis was staying with Gustaf Mannerheim. He wrote of the luncheon menu at the Grand Duke's palace: "Blini with caviar, a wonderful ham with glazed vegetables, dessert and coffee." He amused himself with a stream of counts and countesses, princesses and duchesses, while his workers were taken to the circus. There was talk of furnishing a study for the Grand Duke in Tsarskoje, the site of the Summer Palace. He took the train out, and in his own words "was met at the station in a troika by a coachman adorned with gold braid. All the police on the way to the palace saluted, as did the guard at the entrance gate. I waved my hand, looking high and mighty . . . ."[125]

Louis came home to spend a long, dreary winter trying to make up to his little boys for Eva's absence. It was easy to let depression overcome him, and he even looked back on himself in Petersburg as though in a prostitute's role, going from house to house toadying to the opinions of those who might be clients. But he cheered himself with a palette, and painted a small oil of his younger boy Clas. He took up etching anew, with twelve new plates of Porvoo, and reaped some satisfaction from his furniture making, despite criticism. Competition within the industry was influenced by younger talents now, particularly architects, who were eager to carry on work in which he was the acknowledged groundbreaker.[126] On the other hand, his father Ambjörn had seen Louis's furniture in a Danish publication and for once was suitably impressed.

Dressed in his fur coat, new drawings in his baggage, Louis embarked on the train for another winter Petersburg trip. He was driven in an open sleigh with his host, Commander Ignatius, to the fleet headquarters at the mouth of the Neva River where he stepped aboard the flagship. Louis had no idea of what to expect; the seemingly sparse rooms gave no clue. He began to guess what the procedures would be when he entered a new room where, as Eva later wrote, "a giant table . . . was set with an army of glasses which gave him a dangerous inkling of what lay ahead . . . He would have to try to moderate the liquor serving . . . The doors swung open to a neighboring room where a brass band of horns on a signal from the conductor, let loose a hurricane of tones. To the thunder of military marches, glasses of vodka, wine and foaming champagne were emptied, while puffy Russian pasties, caviar and other eastern delicacies were served . . ." Everything seemed swimmingly, magnificently possible—orders grew in Louis's imagination, supported by toasts and promises of friendship. On the way back, Ignatius was the driver, standing at the back of his racing sleigh. For such an officer there were no speed limits. Suddenly a man was knocked under the sleigh. "To get rid of the unwelcome hindrance, still alive, and carry the man into the nearest doorway was but a moment's work. A few minutes of involuntary delay followed while Ignatius informed himself about the wounded man's condition, and bought himself free by putting down a ten-ruble note on the victim." The trip continued with the same neck-breaking speed while Louis, deeply affected and in a somber mood, listened to the right way of handling a rabble rouser who willingly risked his life for a coin.[127] But these hopes of commercial success came to nought. With the declaration of war between Russia and Japan in 1904, Louis could make no deliveries to the fleet. Only two years later Commander Ignatius was to go down on the Suvaroff in the Straits of Tsushima, in the Russo-Japanese War.

Carl's exile, among among other events, forced Louis to think more seriously about the future. His life looked promising, with many orders from Petersburg. But how steady would they be, and how could they be undertaken at all? It seemed likely there would be chaotic conditions, given the Russian demands, the Finnish conscripts' refusal to report for duty, the passive resistance. How could he neglect letting his boys come to know their country, Sweden, with its peaceful atmosphere, the hockey-playing and skating and other well organized sports for young boys? The boys he had seen on his last trip there seemed ideal models for his sons, attractive in their white sports sweaters in the mornings, later appearing at dinner well groomed and brushed. Such thoughts gave him a sting, while Pehr and Clas sat for his water colors.

The time was not ripe for a change, though Eva urged him to return to his painting. She herself went for a trip to Lugano with her Aunt Hanna and Uncle Christian, while Louis tarred and painted their little sloop Yalf, sailed in Sweden and took his carpenters to Petersburg for the Duke's study. But no sooner had he come home in the late summer than Eva once again found herself under the surgeon's knife in a life-threatening emergency, with yet another long convalescence. She was not well enough until December, 1903, to travel alone to Petersburg. There she would entrain for the Riviera with her friends the von Etters, via Warsaw, Vienna, Genoa and finally Cannes. The Etters had invited her to continue her recuperation in their villa.

Meanwhile, other family members were busy at home, or in exile. Carl was exploring the possibilities of starting a bank in the United States. Sophie was now head nurse at the Hospital for Surgery in Helsinki, and in Eva's opinion would do the demanding work "heart and soul."

At home in Porvoo, in honor of the painter Albert Edelfelt, Louis organized a Museum room with the artist's original drawings, etchings and paintings. At the same time he was designing furniture, etching, cutting linoleum blocks. Best of all, almost, was his election as chief of the Volunteer Fire Brigade, where he was in his boyish element. In still a different setting he was the valued member of a group whose sole function was amusement and dancing. The lady members were chosen for their charms, and Louis was vulnerable. He danced well, his blood easily ignited.

These two, Eva and Louis, shared their work and strong sense of duty, and had a dependence on each other that underlay their companionship. They lived so long together and worked so closely in their early years that an historian of turn-of-the-century artist couples felt their marriage was one of the more harmonious, not as emotionally charged as others. Of their work at the design studio the same author wrote "it was often difficult to differentiate between them."[128] Later, when they no longer shared commissions, they were, according to Louis "helping one another." But despite this professional harmony their marriage was surely not without explosions. His ardent temperament with recurrent depressions, and Eva's caustic tongue, must have caused rifts. They were temperamental opposites, but with similar tastes, connections and interests. A tribute to their resilience and strong affection for each other was the enduring nature of their marriage of nearly seven decades.

A niece remembered in 1992 that Louis had left Eva for two years. Louis's daughter-in-law recalled in 1993 that Clas had, as a small boy, slept in his parents' room when he was sick. He overheard their voices, though they thought him asleep; he wept inconsolably and begged them not to divorce. For his sake they put aside their problems. There must have been other such crises but the world continued to think them a happy pair. Eva knew how to get Louis back, and always did. For her husband it may have been exciting to live on the edge of danger. Perhaps he was one of those men for whom the pursuit of a woman is more interesting than her capture. But whatever the adjustments, surely strenuous for both, the passionate painter and his cool, contained wife learned to live with each other's different approaches to life.

The Mannerheims were scattering, some for political reasons, like Carl and Johan, others briefly coming home before changing their lives for business reasons. But wherever they were, all of them kept the letters going, encouraging each other. There was no stronger bond than that forged in childhood.

In 1903 there was depressing news that Villnäs, the Mannerheims' old castle, had been sold. Its owner, Baroness Mimmi Mannerheim, had been persuaded by her niece, Jeanne, to move to Sweden and buy a manor there. Eva and her brothers and sister reflected that Aunt Mimmi had always been a piece of damp clay in Jeanne's hands. Jeanne was said to have come under the influence of the Swedish estate steward of Villnäs. He persuaded her—"forced" is the word used—to sell Villnäs. The buyer was Oskar Hannus, described as a "financial advisor;" Eva called him a "peasant." Mimmi and Jeanne moved to Sweden the year Villnäs was sold, 1903. The estate steward's heirs are said to have inherited "much Mannerheim silver".[129]

On news of the sale, Sophie wrote to her brother Carl: "One's memory is really the only thing one owns with certainty, a treasure that becomes richer and richer. A scent, a tone or a word can light up a room suddenly like a sunbeam, and at that moment one sees [the home in memory] exactly as it always was."[130]

Louis, at home in Finland, kept sending cheerful letters to Eva on the Riviera, not liking to upset her with the political situation. The carpentry shop was buzzing and the Design Studio, too. A large exhibit of French works in Helsinki interested Louis mainly because of its Pisarro and Monet paintings. Louis thought the future secure, with furniture to make for a chemist, and three rooms in Moscow, and even a chance of a teaching post at the academy in Düsseldorf. But diverting him from such stimulating thoughts was, as always, his own painting. He prepared for an exhibit in Turku to show his paintings, drawings, etchings and book covers. On another front he was the lead as coordinator of the centennial celebration of the national poet Runeberg in February, 1904, with torchlight parades to the great man's grave, statue and home, and a feast with tableaux.

Eva's life in Cannes, continuing through the winter of 1904, was beginning to look up with the arrival of Petersburg aristocrats for the winter. Invitations rained down on her and she was surprised to be taken as one of them, despite not understanding their discussions in Russian. This seemed to make no difference, as she understood the main theme: frank criticism of the régime at home in Petersburg. She was amazed, but took it as a little straw in the wind. The Russians she had met, she wrote, expressed wonderfully uncensored opinions. She thought it possible that the "inner Russia might begin to move."[131]

In February, 1904, August accepted the offer to be head of the AEG Electrical Company of South Africa. He and his young wife Elsie left Finland for Johannesburg.

War news cracked like lightning through the sky on February 6, 1904. The Japanese had made a devastating sneak attack on the Russian fleet lying at anchor in the Manchurian naval base of Port Arthur. In Cannes, Eva heard a young Russian princess moved to tears that her countrymen had not dynamited a group of Japanese instead of taking them prisoner. How kind they were, sighed the princess, and how Christian! And how difficult for Finnish ears to hear, for

Finns were quick to sympathize with Russia's foe. One Finnish writer with wide influence in leftist and minority parties in Russia, Konni Zilliacus, was able to render services to the Japanese during the war.[132] Eva wrote from Cannes on February 15, "One talks of nothing but the war . . . In the long run it will be the poor Japanese who will suffer."[133] No one could imagine a Russian defeat.

And no one, least of all Eva and Louis, could imagine the changes that lay ahead for them.

Eva, the young book artist
By Louis Sparre.

Chapter 18

THE SPARRES RAISE THE FLAG AND THE STRIKE

COMES TO FINLAND; EVA STUDIES IN COPENHAGEN

After her recuperation in Cannes in 1904, Eva waited impatiently to meet Louis in Paris, his trip delayed countless times because of work and exhibits. But at last the boys were put in the care of grandparents, and Louis and Eva settled into Edelfelt's Paris studio. Eva made herself popular with Ambjörn by watching his model submarine, tried out in the bathtub.

Ambjörn, fired with his usual enthusiasm, had been in touch with the British Admiralty about his submarine, encouraged by the Admiral in Portsmouth, Sir John Fisher, and the chief submarine engineer. There was much interest for it also in France, from the head of the "Constructions Navales au Ministère de la Marine." The British Naval Attaché, Commander Ottby, promised to send the Admiralty a report of a demonstration with Ambjörn's miniature submarine model on the banks of the Seine.

The inventor had opened negotiations with a firm in Scotland for building the vessel. All was ready for signature when the project became mired over the question of a patent and was derailed for a moment. At last the problems were solved. Things had turned around in Glasgow. A cheque for 10,000 pounds sterling was on the table . . . . when an engineer fresh from London stepped through the door. Under his arm he carried the copy of a lecture given twenty years earlier to the Society of Civil Engineers in London, wherein, Ambjörn had written Eva in May of 1905, "a Danish Naval officer mused that one should be able to maneuver submarines in a way that was exactly like mine . . . Notice that it was just expressed as an idea, and no person had thought of it since."[134] Everything was off. Ambjörn now dreamed of taking his model submarine to the St. Louis Exposition in America.

At home in Helsinki, on June 14, 1904, just as Eva was working to pack for the country, the telephone rang. She heard her father's voice: Governor General Bobrikov had died at the hands of young Eugen Schauman, who then turned the pistol on himself. The Russian had been shot as he was walking up the stairs to the Senate. The news was electrifying. Bobrikov, Eva learned later, had been taken to Sophie's hospital to be treated—in vain—by Finland's best doctors. The assassin lay abandoned in the morgue.

Deportations followed, and hectoring. But bad news for Russia of the war seemed linked to a policy change: General Kuropatkin was retreating in Manchuria following Russia's reverses in the Russo-Japanese war. Now exiled Finns were permitted to return and partake in parliamentary meetings. Eva wrote her exiled brother Calle in January of 1905, "One hears the exiles may return!"[135] A more depressing result of the war scene was that Russian orders to Louis were cancelled, as were design competitions of furniture. Louis understood that it was impossible to avoid what he found impossible to accept: more standardized production, radical simplification of design. He had, he said, been too busy with the Petersburg clients to give appropriate attention to the Finnish market. Now he foresaw a difficult time for the carpentry and suggested the three partners take over the shop the following January, eliminating his own share in the earnings. His withdrawal was not made with regrets, interested as he was now in purely artistic projects. The pioneer's work had lost its charm, and did not seem to fit in with the current of the times.

Louis now knew what, finally, he must do. He must once more be a painter. Eva and Louis decided to move to Helsinki, rent a studio and apartment roomy enough for the Design office and Liberty agency. To join again with artists, to get his bearings, Louis undertook a trip whose destination was the artists' colony on Cornwall's coast at St. Ives. He left in February 1905. The two wrote each other encouraging notes, Louis describing his trip into the yellow waters of Hull harbor, dotted with stubby red-sailed boats. He loved the foggy atmosphere of the English coast, the great skies with an occasional sunlit streak revealing church steeples and hundreds of boats, or mist wrapped around shimmering silhouettes.

Some days in London with friends were a bracing release from pressure. He learned that an article on his etchings was coming out in The Studio. His visit to a Whistler exhibit stimulated his longing for brushes and paint tubes. Louis knew that he had escaped the disturbing elements of community life, that Eva, at home in Finland, had taken up the burdens so that he might paint. Eva managed the design office, and developed new methods for her own work, new ways of coloring her book bindings. "She kept a very orderly diary of her dyeing methods, from the very first trials to more sophisticated methods."[136] The busy Eva drew textile designs for a linen weaver and patterns for the Friends of Finnish Handwork, and for some of Louis's furniture friezes. She knew that she was pressing her luck, her competence and her willpower.

Louis went on to St. Ives by train, with discouraging icy winds and rain, but found a perfect apartment overlooking town and harbor. Best of all were his contact with English artists and soirées with music. The weather finally brought sunshine and warmth, a view of the mackerel fleet in hazy warm air, waiting for wind with Cornwall's barely discernible coast in the background. His painting senses were roused by the glittering green swell rocking the boats, their red canvases stretched by the wind, everything frustratingly impossible to catch in the shifting weather. Even a leaden, violet-clouded sky excited him, the waters changing from purple to grey green, the sea breaking against black cliffs in a violent game. He was far away from bookkeeping and liquidations. Eva happily announced the acceptance of their textile designs with a "hip, hip!"

Louis, in his ups and especially in his downs, left Eva anxious and wondering how she could prevent his collapse into bitter depression. She followed each nuance of each word, each guilty sense of failure, each longing to sweep the doubts away and give in to his "hunger" for painting. She herself had only the worries of melting snow and boys' wet socks.

Ambjörn observed that Louis had ridden in a "motor-car" in London, but said, "You've only seen one side of it. If the brakes don't function for a moment down a steep hill, one is finished. If one increases the speed, some small unseen stone can pitch one into the ditch . . . . In a word, I wouldn't accept such a vehicle free . . . . if I were given it as a present I'd take it to the pawn shop."[137]

After all the exhaustion of moving, farewell parties after eight years in Borgå, new decorating to do, trips back and forth to Helsinki, Eva gave in to a "wild idea:" taking a vacation with the boys to the north to celebrate Easter in Kajana on skis. Meanwhile from Louis came word that he had weathered a crisis of self-criticism and doubts about his painting. He had felt the months were without results: all that he had done was poorly executed, worthless. His feelings were well interlarded with guilt for Eva's lonely work at home. Two American artists were his companions, firm critics who thought him affected by eight years of furniture design. They advised him to "work very hard" and overcome bad habits, and he himself wrote that he must learn to see nature in a broader perspective, being too caught up in details and irrelevancies which had made his work too photographic.

Louis returned to the new Helsinki apartment from London which again had "electrified" him with its grey painterly fog. It was Eva who took her boy to boarding school in Sweden. The parting was difficult, and one must show no womanly emotions. Pehr kissed his mother in private and quickly dried his tears.

In September, 1905, Louis watched the proud Finnish Guards parading past silent onlookers to the tones of the battalion's own march, for the last time carrying their banners in a military procession to the railroad station to disband. Eva wrote about it to Pehr. "In Finland the Guard is dissolved and Pappa writes that the other night he heard music on the public square at 10 p.m. That was the last of the Guard, whose banner would be brought to the express train to be sent forever to Petersburg. A large number of people had gathered to sing the Björneborg March and Our Country. Another happening is that a large [Russian] battleship went aground at Jakobstad. When the border guards rowed out, they were threatened by revolvers. After this the crew dynamited the ship and escaped in small boats . . . They've found 5,000 guns among the peasants in Ostrobothnia. You can see that this keeps one thinking and one wonders what the outcome will be."[138]

As an artist, Eva's eye never slumbered. "You can't imagine how beautiful it was when we left Stockholm. The horizon was blood red and the city like a grey silhouette." Her sense of beauty outweighed the unpleasant thoughts of Russian naval might on their doorstep. She wrote to Pehr in October of 1905, "Outside the Russian torpedo chasers travel in and out. They have several searchlights to illuminate the city. Suddenly, as we're sitting, there is a blinding light in the room. This would amuse you, and is also very beautiful."

The defeat of Russia by Japan in 1905 caused Russian leftists to call a general strike in Russia. When this reached Finland, organized labor took the lead, but the employers, to "show solidarity," were benevolently disposed and "paid their employees wages for the period of the strike."[139] The "constitutionalists" split with the labor party on the question of submitting reform plans to the Diet for approval. Finnish socialists now issued a "Red Declaration," demanding that representational reform be turned over to a national assembly, to be chosen by universal suffrage. It was at this time that armed militias were organized representing the two sides: the constitutionalists formed the White Guard, the socialists a Red Guard. These Reds showed their true function after Finland's laws had been restored in November, 1905. They then turned on the bourgeois community, not the Russian oppressors. The White Guard represented the country's law, those insisting on upholding the country's constitution, a counterweight to the Reds. By 1906 Finland was close to civil war although each side feared the Russian army might intervene.

In 1905, the strike was still supported by all classes of society, all the political parties. All were as one in fury at their country's crippled future. The Finnish workers, who had dreamed of being joined by their Russian brothers, stripped the police of their weapons, created strike committees and mass meetings everywhere. The post, telephone, gas and electricity were stopped; traffic was suspended, trolleys and vehicles stood still on all city streets. Shops and businesses were closed.

Wild rumors floated about. Eva and Louis saw streams of inquisitive people pouring down their street to the railroad square, already black with a crowd. The two steered their steps toward the same museum where both had exhibited, realizing it had by far the best lookout on the scene.

Now at least twenty thousand people were massed in front of the Finnish Theatre. Eva and Louis had the same thought at the same moment, without taking the time to question where their act would lead. They found the Ateneum Museum's watchman on duty, and persuaded him to turn over the two large Finnish flags, forbidden by the Russian Governor General. Freedom was in the air. The meeting was about to end. Quickly, quickly, before the crowds should scatter they went upstairs to the windows over the main entrance. They opened the windows and unfurled the brilliant emblems.[140] It was like hurling a torch into a lake of gasoline. Shouts of exultation met the flags, a mass moved towards them in their thousands. Suddenly there was utter silence, and the strains of Finland's national anthem rose from the crowds and into the cold October air.

The song had hardly ended when a worker rushed to the entrance, signaling for one of the flags. They threw it to him in the waiting crowd. Instantly the Russian flag on the railroad station was torn down and the old lion hoisted in its place. Before dark the lion flags were rising on all official buildings—senate, university, parliament and congress. Only on the Russian Governor General's Residence did the Russian flag still fly.

Tension was in the air, something between hope and terror. Eva went home, Louis stayed. A deputation arrived at the Residence, demanding of the Governor the restoration of Finland's old constitutional rights. The crowd was enormous. Every nerve was strained, no one could leave. Rumors poured out. The sight of Cossacks on a chance maneuver nearly caused panic; no one had forgotten their charge of three years before.

It was late at night before Eva and Louis learned how the populace had pressed on, bursting through the iron barriers to the Esplanade. People fell on each other as they landed on the deep shelf below the street. Crowded and crushed, they had nevertheless escaped with their lives. Sophie, now head nurse at the Hospital for Surgery, noted in a letter to a friend that they had treated victims of stabbing and bullets, torn and broken bodies, but no one had been killed. She had been amazed at the efficient calm of the workers, and praised those wearing red armbands, the Red Guards. Ever a liberal supporter she cautioned against believing the right-wing newspaper, spiteful and arrogant, she thought, in its views of the workers. Of course it was lucky, she added, that the street bars had been closed. Her father's thoughts were far bleaker, and he wasted no sentimental words on the Red Guards. Had they been in the thousands instead of a few hundred strong, it would have been a disaster. But as it was, the night was filled with omens.

Students, so often the forerunners of rebellion against oppression, were joining the White Guards, and even small children wore white armbands to show where their loyalties belonged. Louis's and Eva's son, seven-year-old Clas, rushed about with his band, but wanting to belong to the "revolutionaries," wore a red one. He knew his older brother Pehr was safely away in boarding school, dying of envy.

Finland was not far from civil war. Sophie had looked on the red armbands with an idealistic eye, but later the flags with a golden lion on a red field were often replaced by the revolutionary all-red flag. By then the Red Guard were planning a revolution against the whole community.

But now, on the last October night of 1905, Eva and Louis waited for more news. Nerves tightened. What would the negotiations bring? How long would Russian patience last? Russian armies were not far away. The whole city was enveloped in darkness.

A friend had come, at last, to tell the sensational happenings: the constitutional delegations were still inside the Governor's Residence, demanding with one voice that the Russian-led senators resign in a body. It was hinted that they might demand the resignation of the Governor himself. Impatience among the waiting populace was rising.

Doors to a balcony over the Esplanade were opened and by the light of two candelabra those senators friendly to Russian rule appeared, flanked by their accusers. The street was black and despite the candle light it was impossible to make out the people on the balcony, where someone waited to be heard. Who could that be? The answer, "a senator," brought a shriek of rage. All waited in the heavy silence that followed. Then a clear voice came from the balcony: a senator reading the document, written in Finnish: "All Senate members in the Treasury and Justice Departments make known their resignation to the people, herewith given to the Ruler."[141] Jubilation filled the night.

The political situation between the parties was volatile. Rumors whispered words like "pogrom" and "military coup d'état". The lion flags were downed by workers. Next Finland's telegraph system was struck, all its machines abandoned. How long, again, would

Russian patience hold? At the end of the week the Tsar's birthday was celebrated by a parade of Russian troops in the market square. On the same day a squadron of four warships anchored in the Harbor. The Governor General did not return to his Residence, but fled to the safety of the "Slava," Russia's most famous warship, where he stayed until the strike's end.

From their windows Eva and Louis could see Russian soldiers emerging from their barracks and disappearing in the dark. There had been rumors of a general slaughter of Russians, alarming enough to send Russian civilians to the protection of the harbor fortress Sveaborg. Eva and Louis could see the warships' searchlights playing all night over the city and harbor.

The next day Eva and Louis heard (one does not know from whom) that the warships had orders from the Tsar to deliver the city to merciless artillery fire and raze it to the ground. The orders were changed only at the last moment, some thought by the help of the Governor General. Others thought the calmer atmosphere had saved them, and the fact that no Finns had attacked Russians.

Eva wrote to Pehr October 30, 1905: "In Russia the workers strike everywhere. No trains leave. In Petersburg it is pitch black, all stores closed. They say some military are going over to the revolutionaries' side. Many rumors, nothing certain. Since yesterday the Finnish railroad goes only to Vyborg. Petersburg is without communication with the outside world. They can still send mail by steamship. Will the unfortunate people finally have an end to this lawlessness and oppression?"

Eva wrote her son as an eyewitness to history on November 2, "One lives with great anxiety. Any moment everything can change . . . Yesterday started with a general strike. Every bar was closed and the workers wandered around the street in gangs . . . Thousands of rumors were spread about cannons, military and other things. People were beginning to arm themselves! . . . This evening we heard . . . that we've got everything. That the Estates will be called and choose a new Senate . . . It's hoped the workers will also agree . . . A good thing it is if the military won't shoot . . . 3 November: Today is the day of the [speech] from the Throne . . . No telegraph yesterday. It was destroyed by gangs. No post. [Eva's letter was being sent from Copenhagen with friends.] No boats have left. Pitch black on the streets. Police are striking. Whoever wants can be a guard on the streets. Pappa today has a white armband. It's a revolution. All schools are closed . . . It's almost like war."

On November 4 the Tsar cancelled the dictatorial decrees that had annulled Finland's constitutional laws. The new signed manifesto was delivered by warship. Louis had a presentiment of the future when on an early November walk in the city he saw the Finnish students' White Guard, several hundred strong, commanded by a captain of the dissolved Finnish military. They made a halt, while the captain spoke to them about the danger of confronting the Red Guards, and that revolvers should be loaded. The column continued on its march, while Louis from his vantage point could see a detachment of the Red Guards, marching to a direct confrontation with the Whites before whose front line they made a halt. Observers melted away, but the captain of the Red Guard saw instantly what was brewing, and shouted: "Retreat! Workers this way to save thousands of lives!"[142] The future was on hold, just for a moment.

The news from Russia was not good. It was a direct signal of the future. Eva again wrote to Pehr on December 4, 1905: "Here a defense guard is being formed . . . Pappa, who also belongs to this guard, is at a meeting tonight . . . In Russia the most terrible happenings are taking place. At all the manor houses the people are living in anxiety, fearing to be plundered and burned. All telegraph, post and telephone connections are severed . . . The population is so raw that they have poured petrol over and ignited flocks of sheep. They have amputated the feet of horses, with other cruelties . . ."

The hated Governor General Obolenski left Finland, the Tsar belatedly having removed the absolute powers of his office.

Finland was almost an outpost, far from the European centers of culture. Nevertheless there was a rich cultural life in the capital city. In February, 1906, Eva wrote to Pehr about a Japanese acting company visiting Helsinki: "What Pappa found the most interesting was to see them fence and fight! . . . Strong, sinuous, with movements as rapid as wild animals'. In the play "The Geisha's Revenge" they wore marvelous old costumes . . . golden armor and great wild wigs . . . yesterday we invited them for tea! . . . The Primadonna Miss Hanako came in Japanese costume. She's no taller than Clas, with tiny tiny hands and a voice like a bird. Clas was so taken with her that he stood motionless by her chair with flaming cheeks. She caressed his hand and he said that her hands were like Japanese silk paper . . ."

One good change in Finland was the appearance of the new Governor General Gerard, a liberal thinker who understood and respected Finland's position, its unique constitution under Tsarist rule, and why it was to Russia's advantage to maintain friendly relations with the little country. Eva wrote Pehr about this new Russian Governor, awaited with some anxiety. But he personally won the trust of the Finns, including the Sparres. Those who moved in society found his family charming and once again could accept his invitations without risking their personal reputations.

Eva saw Louis's decision to concentrate on his painting, to be an artist with all his mind and energy at last, as the only right decision. She had never been able to accept entirely his role as a business man, or even as a designer of furniture. She saw this new perspective as something he had reached by experience, the past years a time well spent which had been both exciting and frustrating. She was not one to waste time on regrets.

In the spring of 1906 Eva left for Copenhagen. She wrote Pehr about it, on board the ferry: "During the winter I've worked at the Ateneum to organize a school for professional bookbinders, something not found in Finland, and I think not in Sweden . . . . A bookbinder would become a teacher in the school and your mother the artistic leader." One has a feeling that Eva felt like a bird let out of its cage. On a scholarship from the Handcraft School in Helsinki, she planned to come back to give lessons to those craftsmen who now had to stay with the same deadly machine work until they died. There were no well trained men to do the handwork of gilding, or any professionals with artistic expertise. She wanted to train a new generation of Finnish artisans.

There is a possibility that Eva's proposal concealed a warning to Louis. Half a century later Eva said that she had once left to teach him a lesson. Divorce was scandalous, but much more compelling was the fact that without money of her own a woman was helpless. Eva's career was well launched, she was recognized abroad, and now, with a trip to Denmark, she could broaden her reach and give her husband a strong signal. She was not dependent on him. It is hardly likely that the differences between them were merely temperamental. Did she issue an ultimatum that Louis would have to curb his interest in other ladies or live without her? Had there been battles over infidelities? One needed only to meet Louis, to know that he was an ardent, intensely romantic man, easily moved, easily empathetic, whom women found irresistible. Perhaps he needed a spontaneous warmth that Eva may not have found easy to give.

Eva and Louis had a marriage that would have been considered normal 75 years later: two careers, two children. Eva was herself a modern young woman inside a Victorian shell. Though she kept to the view of morals as they were understood in her day, she was tolerant and accepting of others with less conventional ideas. Eva was a passionately independent person in all ways: artistic, how she dressed and lived, how her own earnings gave her self-sufficiency. She was shy about promoting herself, but quietly adamant in living by the rules of propriety to which she had been trained. She and Louis were not slavish followers of trends (Louis rejected symbolism for his own art, when it was au courant in artistic circles) but always, even in their old age, fascinated by contemporary art and literature even if not always admiring of it.

Eva had a matter-of-fact nature, a well-trained non-religious acceptance of fate. Her younger son's sudden death in her old age, in 1948, was accepted stoically and without public emotion, while Louis visibly grieved and struggled. Her anger was usually silent. No one understood Louis better than she. She was prepared to carry out her threat, or warning, but perhaps she also counted on his basic dependence on her, and the transience of his passions. He always came back. The Sparre's marriage lasted until Eva's death in 1958. If Eva had issued a warning in 1906, Louis heeded it.

In any event, Eva took her leave. She was treated like a colleague by Denmark's famous bookbinder Anker Küster, thanks to The Studio and other art publications that contained articles about Eva's bookbindings. She, for her part, had seen Küster's marbling, a tightly guarded secret, and his original front fly-leaf stock, designed on handmade Japanese paper. She visited a night school for bookbinders, on the top floor of the Industrial Arts Museum in Copenhagen. Eva noted that courses included, in addition to the curriculum for educating a bookbinder, classes in drawing and hand gilding which she herself planned to introduce to the Finnish artisans. She visited a school for women students of the trade, where the famous Danish porcelain factories and workshops found their workers. She met Copenhagen's most important collector of contemporary bookbindings, who offered an inspection tour.

Among his designs were priceless William Morris volumes printed by the Kelmscott Press. She dined with Björnstjerne Björnson, the Norwegian Nobel Prize winner for poetry and novels, who thought it most amusing to meet a female holder of a scholarship. Not even in progressive Norway did such a being exist.

Nagged by a guilty conscience after leaving Louis alone for a month, she returned to her husband and two young sons, pleased that her suggestion of evening courses three times a week for the education of bookbinders had been accepted. Now she began to teach the courses at the Ateneum, although she never saw her ideas bear fruit.

Louis had rented an old fisherman's cottage in the country, not far from Helsinki, charmingly repaired, painted and furnished by his friend the lighthouse keeper. This good man's daughters made home-woven curtains and rag rugs and even planted a vegetable patch outside. An old boathouse near the lighthouse served as his studio. The only leisure Louis permitted himself was sailing with his boys and Eva in a rented little cutter.

He stretched a large canvas to paint his wife, who sat still for many hours on an unyielding bench-like plank under the trees. He had no time for even a whisper of sympathy, and having just returned from her own lark in Denmark, she was probably silent. In the painting, their little rowboat sits beached in the background near a strip of water. The seated model wears a beige silk blouse with leg-of-mutton sleeves, and a long blue skirt. Sun-dappled light filters through the leaves onto a broad-brimmed straw hat. The composed young face is browned by the wind from sailing, her cool blue eyes gaze steadily beyond the ken of the onlooker, into an unknown future. Her lips are full and sensuous. Ardor under that calm surface is there in the painting of this pensive young woman to whom Louis always returned. For those who were strangers, her sometimes glacial formality, the bite of her wit, her cool competence, obscured the flame that warmed her friends and those she loved.

The Russian drumbeat continued, but hardly touched the summer idyll. The newspapers were silent, though rampant gossip whispered of revolts inside Russia. No one realized how near Finland's borders the explosive future lay.

Chapter 19

THE BARONESS COMES HOME TO LEAD A CHARGE

Sophie wrote to Carl in January, 1899, from her lonely post at the Jokkis estate. She was nursing Johan, who was ill. She found the solitude oppressive and her thoughts were black. In the most despairing of her letters, she wrote of her failed life, her isolation, the memories that could not be erased, her own harshness and the bitter words that hurt those she most loved. She had hurt Carl, she wrote, but knew that her words would be forgiven.

In the difficult experience of taking care of Johan, Sophie had discovered her destiny. She set her sights on nursing and longed to begin.

Earlier, in 1887, Sophie had nursed Gustaf when he was ill with typhus. Like Florence Nightingale, she had nursed her own family members before knowing what her calling would be. Her brothers needed her, and the world was filled with people who were sick and in need of help. She had felt useless at her husband's manor, relegated to a minor role there as hostess.

She was not interested in the hand-holding of patients in hospitals, or reading to the sick, which any number of well-meaning friends tried to persuade her was the role she must play. Sophie had no intention of playing the role of the broken-hearted woman who loses her sorrow in attentions to the sick in hospital wards. She would become a professional nurse, adhering to the strictest standards of competence and the broadest field of practice. Her friends thought her mad. She must get rid of what they called her "ideas." But Sophie now knew precisely what she wanted. She made a study of the best teaching hospitals. St. Thomas Hospital's Training School for Nurses in London had been endowed by Florence Nightingale herself. Miss Nightingale's upper class family had staged scenes of hysteria and anger when she announced what she wanted to be, but Sophie's family was supportive, even if her friends were astonished.[143]

Sophie made the journey to London by way of Copenhagen and Brussels. On her way she wrote Calle, "From now on, I'll have no one but myself in the wide world, but I'm in good spirits." In London, at the Prince of Wales Hotel, she made the decision to use her maiden name, and ordered visiting cards printed as Baroness Sophie Mannerheim. Her time as Sophie Linder had ended. A divorced woman was looked at askance. Armed with her old name and inherited title, there was no need to explain her marital status when she met people socially. The nursing probationers addressed each other by their last names.

Florence Nightingale passed on her gift of money from the English people for her work in the Crimean War of 1854 to St. Thomas's Hospital, an ancient institution of renown, to build a school for nurses. To have been a student here was a recommendation in itself; one needed no further testimonials. The school had opened its doors in 1860 amidst controversy. The Senior Consulting Surgeon had argued only three years earlier that nurses were like housemaids and needed only to learn by experience. Before Florence Nightingale's activities, nurses had, in fact, been women of notorious reputation, sleeping with the patients, having no lodging other than "wooden cages on the landing places outside the doors of the wards," according to the great reformer.[144] It was considered that "ladies" would not take orders or be able to deal with drudgery. Miss Nightingale insisted from the first on the highest standards of personal conduct. Nurses were therefore subject to careful examination before being accepted as probationers. The nurses she trained would become missionaries, teaching the Nightingale system in hospitals.

It was said that Florence Nightingale had seen Sophie's application and taken an interest in it. The fact is that the older nurse's cousin, Henry Bonham Carter, secretary of the Nightingale association, approved the papers and Sophie entered as a probationer in The Nightingale School for Nurses at the end of March, 1899.

Sophie remarked to Carl that she had never before known real work. The hours were from 6 a.m. until 10 p.m., with time for meals and lectures and a cup of tea in the afternoon. What she may not have told him at the time, was that she had rushed to her room after the first lecture to cry her heart out (she said later that she had screamed). Her English was adequate for ordinary conversation, but unfamiliar technical words and the lecturer's speed in speaking to a class of English girls overwhelmed her. Not a word had she understood!

By July of 1900, Sophie wrote that she was learning the work of night nursing and was given difficult cases. To Johan she wrote from St. Thomas's, "I'm now a night nurse, awake by night, sleeping by day. I've been entrusted with several 'desperate cases' and though it's depressing to go from death bed to death bed, it is good experience for me. The last patient died in lockjaw, the most terrible death I could have imagined." Night nursing would become one of Sophie's reforms in Finland, where night nurses were unknown until 1898. Nurses had shared this work with little relief, until Sophie's reform of freeing night nurses to sleep during the day, all based on her London experience.

When the probationary period ended and she put on the real uniform, Sophie was happy to be asked formally by Matron to stay at least two years in the hospital. Sophie could write home that she had at last found something she was fit to do. Matron (Miss Gordon, the formidable head nurse) seemed even more powerful than the reigning Queen Victoria, and her smile was reward enough for the day's hard work. Sophie preferred the girls whose backgrounds were simple, who had no pretensions and didn't drink tea with silly mannerisms. She must, at 36, have been much older than the other beginning nurses, but some of them became her friends for life. She visited one in Wales who had a big robust family. Her young friend later remembered Sophie's talent for compassion, her ability "to look into the soul of the one she was talking to and see everything with that person's eyes."[145]

Nurse Mannerheim served as district nurse, a branch of nursing she was particularly interested in. This function was established during the 1880s, when nurses were sent into the homes of the poor, not as almsgivers, but to teach mothers sanitary and health precepts. In 1887 Queen Victoria had donated to this cause much of her Jubilee fund given by the women of England. Sophie loved the challenge of dealing with the poorest patients in their own ill-equipped homes. She arrived early in the morning with basic supplies of carbolic acid, soap, thermometer, measuring cup, bandages and a bottle of wine. Even candles, matches, pen and ink were stowed in the little suitcase she carried, as she made her way through the shoddiest quarters, sometimes several times a day. Sophie went to work scrubbing every corner of the house—more likely a hovel—and teaching the children stories and songs, encouraging the patients to follow her advice. Once a week the head nurse arrived for inspection and checked to see if there were complaints about the visiting nurse. Sophie's intuition, her understanding of a look, the intonation of a voice, her instinctive liking for people, were the real tools she used in her healing visits to London's most destitute and ailing young mothers.

At the end of three years, having taken the examinations and hardened her competence, Sophie decided to return to Finland. In April 1902 she was aimless no longer, and knew the outlines of what she must do though it was not easy to know how or where she should begin.

She returned as a Nightingale "missionary" Her first job was in a sanitarium for tubercular children at the seashore. During that summer the rain poured down relentlessly. Sophie made up for the lack of sunshine with exercise, improvised plays for the children. She found two little boys to protect, one a 13-year-old who had spent his life in one hospital after another, paralyzed for the rest his 32-year life. But Sophie understood his lively intelligence and helped the boy to find books, so many that he later arranged a small lending library in the countryside where he lived as an adult, earning pocket-money from the embroidery he had learned under Sophie. The other little boy, still a babe in arms when Sophie took him home to care for him, grew up to be a healthy young man. Sophie saw to his education, helped him find a post as gardener and even remembered him in her will with a small house and a bit of land near Turku.

To Carl she wrote in February 1904, "I've sought the superintendent's post at the Hospital for Surgery and been named as such. At the beginning of March I'll go abroad a few months to see some model hospitals in Altona, Breslau, Berlin, London, Edinburgh, and come back home by way of Copenhagen and Stockholm." She added that she would go to Pielisjärvi for the whole summer to practice Finnish. "I'll start my work in the autumn. It won't be a dance on roses, but will be what I've long missed. I'll be fully occupied, with an interest in life. I know you'll be happy for me, understanding that work is what one cannot be without." Pielisjärvi was a Finnish-speaking region, where she could learn and practice the language.

She would need that language to carry out the education of the student nurses. And she knew how much was in disarray and confusion in the nursing world as it then was in Finland.

She had won the competition to be head nurse against more practiced and competent nurses, even though the hospital leadership was aware of creating discord by naming a newcomer who had never practiced in a Finnish hospital. They were at once impressed by her patrician bearing, and had a sense that this young woman, trained in England's best hospital for nurses under Florence Nightingale's guardianship, would not be content to follow in others' well-worn footsteps.

In Pielisjärvi, where no Swedish was spoken, Sophie lived in the vicarage with the dean and his wife. She would bring no Swedish books, write no Swedish letters, but she would not neglect her nursing. The pastor's wife suggested they take care of a little seven-year-old girl, Siri, who had been bedridden for four years, lying in the same bed in the same position for all that time, on her side, her knees drawn up under her chin. The walls of her home were blackened with soot; her bed consisted of a pelt that had become as hard as a board from the accumulation of dirt and pus.

Sophie and the pastor's oldest daughter, Elli, changed the rectory's ironing room into a hospital bedroom. There were no proper beds, but large wash baskets served instead, being more practical because they could be moved out of doors. One basket was not enough, as Siri soon had a companion, another little tubercular child, and even a third. But none was as sick and helpless as little Siri; the others were merely "scrofulous" At her first bath she screamed so heartrendingly that her father fainted, and it took two adults to wash her. The little patient's body had developed fistulas, and one arm, tightly pressed against the body for so long, had literally fastened to it.

By the end of the summer, Sophie and Elli, using special dressings, succeeded in easing Siri's arm and hand, making them nearly normal.

One day Sophie and Elli decided to take the children to the hill of Koli to breathe the healthy high air. Sophie told Siri of the plan. "How would you like to come to Koli with us? There the sun shines and flowers grow, and you'll be well enough to pick them."[146] There was no answer. Sophie realized the child had not yet uttered a single word to them.

On the day they were to go the rain pelted down. The trip was hardly a tempting prospect, for they would have to take a rowboat out to the steamer with the little ones. But when Sophie visited the sickroom Siri spoke: "It's today that we're going to Koli!" It was the first time the child had looked her in the eye and spoken. That was enough. The rain stopped, Elli carried Siri on her back and ran up the path with her, while Sophie and the young people from the deanery followed to the tourist cabin on the hilltop with the other children, baskets, picnic and mattresses. The basket with Siri in it was placed on the hill while the adults scrubbed and cleaned the cabin. Suddenly there was a cry from Elli. Sophie hurried back to find Siri standing on trembling legs next to her basket, picking flowers! Elli and Sophie embraced and wept. From that moment Siri made progress. She could run by autumn and easily use her arm, and even be officially dismissed from the sanitarium as fully restored.[147]

Sophie's work in Pielisjärvi continued without her, for a children's home staffed by the local farm women was organized. As Sophie said to the parson's wife later, the beginning of it all was the rectory's ironing room.

When Sophie entered the Hospital for Surgery in the fall of 1904 as the new head nurse, there was much to be done. For one thing, she would no longer allow nurses to work in the dresses they wore on the street, gathering dust and germs. That was a radical notion. Nor could they wear their new uniforms back out to the street. There was much opposition, but the new head stood firm. Furthermore, there would be no favoritism. Sophie made it clear that she was to be addressed as Baroness by all her subordinates. It was not a piece of arrogance. She explained to a good friend: "One must behave exactly the same way with everyone. If you were my student you too would call me Baroness."[148] There would be no squeaking wheels in her administration. She had seen the respect English nurses had for their superiors. The reforms in Finland would now proceed.

Not everyone liked her perceived stiffness. Her sense of command, inherited by birth and trained in England, could well have been resented by nurses who were older and more practiced than she. She did not encourage familiarity and the distance she created between herself and other nurses was not unlike a description of Florence Nightingale's manner: "There was, in spite of the gentleness, the sympathy, the charming intelligence, something about Florence which chilled . . . she lived on a different plane, out of reach, frighteningly, but also infuriatingly, remote."[149] With the advice and help of one of her professors Sophie learned to temper her high expectations with humor and understanding. And in time she improved the conditions for the hard-pressed understaffed nurses. Nothing escaped Sophie's eye, and a natural diplomacy and compassion guided her way.

Less than twenty-five years before Sophie's arrival as head nurse, there had been no antiseptic solutions at the hospital. Such treatments were first introduced in the 1880s. Until 1889 there were no courses for nurses and even then they had only half a year of instruction. They rarely washed their hands between patients. The doctors operated in the same gowns, stained with blood and pus, that always hung on hooks in the hospital. There was no special operating room nurse. The head nurse had responsibility for preparing the patient for surgery. There was, in fact, no head nurse at all until 1889.

The official part of Sophie's work, in addition to her lectures in both Swedish and Finnish, included administrative duties both morning and afternoon, oversight of the hospital's linens and wash that she counted two days a week. She had to watch over the budget and the kitchen, and being a true Mannerheim was interested in food. She wondered what the patients ate and what, precisely, they had to endure. When she'd made a study of it, she could be found giving the cook lessons in seasoning and preparing meat without overcooking it and boiling out the last bit of taste.

Reforms in methods and education had taken place at the hospital before Sophie's arrival, but she still found the nurses' days impossibly long. They alone, with the help of student nurses, had to take care of the wards. There was only one ward nurse, with student nurses caring for all the practical duties of making beds and washing 200 patients. Sophie extended the student courses of one and a half years to three, so that eventually these young student nurses could be used as subordinates for the overworked division heads. As for night nurses, there had been none until 1898. Before that, the ward nurses had to take night duty, only occasionally assisted by student nurses or women employed for other duties, the so called "night watchers." Sophie's reform, the appointment of subordinate nurses, made it possible to give the night nurse necessary help.

Before this new system could work, still another reform was necessary, one that caused great opposition in the hospital and even in the city. Students had had night duty every fourth or fifth night, which meant that in less than a week they had one 24-hour work day. Now Sophie decided to give the subordinate nurses three months of night duty at a time, the students one month. The night nurses, freed to sleep during the day or do what they wanted, returned to their duties at 8 in the evening. There was much criticism both in the hospital and out, for it was considered inhuman to require them to sleep during the day and be on duty at night. Sophie took a great deal of criticism as a harsh disciplinarian. But she drove through the reform. It was a success: there now was a rested replacement for the day nurse at night.

Above all, Sophie wanted her leadership to be such that students and nurses alike would have the same sort of feeling about their calling as she herself had. Like the doctors, their most selfless feelings would be involved. She wanted them all to love their work, to see it as a calling beyond praise and self-esteem and rewards.

Sophie drove herself as hard as the nurses. She was never on leave longer than they. Each one must feel the responsibility of acting as spokeswoman and exemplar of the profession. It was not they who had chosen the work, but in most cases the work that had claimed them. Anyone who failed to uphold standards would cast a shadow over the whole of the corps.

Sophie was also aware of the material needs of the nurses, how uncomfortably they were housed next to the wards, with a door open to these at all times. It was as unsuitable for patients as for nurses. Sophie wrote Johan in May, 1905, "I'm very pleased to have my way in many matters this winter. I've reorganized the night nurses' work entirely and driven through my program with the assistant nurses. The Hospital for Surgery has money to build and in a few days will start. One of the attics will be furnished for the nurses, and there will be a new, charming location for the senior nurse, who until now has had a rather unpleasant residence. But much remains to make the students' instructions better. This summer I'll try to give shape to my wishes in that respect. It's strange how everything must go according to one's wishes when some of them have been fulfilled. But it's good the field is still so unplowed, and that there's so endlessly much to do." The more there was to do, the happier she was. "One has no one to talk to about all this, but one can't have everything, and must be satisfied with the feeling of perhaps being able to do something useful."

Typically, she considered members of the cleaning staff as important as the nurses. She saw to it that their hours were decreased, their pay raised and housing changed. Heretofore they had lived in the cellar, with many to a room; now new, two-bed rooms were found in the attic and a meeting room was provided. Porters and guards, the keepers of the linen closets, often gave Sophie their confidence. The Baroness was always there. She knew them all and she knew their personal situations and problems. She set up a fund for their sick care and gave it the income from her first book and a sum at her death.

Now she arranged a meeting room for the nurses and subordinate nurses, a pleasant room where they could read the newspapers, even practice the musical instruments they had bought for themselves. Their sleeping quarters were further away from the patients, in the attic of one of the wings.

In November, 1907, Sophie compared herself to the helmsman of a ship. "The sea is agitated, the weather squally, with wind gusts from unexpected directions, and the vessel is heavy to steer, my arm numb from exhaustion, so I'd like to leave the rudder to another. But there's no one else who knows the channel as well as I, and I must stay at my post and struggle until someone will come to turn over the helm to."[150]

It has been said that the head nurse was worshipped, and hated.[151] How could such a paragon draw antipathy? She has been compared to her brother Gustaf in her perfectionism, her total immersion in her calling, her instant observation of facial expressions, those traits in speech or manner which might reveal inner discomforts or anxieties, feelings which must under no circumstances be shown patients. Failure to obey her instructions in these matters could bring on her considerable ire. The smallest detail, a missing button, a crooked hem, a casual attitude of dress or manner, a posture less than perfect, invited criticism and a word of warning. The mere sound of her silken petticoat's rustling as she approached was enough to speed up the work.[152] If a nurse were given leave to go home for an important family event, it was understood that she would have to return on time or give up the course. But the head nurse had the gift of listening. It could happen that one of her nurses might differ with the Baroness as to which area in the hospital she should serve. A good argument could win the point, and their relationship was not affected. If Gustaf was now an army colonel, Sophie was certainly a field marshal in her hospital world. She had the trademark of the oldest child in a large family: she took charge of everything and everyone.

The twig had been bent in childhood. If only her mother could have seen what her troublesome daughter would accomplish! What the Countess Helene Mannerheim interpreted as stubbornness was an iron will, matching that of her mother and apparently often in conflict with hers. She hid her feelings under a proud mask. Sophie grew up in a large family but was often alone, having no companions of her own age. Finding a governess equal to the task of educating her was often an impossible task. A few of her mother's despairing remarks when Sophie was 13 are interesting to read in view of what the child would become. Helene wrote to her sister Hanna Lovén in Stockholm from Villnäs: "Sofi's occupation is my hardest task, because I don't know enough myself to be able to awaken her interest in school subjects, and she is very lazy and stubborn . . . She can play around superbly, and then she's never tired. If she can get a good teacher this spring all will be well . . ." A few months later Helene commented, "We have astonishing bad luck with the governess. A well-recommended German was found judging by her letter to write worse French than Sofi . . . . Sofi is the one who most tries my patience, perhaps also because I expect too much of her. She has a way of driving her will through which irritates and bothers me and yet I often give way. She also needs a person of her own age sometimes . . ."

The problem of Sophie's education continued to trouble her mother, who was ahead of her time in her feeling that girls' learning was as important as that of boys. "Where Sofi will be this winter is as uncertain as possible. I don't know myself what I think would be best for her because there is much to study, but the time is short and Miss S. can't measure up to the instruction she'll get in Helsinki." At last it seemed resolved, for the time being: "With Fraulein I'm quite pleased and if her competence were greater there would be every reason to keep her a long time, for she is quiet and determined and sensitive which little by little forces Sofie to modify her independent spirit." Helene often blamed herself for not understanding her child. "Sofi has become much better this fall but sometimes I think she is pretty cold, or perhaps it's just a lack of sentimentality which I suppose to be coldness."[153] There one sees an early sign of remoteness, also a characteristic of the great Florence. Sophie was already standing apart, seen to be aloof.

Sophie was not content to have patients dismissed when they once again were ambulatory. She made sure that a worker who had lost his leg or arm would be able to afford a prosthesis, that a poor woman had clean and new clothes on her departure, that peasant women without the ability to write or communicate would have news from home. Sophie herself would write the letter, or a husband would suddenly appear from a great distance at the bedside of a wife whose days were numbered. Somehow he had the news and the money to come. A faithful old retainer's family might find at her funeral a wreath marked "from her friend Sophie Mannerheim."[154] She organized the first convalescent home in Finland for those who were once again healthy but still too weak to go back to work. She always seemed to know the right people, and once again her articulate and intelligent plans would meet with understanding and backing.

Sophie, in her capacity as chairwoman of the nurses' organization, was eager to reproduce the kind of housing for nurses combined with instruction that she had seen in England. The initiative for a nurses' residence had been taken in 1899 by another nurse educated, like Sophie, at St. Thomas's. There the young student nurse had visited the bedside of Florence Nightingale who was happy to see a nurse from Finland, and talked to her of the importance for hospitals of a students' residence. The old lady gave her visitor five pounds toward such a Finnish establishment, which must be ample enough to hold all the students. In 1906 a combination student residence and school of instruction opened its doors. Later, Sophie would see her dream answered for a more extensive residence and school.

In 1907 she established a home for educated women bound by work to the city but without the means to live there in any comfort. She talked the town fathers into using a donated summer residence for the purpose, and as usual won her argument.

As chairman of the Finnish nursing organization, Sophie went to Paris in 1907 for the meeting of the International Congress of Nurses, to which her group did not yet belong. Her representation had more than a casual importance, because world attention had focused on Finnish women who had won the right to vote and be voted for in 1906. Sophie was proud to represent her country together with leading nurses from America and elsewhere, all of them pathbreakers. It was her first appearance in these international circles, admired by the British Journal of Nursing for her speech on the Finnish organization's work, and by the American nurse Lavinia Dock, the nursing historian of her time. In London in 1909, the Finnish Nurses' Organization joined the International Congress of Nurses, and once again Sophie captured her audience.

Some details from her nursing life cast more light on her character than long lists of accomplishments, reforms and positions held, medals won. These details are taken without regard for sequence, merely as small sketches. So we can see her arriving to meet the board of directors of her hospital, coat and hat in hand to argue for the ordering of new, modern hospital beds. After all, an international congress of medicine was to take place in Helsinki, and the hospital would have distinguished visitors. Surely, no one would want to show off their old-fashioned, ugly beds? The board members asked: "Who will pay for these beds?" She replied: "I am sure this board will find the means. They are not expensive. See here, I have a comparative chart, this [bed] is cheaper but impractical, this one excellent and can be bought at a discount." The directors objected: "It will cost too much to transport them." She replied that she'd already been to the steamboat office and now had a promise they would charge very little for such a noble purpose. They asked: "and the customs?" She replied that the customs cost nothing; she had looked up what the beds were made of, and these materials were virtually untaxed.[155] The Baroness won her case. Like her predecessor Florence Nightingale, Sophie was a practical woman and her social standing gave her access to those who would listen to her and implement her reforms.

For the children's department in the hospital she had thrown out the dreary grey clothes that made the children look like convicts. Instead, she had ordered red and white checked dresses and shirts. The recuperating children would all learn to make handicrafts, but these must be useful. They might lay the groundwork for future careers, and all the work must be good. The boys learned to tie nets and weave baskets for the flower shop. They learned carpentry and toy making. The girls sewed and knitted and wove, making things that could be used in the hospital. Instead of money which at first made the children work too quickly and carelessly, they earned tools so that at the end of their stay they would each go home with a full toolbox.

Sophie started a nurses' periodical, written in both Finnish and Swedish. She was adamant about making Finnish as important as Swedish in nursing circles at a time when language equality was not taken for granted, when the Finnish-speaking population bitterly perceived their own language to be considered second-rate. She was convinced that in her small country with its two cultures, each was uniquely enriched by the other. The periodical would be above politics and would contain articles about social service, care in the poor homes, and whatever questions about nursing were under review. Specialists contributed their knowledge, and ultimately a book on health care was published.

In a speech to graduating nurses she compared the nurse's duty with a young woman's taking her husband's name and the responsibilities that now belong to all her actions. Every word she utters, everything she does, is a direct reflection not only on herself, but on the new name she bears. Just so, she said, is the nurse's calling: each nurse will cast a light or a shadow on the whole corps of Finnish nurses. But she cautioned them: "baggage we take on the trip to become nurses, like 'offering ourselves up for suffering mankind' I would like to call drivel." There was the caustic Mannerheim tongue speaking, rejecting self-serving sentimentality. But the final questions and summation came from Sophie's heart. "Put your hand on your heart! Did you ever really feel it a sacrifice to become nurses? Wouldn't it have been a sacrifice not to? . . . . No; our life is not a sacrificial one. To us much has been given. May we therefore strive to be worthy of such great gifts. May we never forget to be prepared in this life, so that when our working day comes to an end and the long repose awaits us, we will be ready to welcome it."[156]

Sophie was recognized abroad. In 1920 she was invited to the International Nurses' Congress in Atlanta, Georgia, in those days a 26-hour trip by train from New York where she landed. She spoke to the 3000 nurses at the Congress, and on her return to New York at Teachers College of Columbia University. She was chairman of the International Congress of Nurses from 1922-25, and represented Finland in the International Council of Women in London in 1925. Sophie won the Florence Nightingale medal in 1925 and the White Rose medal in Finland.

She was indeed a towering figure: intolerant of pettiness and sloth, capable of great rage in the manner of a grande dame, fearless, tender, a born ruler. A believer in independence and professional responsibility for herself and all women, she championed small children, the poor and the Finnish language. Sophie Mannerheim, like Florence Nightingale, had the aristocratic assumption of equality with men. Neither woman had felt hindered by her sex in making her own way, in effecting reforms. When confronted by obstacles, they found practical ways of defeating the opposition. Sophie Mannerheim was a constant innovator of imagination and courage, an international figure in her day, taking as her due the homage she received.

Baroness Sophie Mannerheim
Founder of Modern Nursing in Finland

Chapter 20

COLONEL MANNERHEIM GOES TO WAR FOR

THE EMPEROR

When the Japanese made their surprise attack on the Russian fleet in Port Arthur, the Russian Empire was overextended. Russians had pressed on to the Far East, to Siberia's Pacific coast, in the 1850's. By 1900 Russia had made the rich Chinese province of Manchuria its own "zone of interest."[157] Russian troops were known and hated for their brutality. Russians were exploiting the timber industry there, of particular interest to Tsar Nicholas II who had invested his own money in it. Extensive markets for export were developed in Manchuria and Korea. Russians had built the Trans-Siberian Railroad to carry Manchurian timber and other produce to the west, and to transport armies in either direction. The naval base of Port Arthur in Korea Bay was now under Russian control. This port was of the greatest importance to Russia, as she needed a harbor free of ice the year round. That prize had been coveted and won by Japan in the war and peace agreement of 1895 with China. But now Russian demands, greased by bribes and backed by gunboats, succeeded in grasping the prize just before the Chinese were to hand it over to the Japanese. Not only Port Arthur, but Dairen, a large commercial center, and the whole Liaotung Peninsula had come under Russian hegemony. Japan was aroused, suspicious and enraged.

Commanders of the Great Russian fleets and armies and the Tsar's men at home in Petersburg and Moscow had grown careless and too sure that their power could only grow. They assumed no nation was strong enough to challenge them. Russia's army was far larger than the Japanese, and Russia was a great naval power. The Tsar did not doubt that he could easily win a war against people he despised, for he had not forgotten the assassination attempt on him when he had visited Japan as heir to the Russian throne, in 1890. A war might arouse patriotism at home, diminish the discontent, the dangerous stirrings of millions, not to mention the demands of Poles and Finns, who increasingly wanted to have a say in their governance. Independence was not actively desired by most Finns. Actually, it was hoped in Finland that their ties to the old Empire would continue within the historic institutions, and that the Tsar would be protective of Finnish interests, as his oath of office demanded.

The Russian planners in St. Petersburg were not alone in dreaming that their ambitions might plant their imperial flags beyond Manchuria. Indeed, the Japanese feared the ultimate: an invasion of their country by the Russians. From Emperor to foot soldier each man was prepared to die in defense of his country. The British kept a wary eye on the Russian presence, thought to be too near them in India, and had made an alliance with Japan in 1902. Japanese battleships were being built in British docks. In winning the Philippines, the United States had expanded its own role in the future of Asia, and looked on Russian expansion there with displeasure.

No one could foresee that Japanese actions would show the beginnings of the decay, the eventual disintegration of the Tsar's Russian world. No one could imagine that an Asian country could take on a war with a great European power, and win.

At the end of December 1903, when the Tsar was on a hunting trip in Poland at Spala castle, the Japanese Ambassador presented a note. It repeated an earlier suggestion about dividing the spheres of interest in the Far East. The Japanese demanded that Russian power cease its forward march in Asia and recognize Chinese sovereignty in Manchuria. An answer was required by January 7th. Weeks passed; the young Russian heir to the throne had a hemophiliac attack, which always postponed official activities. The reply in February was, Gustaf

Mannerheim writes in his memoirs, conciliatory though "preceded by a particularly arrogant treatment of Japanese proceedings."[158]

Suddenly, on February 5, 1904, Japan broke its diplomatic ties to Russia. Three days later, using surprise as effectively as its swift ships and projectiles, the Japanese attacked Port Arthur. Japanese destroyers silently stole into the harbor at night, despite Russian searchlights covering the waters, despite the observations of patrol ships outside the harbor and even within it. Officers of a Russian ship in the harbor thought the newcomers were the patrol coming home. The Japanese, having seen the whole lineup of Russian ships at anchor, aimed their torpedoes. Three of Russia's largest ships were crippled; the belated Russian responses from shore and ship were ineffective.

At home in Russia, the attack was sneeringly called a "flea bite."[159] The attack was unimportant. How, the Russians asked themselves complacently, could this despised people take on the might of all Russia, with its enormous territories, its Asian subject peoples, its mighty armies and fleets? After all, Russia still had its Northern Fleet at anchor in the Baltic, and it was given orders to sail for this Pacific war 18,000 miles away.

Eva Sparre, writing her brother Carl from Cannes on February 15, 1904, reported that "all talk about the war, which will not bring anything good in its wake. In the end, it will be the poor Japanese who will suffer. It's possible that inner Russia will start stirring. I've met a number of Russians who all have marvelously liberal opinions, and all of them criticize the government. Kuropatkin [the supreme commander] has asked for retirement and has been posted to Turkestan." Eva's letter reflected the pro-Japanese, anti-Russian attitudes in Finland, and later in America, when the Japanese asked Theodore Roosevelt to mediate the peace treaty.

The attack on Port Arthur signaled other planned Japanese movements. A great Japanese army now marched across the Yalu River against Russian troops in Korea. Encouraged by rebels in the Russian ranks, Polish troops at the front had gone over to the enemy. General Kuropatkin, the supreme commander, was forced to retreat. Quite suddenly, the Japanese defeated Russian arms in their first battle. The greatest siege of modern history soon took place, a seven-month siege by land and water, gradually ravaging the Russians' Asian fleet in Port Arthur and its fortress defenses. With the first surprise night attack on the Port, the Russian fleet in Asia had been locked in, though the damaged ships were stubbornly repaired and the defenses often manned by sailors dragging heavy guns up the hills from the ships. But on January 2, 1905, the Russians gave up their long defense.

Before this, Russians at home had looked on the whole affair as a boring colonial spat. Fatally, the Russians had not modernized their armaments. Their few machine guns were far outnumbered by the enemy's. The Russian Imperial armies still dressed as they had in Napoleon's time. Their brightly colored uniforms made easy targets for a smaller but better equipped Japanese army whose earlier blue uniforms had been replaced by khaki, blending with the dusty landscape.

The vast power of Russia had reached its peak and was now on the downward slope, though no one understood this. The Japanese attack was no "flea bite." Russia's standing as a world power was threatened. Using the Trans-Siberian Railroad, more soldiers were rushed to the armies already in Manchuria, but not all the tracks had been laid. The Russian fleet in the Baltic was mobilized, but though the war had begun in February, the fleet did not begin its long journey until October.

Despite the interest of Grand Duke Vladimir, an old friend of Finnish rights, and the influence of the Danish-born Dowager Empress, who worked behind the scenes to diminish "Russification" in Finland, the policy of pan-Russification had the greater influence upon Tsar Nicholas. Although the young men of Finland no longer felt loyalty to the Russian Empire, those Finnish officers, like Gustaf Mannerheim, making their careers in the Imperial army and navy stayed true to their sworn oath of loyalty. But they could not agree with the Tsar's policies of oppression.

By 1903 Mannerheim had had his fill of his post at the Imperial Stables, and saw his opportunity to return to military service in an appointment as commander of the Model Squadron of the Officers' Cavalry School in St. Petersburg, a good career move. This was a demonstration squadron for commanding officers' exercises and for trials of new kinds of equipment. Gustaf reported to his brother Johan that it was the only squadron in the cavalry whose chief was a colonel, and could thereafter command a regiment. The timing coincided with Gustaf's own doubts about staying in Russian service. With Carl's exile and Johan's departure from Finland, Gustaf had given serious consideration to resigning his commission, in anger at the Russian policy of oppression and the treatment of his brothers.

When the Japanese attacked Port Arthur on February 8, 1904, all plans for changes of career were abandoned. He had written Johan, after the news of the attack, "More and more I'm thinking of going to the war theatre. I need a change of scene, not to mention the necessity for a military to see a war. All this between us."

Mannerheim was not ordered to the war front. It was he himself who made the decision to seek war service. His action came as a shock to the family. But they surely heard the cri de coeur of a man trying to resurrect his own sense of worth by breaking completely with the past, taking part in a distant war and perhaps actually seeking death. They understood that he had just lived through the experience of an unhappy marriage and its disintegration; his wife had left him, taking with her their two small daughters. She had left him once before, but this was the searing end. Now what he saw as a duty coincided with an opportunity to change the direction of his life, perhaps to win honors with the hope of enhancing his career if he survived. The melancholia and sense of failure that Gustaf felt is reflected in a letter to Sophie of 1903. He speaks of his loneliness and feeling of uselessness. He had already written Johan about his thoughts of joining the Russian war effort; to his brother Carl he wrote that his existence in St. Petersburg had become unbearable.

Many in Finland saw his decision as approaching treason. Two of his brothers were in exile, harassed by the Emperor he was to serve. Aunt Hanna had written, in 1903, "I know Gustaf's feelings are warmer than the controlled surface he lets show, but I regret the more that he will not stay with the Imperial Stable. There he would perhaps not have the constant reminder that he is working for the enemy."[160]

Gustaf wrote his father and brothers that he was sworn to defend the Empire, now under attack, its first important battle already lost; his decision did not imply approval of all the Russian policies. In serving he would gain experience in his chosen profession, and perhaps, if he distinguished himself, he would have the authority to be heard in matters important to Finland. His thinking was part idealistic, in adhering to his officer's oath, in part practical—perhaps one might call it a sixth sense. The family, despite their strong opposition, accepted his decision and closed him into their circle.

At last Gustaf's orders to leave for the war front came through in October, 1904. "It cost me dear to say goodbye to father and the sisters," he wrote Johan. His letters from that time reflect his own broad interests. This seemingly aloof, unfeeling man expressed in his letters to his father, brothers and sisters what no others, however trusted, would hear. To Sophie he would write of his heart's concern for a woman. Johan, the brother closest to him, and an expert on horses and farming, would hear about stallions, Mongolian horses, Gustaf's enterprises at his wife's estate—buildings for a dairy and cheese production, a fish hatchery, the breeding of horses and pigs. His sister Eva would hear details he knew her artist's eye would seize on: a young Chinese officer dressed in a silk mauve and black uniform. To his brothers he gave sartorial advice; Gustaf was a demanding client of boot-makers and tailors. To Sophie he wrote, admiring her lessons in Finnish, though he found it amazing she could learn this difficult language in half a year. In his letters to Johan, Gustaf worries about his wife, Nata, and his will, deeding her the money he is saving to support her. The love for his Finnish family is obvious in every letter; they have replaced the marriage and family life he did not have.

For his coming adventures in Manchuria, Gustaf bought three horses in Moscow. One of them, his beloved five-year-old throughbred stallion Talisman, was to carry him through the most important battle of its time, a battle that would reveal the Tsar's crumbling authority within the Empire. In the old Russian ceremony of sending its soldiers off to war, a saint's medal was hung around Gustaf's neck at the railroad station in the presence of the Chevalier Guards officers, before he boarded the long, hot, dirty and very slow train to Manchuria.

As the tracks had not been laid down around Lake Baikal, Gustaf crossed it by boat, then crossed Siberia by train again. While waiting in Harbin for his horse Talisman to arrive by separate transport, Gustaf took a side trip to Vladivostok. The city is on a peninsula overlooking Peter the Great Bay in the Sea of Japan, hills rising from the water. It was a sizeable distance, though two and a half days seemed short compared with the trip he had just undertaken. Gustaf had a number of reasons for wanting to go there. In 1860, when it was founded, his great-uncle, Leonard Jägerskiöld, had an early hand in developing its Russian position there as an outpost, a naval base and port for fishing fleets. A part of the city was still named for the Finn, with his prescient ideas about the future of Japan as a world power, and Gustaf had long been curious to see it. To Sophie he wrote, "The location is imposingly lovely . . . the most gorgeous site I've ever seen."[161] Although he was always sensitive to natural beauty, Gustaf had still another purpose for his trip to Vladivostok. Sophie would learn his heart's reason, written on postcards. "A friend of mine, to whom I'm still just as attached, has a hospital near Vladivostok, and was kind enough to come into the city during the two days I spent there. I am so glad to have seen her before going to the war theatre. This is only between us two."

He trusted only Sophie with a hint of his feeling for Countess Betsy Sjuvalova, a member of the court society and influential in the intellectual circles of St. Petersburg. In the salon famous for witty conversation, where Betsy shone, Gustaf met politically lively men and women interested in social reforms. He is said to have absorbed their ideas for later thoughts of his own. For more than ten years it had been rumored that the Finnish baron and the Russian countess would marry, though she was much older than he. She was a widow, and Anastasia's running away had made him a bachelor. Anastasia had complained that Gustaf was cold and reserved, but it seemed clear that with Countess Betsy he could not be called aloof.

He wrote his father in November, 1904, telling of his train trip. "The trains with their dust, uneven temperature and endless stops are a real nightmare." He had dressed in his "long-haired goatskin cap," waiting for another train on the everlasting trip. Under those caps, he wrote, were members of nearly all classes, from Petersburg's "drawing-room officers to the most decadent alcoholics in the final stages, begging a tip to get drunk."

Gustaf is known to have sought help and medication at a Vladivostok hospital, thought to be the one Betsy supervised. His body was on fire from lice bites after the month-long train trip. The two days in the Russian port city were a civilized intermezzo, a solace for mind and body. He luxuriated in two nights in a hotel. He had what he craved—a wise, warm and affectionate woman's company.

The dazzling Betsy and Gustaf kept up their friendship for many years. He traveled to distant places to meet her. A woman who was widely admired for the finesse of her wit, her wisdom and beauty, she could often make up for what he had missed in his personal life.

She was said to have been a greater support to him than anyone else, and her help extended to promoting even his friends and family into her elite circles. Louis Sparre painted her portrait, and from his furniture factory in Finland designed and made chairs for her formal dining room in St. Petersburg.

From Vladivostok, rested after his visit, Gustaf returned to Harbin to receive Talisman. At last he arrived in Mukden, now called Shenyang, the capital of Manchuria, a Lieutenant Colonel transferred to the elite 52 Nezhinskiy Dragoons Regiment with its brilliant blue uniforms.

Many disturbing details struck him. He was aware that here in Asia, Russian officers were distrusted by their men. This was not true in European Russia. He knew that the Russian army had no experience of modern war. He knew that Kuropatkin, head of all the armed forces and hated in Finland as one of its oppressors, was scorned for his life aboard a luxurious train, surrounded by "society officers." More dangerous still, Kuropatkin was jealous of an important and popular Finnish general under his command, General Gripenberg, and did what he could to undermine him. Eventually, Kuropatkin would be held responsible for the Russian catastrophes, and removed from his high post.[162]

Gustaf also noted the heavy drinking in the officers' quarters at night. "Brandy drinking has diminished, thanks to my influence," he wrote his father in December 1904. "It seems comical to have become a sobriety and morality preacher. That this is needed, you can judge from the amount of drinking in our cabin: 82 bottles of brandy in 18 days." One more observation troubled him: the destruction of Chinese villages by Russian troops, soldiers stealing and leaving nothing standing, hoping to enrich themselves, or to gather fuel. Gustaf's Dragoons were liked, because they had respect for the Chinese and their property. (The Chinese buried their supplies—even live oxen, with hay-covered openings—to prevent stealing.) But Gustaf's commanders were strict with their men, as he wrote Eva.

Soon after his arrival, Gustaf sought permission to visit the Russian outposts, and spend the night two thousand feet from the Japanese trenches. He was still dressed in a spotless uniform, which aroused the suspicion and irritation of the battalion chief. Who was this man in an elegant uniform, nudging the rules by sporting handsome yellow leather leggings, his clothes expensively tailored and newly bought? Gustaf found himself under arrest and on his way to the chief of the infantry division. But his guards lost their way in the dark, and brought him instead to the Cossack division's staff where he was greeted with high amusement. The next morning he heard about a Japanese discovered prowling in Russian positions. He realized it was himself, taken for a spy! He wrote his father about this in a December, 1904 letter. His adventure was reported in the Finnish newspapers, giving his family exquisite mirth. Shortly before, the Russian Baltic Fleet, on its way to the Asian war theater had mistaken some innocent British fishing trawlers in the North Sea for disguised Japanese warships. Tragically, the Russians fired on them, killing several fishermen and of course destroying their boats. Gustaf's father, at home in Finland, thought it was not surprising. After all, a Russian battalion commander had taken Gustaf for a Japanese. The absurd mistakes caused joy in Finland, and as far as Gustaf's family was concerned were more signs of Russian disintegration.

A German military observer sent to the front has left a picture of Gustaf at this time. "A distinguished, unusually handsomely mounted Lieutenant Colonel in the 52nd Nezhinskiy Dragoon Regiment's blue uniform rides next to me. For his rank he has a strikingly supple, youthful bearing . . . [He is] a Guards Cavalryman from Petersburg: the Chevalier Guards, the Tsar's Life Regiment. The Guards majors are given one rank higher, lieutenant colonel, in regiments of the line . . . A magnificent horse has made the journey with his master, a reminder that the Tsar's Life Regiment is mounted on particularly imposing horses . . ."[163]

Gustaf wrote home about his experiences at the front. For a time calm reigned while both Japanese and Russians were quartered in the same village. By silent arrangement, each side, unarmed, fetched water from the same river. "The other day," Gustaf wrote, "one of our officers amused himself by starting to sing, and when he was finished he was rewarded by applause and shouts of 'encore!' from the Japanese fortifications." Gustaf noticed that Japanese taken prisoner were well equipped with woolen sweaters and leather garments.

When he was reconnoitering a village to see if it was occupied by Japanese, he had his ordeal by fire; bullets whined past just as he had reined in his horse to look through binoculars. Two soldiers were badly wounded, and Talisman was shaken. Gustaf had to use "full force" to prevent him from shying. He remarked that according to Russian Caucasian tradition, the wounded would have considered it a breach of honor to have complained. They were carried on stretchers swung on two long poles, the Chinese bearing them with "mincing steps and slightly bent knees."

When Port Arthur capitulated to the Japanese in 1905, it spelled opportunity for Finnish patriots at home: the enemy of their enemy had become their friend. A future general in the Finnish army of liberation, Hannes Ignatius, wrote in his memoirs that he and members of the Kagal passive resistance met in Stockholm in the spring of 1905. They had two purposes: to discuss what support Finland might have from Swedish authorities when the expected revolution erupted in Russia, and to negotiate with the Japanese at their legation, seeking the transfer of weapons for the Finnish cause. (Ignatius had little patience with the passive resistance, being at heart an activist, but he did not espouse working with the revolutionaries in Russia, all of whom he distrusted.)

The Japanese expressed interest, and wished to have information on the mood in Finland; they wondered if an uprising in Finland could be counted on. The Finns could give no guarantee, but if revolution came to Russia it might create the opportunity for a revolt. The Finns asked the Japanese to assure their independence in any peace treaty, but declined old rifles offered them at a cheap price. No Japanese officer could presume to promise any support of Finnish independence.[164] The fact that early supporters of Finnish resistance and independence were negotiating secretly with the Japanese suggests the conflict of loyalties troubling Gustaf's family.

Carl wrote Johan on March 2, 1904, from St. Louis, Missouri, "I was happy to hear that you and your family, including house pets, had escaped across the Åland Sea and that you now are arranging your new home in freer circumstances." This was a reference to Johan's departure from Finland, preventing a move by the Russian regime to exile him. Carl continues: "That I, too, will stay in Sweden you've probably heard . . . What you write about Gustaf grieves me greatly." [He was writing about Gustaf's decision to serve the Russians in their war with Japan.] "I hope what he said to you was the expression of a momentary frame of mind, and that he'll listen to his better feelings, which surely will forbid him to fall for such an affront against his compatriots. Do what you can. Gustaf is worth more than going to waste this way, physically and morally."

Carl continues, writing about American viewpoints: "It has been wonderful to follow, from here, the Japanese successes. A more united anti-Russian atmosphere one can't imagine. And their perception is absolutely correct, for the feelings are hateful, not against the Russian people, but against the Russian government. Such a mighty movement may have practical significance if conditions continue to develop favorably." The anti-Russian sentiments Carl found had their origins in the perceived threat to U.S. interests by Russian economic operations in the Far East. American politicians and businessmen—owners of cotton and flour mills—saw the Russians, backed by money from France, as a menace to all powers expanding economic efforts in North China. Theodore Roosevelt made it clear to France and Germany that if their support of the Tsar continued; he would take Japan's side. England, he knew, would act in the same way. This would mean war.

Gustaf had been given an important reconnaissance task under the First Siberian Army Corps, a corps that took the heaviest attacks of the Japanese attacks on Mukden in March of 1905. It would be the bloodiest battle fought before World War I. As the historian Jägerskiöld writes, each of the adversaries had a world position at stake: Russia, her eastern Empire; Japan, her new posture as a world power.

Mukden, on the Hun River, lies northeast of Port Arthur and the Liaotung Peninsula. The great siege of the port city had won more than a victory for the Japanese: now General Nogi's triumphant troops were freed to increase Japanese forces encircling the Russian troops south of Mukden. This would become another surprise attack. In fact, Gustaf, following orders to make a reconnaissance westward without getting drawn into a long battle, had encountered several Japanese cavalry squadrons armed with machine guns, and traded fire with them. He sent messages to headquarters that the Japanese were making movements to envelop the Russian troops. Afterwards he realized he had seen General Nogi's cavalry.

In January, he had also taken part in an offensive against Sandepu, south of Mukden. He saw action under General Gripenberg in the only operation that gave some promise of success. "It was a matter of rolling up the enemy's left flank to create the possibility of a deep thrust against Japanese supply lines."[165] But here General Kuropatkin, the Commander-in-Chief, interfered, removing one battalion after another, and took other units for his own use elsewhere.

Gustaf saw how successfully the Japanese used the terrain, how invisible they were in their khaki uniforms, how cleverly they protected artillery positions, while the Russians fired from open emplacements. Already in 1903 Gustaf had written to Sophie that Russia's chances in a coming war with Japan were not promising, and foresaw that the Russian military would face first-rate Japanese soldiers.

General Kuropatkin's counter-move to the Japanese encirclement that Gustaf had observed, was to retreat north. 200,000 Japanese troops had maneuvered to encircle the defending Russians, 270,000 strong and superior in cavalry and artillery. But instead of moving under the cover of darkness, the threatened wing did not march until morning and sustained heavy casualties. The retreat became, at times, a rout.

Gustaf sorrowfully wrote about the death of young Count Kankrin, his aide, killed by a bullet through the heart "the moment he turned to deliver an order . . ." Gustaf had suggested him for the St. George medal, the highest medal for valor, which he would one day win himself. Now, as he wrote, there was only time for a wooden cross to be raised on his grave, and it was Gustaf's sad duty to give the news to the young man's family.

He himself would come through the battle without a singed hair, though wild rumors were published in the press that Gustaf had been killed, or at least wounded. But the loss of his beloved Talisman was never forgotten. He writes of his horse, drilled during the stormy winter months: "he had a classical swiftness and talent for schooling . . . . To these qualities are added an excellent and rather fiery temperament, a good gait, a sustained trot, an elegant canter, and much pleasure in his fodder. If he hadn't been horribly mean with other horses, he would have been the ideal horse. The ones I have left are far from perfect, being nervous and fearful of bullets." Talisman had been struck by a bullet. "Fatally wounded, the noble animal carried me until the battle's end, completing his task before he collapsed and died, to my great sorrow."[166]

Behind the recently fortified defenses, there were Russian optimists who thought themselves invincible, but for many, morale had plunged because of the preceding defeats. The machine guns, whose absence on the Russian side Gustaf had observed, enhanced Japanese power: they had almost 1,000 to the Russians' 56. Lack of planning led to a chaotic situation. Gustaf writes of the battle of Mukden, "I was witness to troops who had fought like lions, whole regiments which in the passage of some hours had melted away to a few hundred men, but I have also seen scenes which I can't remember without pain. The completely unprepared retreat can't be described. Whole troops, or divisions of troops, were as though crazed and in many places the unplanned retreat became a frenzied flight . . . [It was] decided so quickly that the baggage train left at the same time as the troops, which made for indescribable crowding. The whole terrain was bombarded by artillery crossfire."[167]

Gustaf lost officers and men, half a squadron the first day. They had been seen with their sabers, "hacking their way through two enemy bodies of troops in Mukden itself, which was seething with Japanese. We don't know what happened to them for no one has returned."[168] He described the infantry's battle with the Japanese as a slaughter.

It was during this battle that he developed his thoughts about army volunteers. "One shouldn't permit young educated men who do not plan to devote themselves to the military profession, to join as ordinary soldiers, for the service they give is not worth the sacrifice of their young lives and promising futures."[169]

Although the Japanese did not gain a definitive battle victory—the front was stabilized 170 kilometers north of Mukden—Kuropatkin was dismissed. (Nevertheless on his return to Russia he was given a new command.) With the defeat, land operations had virtually come to an end. Gustaf worried about the return of the army, and how it would be greeted. "For officers it will not be pleasant to return and bear the shame for all our defeats," as he wrote Sophie in June, 1905. He observed with amazement the promotion of other generals who had shown poor leadership. The political system remained unchanged until Mukden; bureaucracy still reigned in St. Petersburg. The Battle of Tsushima Strait was only months ahead.

A Finnish doctor serving at the front observed Lieutenant Colonel Mannerheim. "Under these difficult circumstances he behaved with a confidence and courage which impressed the soldiers. They felt they were under a leader, and they obeyed." The German military observer wrote that he had ridden at night through the deserted city of Mukden and saw the infantry's last man to man battle against the onrushing Japanese. "The Dragoons gather at the railroad station. The Finnish cavalry's march resounds through the vicinity and the Nezhinskiy Dragoons with their blue uniforms charge forward with Gustaf Mannerheim and his officers at the fore. The infantry has had a needed breathing space." In the terrifying atmosphere with its total confusion and false rumors, riding horses and pack horses were lost; the Commander in Chief's baggage train had disappeared as had his records. [170]

During the battle Gustaf escaped injury. But in the Mukden retreat he was ill and had a high fever, so ill that he felt ready to lie down under the artillery fire. After the retreat, he traveled for 72 hours, partly on horseback, partly on an improvised hospital train, where he was one of about thirty officers who were virtually attacked by retreating soldiers trying to find safety on the roof, on platforms and even wheel axles. The soldiers on the train were packed in three or four layers, with boards between. Writing about the retreat, Gustaf was careful to point out that Russian soldiers had fought with courage, as the many dead silently attested. Gustaf's old school friend and doctor was with the Finnish ambulance when he arrived, and operated on a painful swelling of his ear. Others reported to a Finnish newspaper that Gustaf was so exhausted by overexertion that he could hardly move.

When he returned to service, his duties took him to Mongolia where he was to discover what he could about Japanese infiltration. This was important to the military because the population had partially closed ranks with the Japanese. One objective was therefore to encourage ties to Russia, and also to find out more about Japanese political moves in the area.

Gustaf commanded some units of improvised Chinese militia on a reconnaissance raid behind Japanese lines. He characterized them as highwaymen. For centuries they had ruled the local population, "murdering and burning those who don't pay them bribes. They ride their seasoned, fiery and spirited little Mongolian mounts . . . In the saddle they looked well, youthful and jaunty." Rifles and often a few hundred rounds of ammunition "were carried as easily as a riding whip," and Gustaf admired their nimbleness as compared to "our unwieldy Dragoons." One of the "robber band" reminded him of his Swiss governess: "His appearance under a large Panama straw hat with long colored ribbons and velvet flowers appliquéd on the brim looked astonishingly like Fräulein's," added to which "he had an enormous blue umbrella fastened to his saddle."[171]

Gustaf never failed to notice courage, and saw his Chinese cavalry's bravado with an admiring, if ironic eye. "Even when retreating, they shoot with the gun aimed backward over the shoulder and without turning . . . One might easily get an unintended bullet . . . ." Eva wrote a September, 1905 letter about Gustaf to her son Pehr: "The Japanese have used them [the Chinese militia-highwaymen] in their service, and now the Russians have followed their example."[172] Gustaf had written her how he and his men had nearly been surrounded by the enemy. While on Gustaf's errand, they had gone swimming, and he joked that it would be a fitting moment for an attack. Just as they were pulling on their clothes, shots whined; the enemy were on three sides! The Japanese had hidden behind the sand dunes. During the night, Gustaf changed directions and made a forced march over the dunes to shake off their followers.[173] As for his project, Gustaf mapped many miles with information about where the Japanese were stationed.

The Russians had relied on their fleet. But the Northern Fleet's fate instead proved the final straw. After a six-month trip to Asian waters, the ancient, decaying ships from the Baltic at last arrived in Tsushima Strait. The vessels were filthy, being overloaded with coal, far from supply bases, and many of the men were ill. Revolutionary elements among the sailors made treacherous use of the growing demoralization and planted their seeds. The men literally prayed to reach the Russian harbor of Vladivostok and safety. But the Japanese were lying in wait for them in a Korean harbor on the Strait and had carefully followed their numbers and condition, observing them in every harbor they had visited on the voyage. They recorded their movements at sea by means of the new telegraphic technology. Japanese battleships, unlike the Russians', were modern, their men disciplined, single-mindedly ready to die for their Emperor and Japan.

The Russians lost their Admiral, and in the confusion were commanded next by an admiral who had no idea that he was, in fact, in command. They fought until the admiral proposed to surrender to save his men. The sadistic Japanese Admiral Togo continued to fire on the remaining ships despite the surrender flag. Only when the Russian ships stopped their engines did the firing cease. Gustaf wrote Sophie when he heard the news, "[Admiral] Rojestvensky's defeat at sea is undoubtedly the Japanese most dazzling victory, and above all a victory that will decide the war." In this action of May, 1905, one of the greatest naval battles of history, the Russians had lost eight of twelve battleships, and four were captured. Nearly 5,000 men were killed or drowned, 7000 taken prisoner and nearly 2000 interned in neutral states. The Japanese lost three torpedo boats, 110 men killed and 590 wounded.

The future Admiral Yamamoto served in this Japanese victory as a young naval lieutenant. Thirty-seven years later he designed the attack on Pearl Harbor. He had watched and waited, modeling his surprise on the operation at Port Arthur.

The flag that fell from the masthead of Akagi, the Japanese carrier, when the planes were landed to destroy the United States Pacific fleet in 1941, had flown also on Mikasa thirty-seven years before. The Japanese thought far ahead, even saving the battle flag.

In November of 1905, Gustaf was ordered to St. Petersburg—not, as he had feared, having to watch over the troop transports' departures from Siberia during the long winter. He returned, relieved that he had made the right decision, despite his family's and friends' doubts. He had distinguished himself and could argue that in serving in the war he had in no way harmed Finland's cause, whatever misgivings his family might have had on that score. (His father longed for peace, for Gustaf's sake. When rumors of unrest and murders in the Russian military reached the Mannerheims at home, they calmed their fears by remembering Gustaf's excellent relations with his men.) He had seen at first hand a great power's army in action under stress, noting the valor of ordinary soldiers, as well as Russian weaknesses in weapons and equipment, the pervasive cases of vodka, the reliance on high generals who had no idea of modern warfare.

On the way back—a trip of 31 days—it was obvious that discipline within the army was vanishing. All along the Trans-Siberian railroad, stations and depots were controlled by revolutionary soldiers. Anyone who tried to maintain discipline was shot down. Locomotives were sometimes uncoupled and joined to a troop transport. There were no buffets, and "if the sturdy Siberian women hadn't displayed their freshly roasted chickens and squabs, hardboiled eggs, fresh butter, cheese, milk, huge white loaves and black breads—witness to Siberia's abundance—starvation would have menaced the returning men."[174]

Gustaf remarked that the Monarchy was spared, for the moment, by the corps of Guards in Moscow and St. Petersburg. "The last assertion may seem like a joke, but the relationship is explained by the cavalryman's care for his horse that took up his time and prevented him from discussing politics and making conspiracies."[175]

As Gustaf wrote, "he who wanted to learn from what he saw and heard had now . . . acquired knowledge about how one should not proceed, whether regarding diplomacy in the years preceding the war, war preparation, or the actual strategy and tactics of the war itself. Further, the Manchurian campaign had manifested . . . that war no longer was a concern only of the armies, but of the whole nation. In this the Japanese had given the world a salutary example of unison and willingness to sacrifice."[176]

On his return Gustaf learned that he was on the list of officers who would be regimental commanders, something that, next to winning the St. George Cross, he wanted more than anything else. (He would not win that medal until World War I.) The full colonelcy dated from February 19, 1905, during the days of the Mukden battle. He won his advancement "for excellence in the affair against the Japanese."[177] Gustaf wrote to Johan that he was to have an audience with the Tsar, a clear mark of attention at the highest level.

In the summer of 1905, President Theodore Roosevelt mediated the end of the Russo-Japanese War in Portsmouth, New Hampshire. Both sides were bankrupt; the war came to an end when their financial backers tightened the purse strings. Japan had asked for Roosevelt's help in mediating the war's end. With the Portsmouth Treaty, Japan controlled Korea, though Russia recognized Korean independence; Japan respected America's domination of the Philippines; Manchuria once again became a Chinese region. Above all, the Treaty marked the rise of Japan as a dominant power, and the waning of Russian power in the Far East.

General Kuropatkin

Chapter 21

AUGUST AND HIS CAREER IN SOUTH AFRICA

August, youngest of the seven, had spent his first eight years in Finland at Villnäs, the family seat. With a child's keen sense of smell and color, August would have remembered the fragrant amaryllis plants and lush white camellia trees taken up to the drawing room in winter from the greenhouse, to cheer the dark winter days. August must have noticed that his world changed when his father, Carl Robert, infrequently returned. There was the unmistakable scent of cigar smell, and an unusual, chilly formality. August was too small to be thrashed with the leather belt used on his brothers, but contemplated his sins in his mother's room, with its cornflower blue and white tiled stove.

One bit of history that must have stayed with him was reflected in a letter from his mother, mentioning the outbreak of war in the Balkans in 1877 between Russians and Turks. Russian conscription of Finnish soldiers was a reminder of oppression. Helene wrote bitterly that "our people have a heavy burden in this poor, unplowed land, without sending their sons against Turks and Tartars, [though] if it's a question of defending one's country, I think patriotism will grow like weeds." August surely would have remembered, at five, going with his brothers and sisters to see the Finnish soldiers come home. As Eva wrote, it was a nightmarish sight they never forgot: the threadbare troops, their marching tread, the tattered, fluttering banners.

August must have been made aware of his family's changing fortune, when their home with all its treasures was put up for auction in 1880. One memory that surely left a scar was the long hour's wait, with three of his brothers and sisters, at the door of their dying mother's room, one icy January day in 1881. Sophie could not get home in time. But soon she filled a mother's role in August's life, and later was his confidante.

August sailed to Stockholm after his mother's death, to live with her sister Hanna. She called him her borrowed child, saw to his schooling, comforted him when his sister and playmate, Annicka, died in Russia. Aunt Hanna sent him home on holidays, welcomed him back to earn his engineering degree and work on his first post at an electrical company in Stockholm.

August moved to London in 1896 to a branch of the electrical company he had worked for in Stockholm. At a Christmas party August discovered Ambjörn Sparre, Eva's father-in-law, in circumstances that were amusing and surprising. Expecting English reticence, he found rakish dancing, drinking, singing, terrible piano playing, much kissing and game playing going on until 4 a.m.

Ambjörn, the most interesting guest at the party, talked to August about his newest invention. With his fascination for transportation, from balloons and dirigibles to his thoughts of aircraft, he had invented a new kind of resilient bicycle tire of compact rubber. (Earlier bicycles ran on iron-tired wooden rims, the so-called "boneshakers".) The attention paid his tires at their exhibit in the Crystal Palace in 1893 was encouraging. The following year the tires were noticed by the French army at the Salle Wagram exhibit, and if the samples tried out at the bicycle factory proved satisfactory, Ambjörn expected delivery orders. Surely the Russians, whose military committees were the same as the French, would order deliveries! The "bicycle fever" sweeping Europe and the U.S. in the 1880s and 90s proved it was no longer a rich man's sport. For Ambjörn it was just another great opportunity. Everyone would exchange their old tires for Sparre's!

August, like two of his brothers and his sister Sophie, was charmed by the inventor. (Johan Mannerheim, in a letter of 1894, wrote from Paris that he was staying with the amiable "old man Sparre.") August admired Ambjörn's cheerful optimism, his stubborn resilience after failures, never bending or breaking, always finding new ways of starting over. He had been Ambjörn's representative for an English telephone company while in Stockholm, but when the affair did not catch on, he went to London to work with an electrical company. He also agreed to test Ambjörn's new tires, driving 250 miles, to Bath, Salisbury, Southampton, Portsmouth and back.

Ambjörn had indeed invented a useful and popular concept. But, as happened more than once, someone else had been there first. In this case it was the Scotsman, John Dunlop. Ambjörn's improvements on the older bicycle included a precursor of the free wheel (the rear wheel that turns freely when pedals are stopped or rotated backwards), but Dunlop invented pneumatic tires earlier, as well as the free wheel.

Ambjörn went back to Paris, to his apartment at 16 Place de la Madeleine, and August set out for Berlin, to begin work at a large and well-known concern, A.E.G. Electrical Company. Soon after, on his brother Carl's advice, he came home to Finland to head the company in Helsinki.

Aunt Hanna had done more than house and educate August. At 18, the young engineering student was introduced to the love of his life, a 15-year-old school girl, Elsie Nordenfelt. The two were later married in Sweden in 1900. Finland was their home for the next few years, with happy memories of sailing August's sloop Dolly in the Finnish skerries. Elsie was surrounded by her new family: Sophie home from her training at St. Thomas's in London; Carl in his law office; Johan the estate manager at Jokkis, Finland's largest corporate domain; and Gustaf, a frequent visitor from St. Petersburg. Eva found a house for August and Elsie in Porvoo, the medieval cathedral town where she and Louis lived and worked.

August once had written Sophie that his first memory of her was at their grandmother's manor, Sällvik, where she had taken the two youngest, to care for and teach after their mother's death. August recognized the role she had always played in his life, and that "we brothers and sisters have been fortunate in how well we understood each other." It was a typical Mannerheim understatement. While most of the Mannerheim marriages endured—August's certainly among the happiest—the brothers and sisters never lost their closeness. They were able to sense each other's thoughts at a distance, sometimes frankly writing of an unhappy time in a marriage. August himself, his young wife at his side, unburdened himself to his brothers and particularly to his oldest sister, when, at 37, he knew that he would die.

1904 was the year that changed August's life. He accepted a post as head of the same electrical company in South Africa that he had worked for in Berlin. In May, August wrote Johan from Johannesburg after a 46-hour train trip from Capetown. "The whole countryside is velt, a sea of grass, now reddish yellow. The highest plateaux are 6000 feet above the ocean, and from there the most enchanting view stretched as far as the horizon. It is winter here, with drought and sunshine and red dust that blows everywhere . . . The days are quite warm and I'm glad to have a Panama hat. But in the mornings one sees frost on the ground. There is no real cold as we know it, because rose trees are in bloom and all the fruit trees are green."

August's task was to outfit the gold mines with modern equipment, and to lay out electrical transportation deep in the earth as well as on its surface. As Elsie wrote, "it was a whole new world that offered unusual and exciting experiences. We met people of different races—blacks, Hottentots, bushmen, Indians, Chinese, Arabs, Japanese as well as Boer families, charming refined Englishmen and real gangsters, millionaires, black princesses. Everywhere, August was appreciated, even loved, not least by his employees. August succeeded with his charm, tact and good judgment in forming enduring contacts with such personalities as South Africa's High Commissioner, the mine magnate Sir Lionel Phillips, Col. Frank Rhodes, Rudyard Kipling, and among others the loyal black man who carried Livingston's lifeless body through darkest Africa. We joined a merry social life—long trips were taken by car, train, oxcart, even hammock, in a land so enormous that the little part from Capetown to Johannesburg is just as far as the distance between Ystad [in southern Sweden] and Haparanda [in northern Finland]."

August wrote in January of 1905 to his sister Sophie, "You sent as a Christmas present a cool sea breeze and made me think of a lovely trip in Dolly . . . . It's good to live in a free country" he wrote, thinking of life in Finland where rights had been violated, and patriotic men were exiled.

Carl wrote from exile in Stockholm that deportations and detentions were going on at home and gave August and Elsie news of their brother Gustaf. In February, 1905 Carl sent August news of Finland. "The revolution, begun so brilliantly in Russia is probably waiting for a greater defeat in Manchuria . . . until now, Gustaf has managed, more by good luck than skill. He took part in Mistjenko's failed attack recently." [Col. Mannerheim, serving under General Mistjenko, was ordered to reach the coast, take the Japanese harbor with its ships, and dynamite the railroad between Port Arthur and Mukden. No one knew that the Japanese already controlled Port Arthur or that General Nogi's army was marching north against Russian positions. In the battle that ensued, troop trains from Port Arthur could be seen, the Japanese waving and shouting "Banzai!"]

August and Elsie made a six-month visit to Finland during their five-year life in South Africa. But by 1909 August's health had begun to fail, and it was impossible to renew his contract. They sailed back to Elsie's parents' home in Sweden by way of a trip around the world—to India, Burma, Malacca, China, Japan, Hawaii, crossing the American continent, from San Francisco to Yellowstone, Chicago, the obligatory Niagara, and New York. Despite pain and strains, August was jolly and thoughtful, making plans to see all that would be interesting and amusing. But his stomach cancer was relentless. After surgery, he came back to Elsie's parents' home, Höganäs, where his brothers and sisters could visit him. Eva wrote of her brother's activity, keeping up his work and interests until the last days. Finally, as she wrote, all the brothers and sisters visited, even Gustaf from St. Petersburg, each one able to see him and say goodbye.

More than four decades later, his widow remembered his courage, tenderness and the fortitude that marked him. He could be a tease, like the other Mannerheims, she wrote, but his humor, warmth and selflessness, his demands on himself, his chivalry, made each hour with him a feast.[178]

August as a schoolboy

August and Elsie Mannerheim

Chapter 22

GUSTAF CROSSES ASIA ON HORSEBACK

Gustaf Mannerheim was visiting in Helsinki in early March 1906 when he received orders to report to St. Petersburg. In his Memoirs he states that the assignment given him by the chief of the general army staff was a surprise, but one of his biographers says that he used every influence he had to get it. Another says that he had probably considered the possibility for some time. He did not have to accept the new mission: this was an invitation, not an order. He was to consider being an agent for the Russian High Command, to provide intelligence for secret plans of war with China, traveling on horseback across the entire Asian continent. As always, his close family knew as much about his plans as he could tell them. His sister Eva Sparre wrote her son Pehr in May, 1906, saying she had just seen his uncle Gustaf for the last time before his return to Asia.

Mannerheim kept a journal almost daily in Swedish on his long trek. The book that was published in 1940 is called *Across Asia on Horseback*, (*Till Häst genom Asien* in the original Swedish). The foreword to the shortened version of the book, published in 1942, gives an excellent overview of this pathbreaking expedition. Kaarlo Hildén, the editor, has summarized Mannerheim's collections, excavations, the manuscript fragments found, his photography, meteorology efforts, mapping, and how the trip was financed. My translation of the pertinent parts follows:

The Chinese realm, which his trip would largely cross, extended at that time over a larger territory than now. But despite its vast area it was in an exhausted state and had, at the beginning of the century, endured humiliations. These hard times had aroused a movement aimed at initiating a new order in the kingdom. It included building railroads, reorganizing the defense, modernizing the school system, founding newspapers, abolishing the all-powerful and corrupting influence of the mandarin class and strengthening the authority of the central administration. A seething fervor of reform could be traced in many parts of the country; it seemed that China had at last awakened from her thousand-year sleep.

Mannerheim was to take his trip during these times of upheaval. He would have to discover to what extent the reforms had been realized, above all in the country's remote provinces, and assess the attitude of the people and responsible officials toward the reorganization. In addition, he must collect statistics on housing, roads, cultivation, maintenance of cattle, and access to minerals, to give a comprehensive picture of the conditions in the Middle Kingdom. His program included military information on fortifications and military organization.

The directions from the general staff were extensive. But on Mannerheim's own initiative the expedition's program had an even more comprehensive and many-sided purpose.

At the beginning of the century central and eastern Asia were little known in any scholarly way. Several expeditions had accomplished purposeful work outside the cultural boundaries; the 'white patches' had become smaller and the outer cartographic features had begun to take shape. But much remained to be done; the detailed information available was scant, and even approximately dependable maps were not accessible.

The expedition's leader knew that he could collect new and valuable material that would enhance knowledge of innermost Asia's geography and ethnography, both prehistoric and within historic times. To realize these pursuits he talked with Senator Otto Donner, through him the Finnish-Ugric Society [of which he was Chairman], and with a delegation from the Trustees of the Antell Collections in Helsinki. The delegation briefed him on collecting archeological and ethnographic artifacts, and material and manuscripts for the National Museum in Helsinki.

Donner also instructed him to take note of stone figures, inscriptions on stone slabs, excavate Turkestan's ancient ruins and collect articles, historical documents and manuscript fragments, as well as observe the little-known peoples and tribes of northern China. The program was realized. Not only militarily useful, it became also an expedition of scholarly research. Mannerheim led his caravan where no one, or perhaps only a single traveler, had been. He sought little-known areas to follow as fully as possible the military and scholarly objectives.

The expedition traversed many landscapes of the enormous continent. As variegated as the terrain were the settlements, adapted to the varying environment. The path led through cultivated districts with populated cities, villages, fortresses, cloisters and temples, through areas where mile after mile small groups of yurts or single hovels were signs of human existence, through regions where untouched nature was the dictator. The traveler met many peoples and tribes, some of which belonged to predominant rulers in the heart of Asia, others the remains of tribes, which with their special cultures, concepts and primitive tools had maintained themselves in isolated valleys far from the great thoroughfares.

On long stretches the caravan traveled through nearly inaccessible regions, where precipitous chasms opened next to the narrow icy paths, where rocks and ice blocked the way, where horse cadavers and skeletons bore witness to earlier caravans' risks.

Mannerheim was not content to relate the main course of events. Exhaustively and with scholarly precision he tells of the geographic surroundings, of surface formations and geologic constructions, of hydrographic conditions, of plant and animal life, of mineral assets. He tells of cities and towns, their appearance and historical reminiscences, of traffic routes and commercial ties, administrative and cultural conditions, defense facilities, military weaponry practice and marches. He leaves detailed information about provincial towns, cultivated acreage, yield of different grains, number of house pets. He gives an account of the cloister communions' variegated temple buildings, the pilgrims' strenuous life and the monks' spiritual practices; he describes surviving relics, and gives detailed attention to aboriginal tribes' usages, their dwellings, dress, justice system and community life. He tells amusingly and with an apposite stroke of the brush of the remarkable persons he met, of viceroys and imperial princes, mandarins and army leaders, holy men and native sovereigns. He accounts for his investigations and their results; he relates the journey's dangers and difficulties, his own adventures and experiences. Unceasingly, he inserts in his account his own sober and critical view of circumstances and phenomena.

The journal therefore provides on the one hand well-documented, researched sources, which meticulously illuminate conditions in central and eastern Asia just after the turn of the century, and on the other hand a depiction of the long journey's motley adventures.

In addition to his journal, Mannerheim brought home important collections. A significant part of these is among the ethnographic artifacts. The so-called Sarts of West Turkestan take precedence. Their implements typify the Asian bazaar life, musical pieces and instruments, house utensils, tools for weaving rugs and for the street barbers, who also acted as surgeons, clothing, and agricultural implements. Numerous artifacts throw light on the Abdals, a striking people, who according to Mohammedan tradition originated in Turkey. Expelled from their country, they were haunted by an ancient curse and forced to pursue begging.

There is even a large collection of Tibetan artifacts, which mainly relate to Buddhist ritual, principally musical instruments (drums, bells and horns), as well as other attributes of the lama cult like thunderbolts, wreaths of roses and prayer wheels. The collections derived from the Yögur tribes are very valuable, almost unknown to scholars, which give a detailed picture of these interesting peoples' daily life.

But the collections do not refer only to the still-living peoples and their cultures. In accordance with his instructions, Mannerheim carried out, whenever possible, digs where ancient cities had been located or where ruins still told of times long past. Mannerheim brought several artifacts of great value to his collection in this way. The archeological collection was supplemented by purchases. It includes many terracotta figurines representing camels, horses, dogs, birds and other animals, fragments of clay pots and reliefs, numerous bronzes of Buddhist artistry, bronze seals, as well as precious and semi-precious gems engraved with images, some of great interest to art history.

Ancient cultures are elucidated also by stones with engravings and written characters attentively observed by the traveler. He found many ancient and heretofore unknown relics which were cast or photographed. The old document fragments are in the same category, safeguarded by Mannerheim, of interest in terms of language science. Many of them were found in the natives' fields, torn to pieces and used as fertilizer. It is worth noting that among the fragments there is one in Mongolian quadratic script, in use during Kublai Khan's time. This particular fragment is of special interest as it is the first known print of this genre in existence. In addition, Mannerheim came across a number of handwritten historical documents such as täzkirs [sacred documents bought in southern Kashgaria], ancient Chinese books and maps.

Mannerheim also made anthropological observations. He investigated no fewer than eight peoples, whose anthropological particulars had not been noted earlier. These included the Abdals, who supported themselves by begging, the remarkable mountain people Shiksu and Pakhpo near Kargilik (Yecheng). Furthermore, Mannerheim has addressed information about the

Kalmuck's, Kirghiz's and Turguts' somatology. He gave not only detailed descriptions of the peoples' bodily particulars; he also carried out precise measurements with modern implements.

Finally, the research recorded a great number of precise maps. The itinerary maps drawn by Mannerheim, based on measurements, observations and findings from horseback extend over a longer than 3000 km. band. The areas had earlier been mapped defectively or not at all. These maps now acquired great value as they complemented the mapping Sven Hedin's expeditions had carried out, and fill in the 'white spots' which otherwise would have appeared in the monumental atlas of inner Asia published by Dr. Hedin. To the traveler's cartographic work are attached 20 or more detailed city plans, hypsometric estimation of heights as well as careful meteorological observations.

Mannerheim carried back from his trip circa 1500 photographs, a summary of the work he did during his long expedition. He worked within many disciplines—geography, cartography and meteorology, sociology and religion, ethnography and anthropology, archeology and history. His travel program had acquired a larger scope than the original plan. But it would be wrong to suppose that this expansion resulted in superficial research and observations. Many authoritative scholars, familiar with the expedition's results, have praised them. Seen in the light of his notes and collections, Mannerheim is by no means an amateur who collects information and souvenirs as they turn up, but a person deeply interested in scientific questions, a conscientious and critical observer and a systematic researcher. It is the more surprising when one realizes that Mannerheim's studies had not been grounded in scientific research, that he had a relatively short time to prepare for this program and that the trip was assigned to military objectives.

For nearly 30 years the expedition's results seemed forgotten. Mannerheim left a detailed report with high officials, but it was written in Russian and not available in book stores. A travel report for the general public or for scholars was not published. The voyager's intention indeed was to work his notes for publication, but new, demanding commissions have hindered the realization of the project. For his reason a 'research-traveling Mannerheim' does not exist in the general perception.

In the fall of 1936 the Finnish-Ugrian Company took the initiative to publish the collected material. To the Company's great pleasure the Field Marshal promised to take part in the drafting. It was decided that the work would be published in English, to reach the scholarly world. The first part, the traveler's journal, was made public while the Finnish people were fighting for freedom in the winter of 1940, and the Field Marshal led the defense from his headquarters. The book's foreword bears the date 'Finnish Army Headquarters, February, 1940.' Immediately after the peace agreement the latter part of the work was published, containing research based on Mannerheim's collected material. Altogether, the work *Across Asia from West to East in 1906-1908* is over 1000 pages with circa 700 illustrations, and has an atlas of 15 large-sized maps.

In geographic journals the work won recognition as a great scholarly achievement. The Swedish Company of Anthropology and Geography gave the Field Marshal its distinguished Hedin medal in gold, and the Geographic Company in Finland decided to present the first examples of its newly established Fennia medal in gold to the traveler, as a respectful acknowledgement of his important contribution to Asia's exploration.

The voyager's journal was written in Swedish during the trip. In the spring of 1940 it was published in Stockholm in the original. As the book was sold out quickly, there was a thought of publishing it in a new format, this time shortened, to make the account available to the general public . . . The author's style has been maintained. The illustrations are largely as they were in the original edition.

In our perception of him, Mannerheim appears chiefly as the Commander of Finland's military during three wars for freedom, as a statesman during anxious times, as the unifying symbol for the country's independence. Notes and investigations during the ride through Asia, which only recently have been made public, admit him to a place of honor also as a scholar. They constitute an impressive contribution to the century's task of capturing the earth's greatest continent for the arts and sciences.[179]

It was in May of 1906 that Gustaf wrote his brother Johan about his political thoughts. "The situation in Russia gives one serious apprehensions of lawlessness or revolution, which may have fateful effects on our own conditions. I begin my journey with anything but a light heart under these emerging circumstances."[180] The Russian Revolution of 1905 with its strikes, riots, assassinations, naval mutinies, forced the Tsar to grant civil liberties and a representative Duma. But the Social Democrats (actually communists) were bent on continuing the revolutionary movement. The government suppressed the insurrection ruthlessly; the Duma's power again was limited. In Finland, in the spring of 1906, the Tsar's bill was passed forming a unicameral Diet to be voted through universal suffrage, extended to women.

Gustaf's mission was to ride through Asia on horseback with a small retinue. Two Cossacks were promised him and other servants as he needed them, a cook and a Chinese interpreter. The trip would carry him on his new favorite horse Filip, approximately 14,000 kilometers, or more than 8,000 miles of wild mountain ranges in killing snowstorms. He would ride in burning heat along two deserts, often following the Silk Route that Marco Polo had used in the 13th Century. His travels would take him from Russian Turkestan through the ancient Kingdom of China to Peking.

Why did this tempt him? How could he risk an absence of two years so important to his military advancement? He writes in his Memoirs that he now was in line for a regimental command. If he accepted the long assignment, he might be passed over. Mannerheim must have calculated his moves carefully. Certainly he was an ambitious man, not only interested in research on Asian tribes and some limited archeological digs but perhaps actually contemplating a change of careers, as his biographer Jägerskiöld speculates. Fame was the stuff of his childhood dreams, perhaps even expected of him by his family. His admired explorer uncle Adolf Nordenskiöld, first to navigate the Northeast Passage, was an inspiration, too. Why not trust his own connections and diplomatic ability to argue his case, later, for a regimental command? On this point he might have thought a later time favorable, because at this time of Russian oppression a Finn in high military service could too easily find himself conflicted. Finally, his personal situation was still a painful subject; his wife Anastasia had left him only a few years before. Such thoughts must have led him to want the assignment.

His commission must be understood against the background of Russia's historical interest in Central Asia and China, its sparring with the British in India, and its future ambitions which were not at all diminished by its losses to the Japanese.

In the 1860s and 70s the Russians had occupied western Turkestan, and in a military drive some ten years later had completed the capture of the trans-Caspian area. Earlier, the British had stayed the Russians' advance toward India, and now, following the Russo-Japanese war, the British again feared Russian encroachment. Britain had allied itself with the Japanese who were pledged to defend India if Russia attacked.

The Russian general staff was directly responsible to the Tsar. In St. Petersburg there were secret thoughts of attacking the newly aroused China, heretofore sleeping in its old ways, but now pressing forward on reforms inside the ancient Kingdom. These had been inspired by European advances on Chinese territories as well as by their own losses to Japan. As Gustaf Mannerheim succinctly summarizes it in his Memoirs, the great reforms called for a tightening of authority in the central government, uprooting the vast and entrenched misuse of power by the mandarin class, restructuring the army and education, and expanding the railroad network. A very important matter was the goal of reducing opium smoking with its destruction of vigor and will.

The Russian general staff wanted to know how well the Chinese reforms had succeeded. They needed to explore the sparsely settled areas beyond the borders of Chinese Turkestan and northern China. They needed military statistics; information on local attitudes with respect to Chinese policy and towards Russia; the extent of Japanese influence; geographic and weather information; revised maps of roads and new uncharted ones drawn with a view to the movement of cavalry and other troop detachments. They needed someone with the skills of a geographer, cartographer, meteorologist, photographer, and diplomat.

In his Memoirs Mannerheim writes that Colonel Kozlov, seen as a leading Russian expert on Central Asia, was unwilling to share his knowledge with Colonel Mannerheim. This suggests to Mannerheim's biographer Jägerskiöld that Kozlov recognized a rival. There were other officers as high in rank and experience as himself, but in the end Gustaf Mannerheim was chosen: he had proved his courage and resourcefulness in the Russo-Japanese War. Perhaps, too, he was better disguised for his spying as a Finn than were his Russian contemporaries.

The real aims would be concealed with an interesting "cover" for his identity. Mannerheim would travel as a Finnish explorer, making some of the almost unknown tribes in this vast region his specialty, trying to get their leaders' interest and help in recording their history and customs, measuring their unwashed bodies, asking for the favor of some of their articles of clothing when what they wore was all they had. All this he had to do, gaining their trust in addition so that he could glean information useful to the Russian military. In his cover role as a student of anthropology and archaeology, he would be furnishing Finland's National Museum and scientific societies with carefully recorded observations. He would need every scintilla of leadership and understanding of human nature that his character and experience had given him, and he must be fearless. To ascend the mountains of the Chinese Tien Shan, and descend their icy slopes in winter, to cross stretches of the Takla Makan desert and the Gobi, to visit high mandarins of hostile tribes would be a test of his courage.

His challenge was to study the possibilities of military success for the Russians in this wild and enormous stretch of land. In case of a war between Russia and China Mannerheim's superiors needed to know which Chinese tribes might be friendly to the Russians; which ones enemies, wanting to be ruled from Peking. His work could determine where a Russian attack might begin. He would meet important mandarins and must be able to understand how far the new Chinese reforms had influenced their distant provinces in central Asia and Chinese Turkestan. He must bring back vital information about the condition of the roads. He would need to be seen as a gracious European, not as a Russian military officer, although it would be clear that he had a privileged position and knew the Tsar.

To prepare himself for his cover, Mannerheim had the benefit of Finland's long tradition of research in Asia dating back to the latter part of the 18th Century, when a Finn, Erik Laxman, had been a brilliant scholar in Catherine the Great's St. Petersburg. Mannerheim became a member of the Finnish Ugrian Society in Helsinki, whose chairman had promoted several Asiatic explorations. At the end of the 19th Century, the Society was a leader in research on the Samoyed and Finnish-Ugrian peoples in European Russia and Asia.

Mannerheim's biographer Jägerskiöld mentions some specific preparations not listed in the Mannerheim autobiography. In Petersburg he learned the methods of making casts and impressions of sculptures and inscriptions. He studied the literature of earlier Asiatic explorers, starting with Marco Polo, whose route he would follow. He had the advice of his uncle, the explorer Adolf Nordenskiöld, who had discovered that long-sought water passage to the north of Europe and Asia between the Atlantic and Pacific oceans. On ethnographic research methods he consulted with his cousin Erland Nordenskiöld, son of the explorer, educated as a scientist, later a specialist in South American explorations. Another helpful guide was Sven Hedin, the Swedish geographer who himself led expeditions to Central Asia, the Gobi and Tibet. Mannerheim would use his maps. A delegation urged him to collect archeological and ethnographic objects for the National Museum in Finland. One of Mannerheim's biographers, Jägerskiöld, guessed that he may have considered changing his life at this point, devoting the rest of it to scholarship and research.

His real goal must of course remain secret. He was to be known as a Finnish baron (and therefore a Russian subject) with ties to Sweden. Mail to him from Russia and Finland arrived in Asia via Sweden, where the letters were to be put into new envelopes, with Swedish stamps, to fool Chinese authorities. His own letters would reach his father by way of his maternal Aunt Hanna Lovén in Stockholm. His father would copy those parts of his letters with military information, and send them on to someone called "Uncle Feda" in St. Petersburg, a code name for the Russian Chief of Staff. Mannerheim's diary, notes and surveys would be written in Swedish. Under the auspices of the French Ministry of Public Instruction, a famous French sinologist and explorer, Professor Paul Pelliot, would be his traveling companion. The professor would prove an irascible and unpleasant man, interested only in feathering his own nest, and charging Mannerheim for more than his share of the journey. The plan was to engage Mannerheim's brother-in-law, Louis Sparre, for the trip as recording artist, but Pelliot's demands that he pay a quarter of all expenses ended that possibility.

Among the things Mannerheim had to buy was a supply of gifts. He had to be prepared for men of sophistication as well as for childlike people and their families. His presents included Finnish "puukkos," razor-sharp knives with handles on which to engrave a name; compasses; sewing needles and thread; perfume; candies; colored pencils; little music boxes and stereoscopes for pornographic photographs. A good camera would be essential, both for giving photographs of themselves to his Chinese hosts and for recording his travels. He learned to develop and print film.

The financing was provided by a grant from the General Staff, his pay, and borrowing from his brother and sister, Johan and Sophie Mannerheim, against promised grants by Finnish ethnographic societies and the Secretariat of State for Finland. The Finnish-Ugrian Society gave Mannerheim a stipend.

Before he could begin the real part of his journey he had to reach Tashkent, the capital of Russian Turkestan. He entrained in St. Petersburg in July, 1906, for Moscow, and continued to Nizhny Novgorod. He could have taken another train, but preferred a boat trip to Astrakhan in the summer heat. Here, on a stormy night, he took a paddleboat south on the Caspian to Petrovsk and then along the coast to Baku. From there he crossed the sea to Krasnovodsk on a steamship.

The first letter about his trip was written to his father in July 1906. "Yesterday my trip on the river came to an end . . . . The river is magnificent. During the course of five days, one travels at a speed of 25 versts an hour, and with a few short stops there is a series of varied landscapes to admire. The cities I sailed through, Kagan, Samara, Syzram, Saratoff and Tsaritsin, made a miserable impression. Typical Russian provincial towns, squalid, poorly built, wretched communications, defective roads full of drunken ragamuffins and beggars. Sarataoff is called Volga's capital city with a population of 200,000, but, except for a couple of streets, looks like a large village . . . I'd like to have visited Astrakhan's world renowned fisheries. The city leaves a very different impression than the other Russian ones I've seen. I felt I was standing with one foot in Asia. It's not so strange, when one realizes that the population is made up of Kalmucks, Kirghizes, Armenians, Persians, etc. The first thing one notices when coming into port is a Buddhist temple, something I had no idea existed in European Russia . . . . Last night we were in heavy storm which made our paddleboat creak in its joints and roll like a modern propeller-driven ship."[181]

A miserable train carried him onward through the oases of Bukhara and Samarkand to Tashkent, a trip of three days and nights in the torrid heat. There were official visits to the Governor General to clear his trip and receive information about the roads, and, not least, to buy a collection of rifles as future gifts to important mandarins and khans.

He returned to Samarkand, the "jewel of Asian cities," chosen by Alexander the Great as his residence in Central Asia, leveled by Genghis Khan, raised again from the dust to be the brilliant court of Tamerlane in the 14th Century. Here two Cossacks who had been carefully selected among many volunteers reported for duty on their own horses, willing, they assured their leader, to make an arduous trip with him that would take at least two years. At the railroad station they were given an elegant farewell by their Cossack regiment's officers and the regimental band.

At Os the rest of Mannerheim's retinue would all meet for their trip to Kashgar, including a Chinese cook, an interpreter, and the caravan of 75 horses and packhorses that were mainly for the use of the Frenchman. The hardworking animals would have Mannerheim's admiration and concern. Each must carry 260 pounds divided in beehive-shaped baskets tied one on each side of the withers, bearing their burdens over icy mountain ranges, sinking to their bellies in snow, sometimes falling between crevasses, occasionally rescued when possible, their baskets never taken off. He noticed with some horror that the horses were never unsaddled.

On August 11, 1906, they left Os for Kashgar, three hundred kilometers beyond a mountain chain and the first pass through which one entered Central Asia. Coming toward them as they departed were nomad families of the Kirghiz tribe, their women dressed in gaudy colors, often carrying on their saddle a baby in its cradle, shaded from the sun by crude curtains. Mannerheim made notes on horseback.

Two weeks after leaving Os he described how they rode along a riverbed, the water reaching the tops of the saddles, the slippery slopes of clay treacherous to the horses, always in danger of slipping into the turbulent water. Leaving the river, they followed the road up among the naked hills of clay and over rough stones. Skeletons and half-rotted cadavers of horses and mules were not an encouraging sight. His horse Filip shied at first, but later was so blasé that he hardly deigned a glance. Mannerheim shared his bread and melon with his interpreter Lio.[182]

Beautiful sights lay ahead. Mannerheim notes in his Memoirs that "the steep hills looked in the evening light as though dressed in deep green velvet . . . Through the valley coiled a red river, in the background a mighty mountain chain with dazzling white crowns . . . Down in the valley, I determined that the river owed its rich color to red sand."[183]

They were in the Kirghiz country of Turkish-Tatar nomads. After eleven hours of unbroken climbing and struggling they could settle into relative comfort in the welcoming Kirghiz huts of the valley, dressed inside by rugs and silk blankets with pillows, their beautiful saddles on display, the reins decorated with bronze and turquoise. The chieftain greeted them warmly, and Mannerheim noted with respect that these people had a "culture" of horses, even the simplest of them keeping their animals exclusively for races and breeding them for speed. He was treated to a wedding feast, involving a rough game. A ram had been slaughtered, its body smeared with oil. This grisly cadaver represented a girl, fought over by rival participants who grasped the slippery token with both hands, a horsewhip held between the teeth, galloping away with fiendish speed, only to be caught by another. It was, he wrote, a form of wild wrestling on horseback.

In Kashgar where he arrived August 30th, Mannerheim took care of official duties, and several were rewarding. The British consul general, Sir George Macartney, spoke Chinese fluently, his mother having been Chinese. He let the traveler borrow a Chinese grammar of large dimensions, equipped with its own table. Mannerheim's "cover" was a success: Sir George simply reported the arrival of Mannerheim, a Finn.

Mannerheim was not sorry to say goodbye to the French scientist Pelliot here. He had been a fractious and egotistical companion, putting on airs, jealous of his dignity. But Professor Pelliot would find an extraordinary treasure, a library of manuscripts from Turkestan's great epoch, before the Turkish conquest. Mannerheim was happy to go on alone, leaving this crossroads of Chinese, Indian, Hellenic and Roman cultures that Marco Polo had chosen for his point of departure for Yarkand.

After a month in Kashgar, Mannerheim made a side trip south, starting in early October for Yarkand and Khotan, equipped with a new pass for travel in China, and a Chinese name. As he described it to his father, the highest Chinese official in Kashgar used the first two letters in his name, Ma (meaning horse), to which he added two more characters representing thoughts, Ma-da-han, or the Horse that Springs through Clouds. This would make a big impression on all the officials. Now the trip was easy. One could almost have made it by car, he remarked in 1950. He admired the Afghan caravans because of their beautiful horses, so well cared for and decorated with amulets fastened on glass necklaces. His cook Ismail, "though unfailingly filthy, was a treasure!"[184]

Mannerheim stayed in Yarkand for some weeks, finding it livelier than Kashgar. He went to dinner with the district mandarin and was treated to snails, pork cooked in sugar water, shark fins and hundred-year old eggs, among other delicacies. The mandarins were exquisitely polite, giving the travelers presents of fodder, sheep, chickens, and rice, while Mannerheim was embarrassed that he had only cheap presents. What, he asked his father in a letter, does one give to people earning forty to fifty thousand rubles a year illegally? He felt better when he found in his luggage silver watches and chains, strong perfumes, music boxes, one hundred boxes of English cigarettes with gilded mouth pieces, perfumed soap and Russian sweets. He was interested that the chief mandarin posted a "guard of honor" at his door—perhaps to keep him under surveillance.[185]

On leaving Yarkand for Khotan in November, Mannerheim found the desert bitterly cold at night and was grateful he had bought a little stove which could be folded up. He threw everything on himself at night, "short of suitcases and plates."[186] Water came from a well so deep that it seemed bottomless, fetched with a little leather pouch tied to an endless rope.

This was rich ground for archeologists, and Mannerheim regretted that he had not the time or equipment to dig, and no camels. Under the Taklamakan sand near Khotan, local diggers hoped to find jade and gold fragments from Buddhist statuary, but these "diggers for happiness" lived in misery. Most who had come with money left it there and drifted downward in society, becoming collectors of fuel (donkey dung) and opium chewers. Mannerheim found trophies telling of Muslim pilgrimages and religious wars for a thousand years. Each burial ground had its own history recorded in ancient scrolls, guarded by the mullahs as treasures. Whole towns had been buried under the desert sand.

Mannerheim made note of a tribe he called Abdals, from whom he bought books to throw light on their history, and spent a few days with them. Bearded and dirty, they honored him by singing their begging songs and playing guitars, their voices cracked and hoarse, croaking lilting love songs despite their unscrupulous custom of taking and trading women, whose value seemed too small to calculate.

Returning to Kashgar, he spent Christmas with a Swedish missionary who brewed ale and cooked fish in imitation of the traditional Swedish Christmas dish. There Mannerheim could take care of his people, and attend to those who were ill. He expanded his retinue with two Turks and one Chinese, of whom "two stole lightly" from him.[187]

On January 27, 1907, he headed east and northeast to Aksu. The Kirghiz people gave the travelers shelter in a tent only ten feet in diameter, shared one night by twelve adults, four children and forty sheep. The more people, the warmer! It was quite comforting, Mannerheim wrote, to have the woolly creatures near one in the fearful cold.

In Aksu, important militarily to the Russians, Mannerheim arrived on March 2 and spent a night in a house chosen by the cook Ismail, while the owner was away. She seemed to find it entirely natural on her return that her family would occupy the least comfortable quarters. Mannerheim of course was embarrassed, and on his departure offered her money. With one hand she proudly refused it, but accepted with the other!

The district's chief mandarin was a military man, a general, whom Mannerheim particularly liked. However, the two could only discuss limited topics, because the new interpreter was far from expert. However, Mannerheim was invited to meet ten mandarins for a dinner lasting from 11:30 a.m. until 6:30 p.m., interrupted briefly for target shooting. Etiquette was not forgotten for a moment. The soldiers marched in a group, muskets on shoulders, standing and curtsying deeply before the general, their right hands just touching the floor. The host arose, followed by the rest of the mandarins, and the guests took up their positions in the shooting line. Mannerheim couldn't resist mimicking the ceremony, much to the amusement of the guests. One of his biographers remarks that the Chinese had guessed his real identity, as they were careful to show him their garrisons, and the shooting ability of their soldiers.[188]

During dinner amateur theatricals were offered, and Mannerheim could only imagine, he wrote his father, that if he had asked them to play Hamlet or La Vie Parisienne, they would have performed with pleasure. The Chinese general led Mannerheim to his three wives, dressed in magnificent robes, staggering in on their tiny bound feet with their children and servants. Even the wives and daughters demonstrated their talents in target shooting. Mannerheim confessed he was a "broken man" when at last he could return to his quarters and fall asleep.[189]

Now it was on to Kuldja, a dangerous ride through the Muzart Pass in the Tien Shan. Thanks to the general's help in arranging his purchase of necessities, Mannerheim could start with eight extra horses in addition to the usual thirteen. There was a heavy snowstorm. Not only the guides, but the men who had led caravans over this route for years went astray. Ever rising along the Muzart to the foot of the glacier, their path crawled between huge blocks of stone sometimes crashing down from the mountain.

Some places had to be traversed on foot. Filip, his horse, "is fascinated by the beautiful landscape and always wants to go along the outermost edge, which is less than comfortable. I'm beginning to suspect he might have suicidal thoughts." The horses had to be led over twenty or more steps cut into the ice, along a zigzagging glacier luckily often covered with gravel and stones, otherwise treacherously slippery. When the Cossack's "comely horse" fell into one of the crevasses, it took five men to lift him out. His rider was feverish and could hardly keep to his saddle. At fourteen thousand feet they had not a piece of wood to make a fire in case of a snowstorm, yet it would be impossible to ride at night. At last they found the pass just before nightfall, and from this point they descended between two mountains, the divide threatening to fill up with glaciers. "Tongues of fir trees pointing up toward the mountain's crest" reminded Mannerheim of his northern countries. [190]

After fourteen hours of unbroken riding they reached a shelter already holding many travelers, simple wooden buildings divided into huge spaces and hardly adequate protection from the snow and wind. One man had lost his wife and daughter—exhaustion overcame them and they froze to death, abandoned next to a boulder. "He who gets tired goes under, for no one can reach out a hand for fear of slipping down also," was Mannerheim's comment.[191] He worried, as always, about the animals, the faithful packhorses and his beloved Filip. There was another mountain pass in a snowstorm, followed by rain. But two days later they had arrived, Mannerheim's packhorse safe with his instruments. Now they had reached the northernmost part of the trip, Kuldja. They were in the Ili Province, separated by deserts and mountains in all directions from its neighbors.

This province, too, was of interest to the Russian military. The Mongols had moved forward here during their wanderings from the Asian steppes, and nomads still traveled by this route. Mannerheim had to study the terrain thoroughly and gauge the accessibility of the roads, the availability of water and fodder in the valleys. In some future Russian march against China, the roads leading southeast from Ili could be important to troops in various branches of the service.

Here he tried his hand at a dig, given tips by the Russian consul, who was himself interested in archeology. He made no wonderful finds, only a few clay jars and coins and a burial ground. One of his Cossacks had already been sent home, and now the second one was replaced. Lukanin, the new arrival and much admired in time by his master, learned Chinese, something Mannerheim had found next to impossible. Lio was replaced by Chao, a sixteen-year-old boy who proved to be a competent interpreter, and in addition could cook.

Their ride to Urumchi, capital of Sinkiang, was through huge snowfields. The horses sank so far that only their heads were above the snow. Many stretches had to be made on foot, the men, not the packhorses, serving as bearers. At night, Mannerheim's trench coat covered the ground, and a saddle was his pillow. There was no fuel to burn and no crumb of bread. But there was hunting. He killed a mountain ram, providing food for his little troop.

"The concept of time becomes more tenuous the further East one gets," Mannerheim observed. There was little time for philosophizing, though one has the impression that he was much affected by the eastern sense of timelessness, its fatalism and acceptance of life's harsh turns. But he had to be practical: his "poor animals look more like ghosts than living beings." The goal now was to arrive safely at Urumchi. They traveled there by night over the Tien Shan, to avoid the hot sun in the deserts between. [192]

In Urumchi where he arrived on July 24, 1907, Mannerheim found his life hampered by Russian bureaucracy. The Consul was jealous, and disliked "reports other than his own sent off." Officialdom was rather pleased to see the traveler "fuss and poke about and believe incorrect information." However, there were compensations. The Consul offered him a magnificent apartment, a "bed with sheets, a generous table, shade and quiet." Mannerheim's interpreter was "nailed to his bed" for many days, while his master was busy buying new horses.[193] Now he would continue on accompanied only by Chinese, except for the doughty Cossack, Lukanin. Ismail left here, too, well liked by Mannerheim despite his filthiness. He would miss his person and his pilafs. Now only one horse of his original group remained, his own Filip.

After a month he left Urumchi with his Cossack and Chinese. They traveled along the old Silk Route, crossing over the Tien Shan to Turfan, where Mannerheim would make a report to "Uncle Feda" carefully written in buried in travel talk, copied and sent on by his father to St. Petersburg. He measured heights and distances and described roads. On their way his party met a caravan of five hundred camels led by Chinese on foot from Kuldja to Peking. Mannerheim marveled at the silent discipline: they were carrying ammunition and weapons, with very few officers. "Here and there an officer or gunsmith was mounted on a camel's back, head bobbing in time to the animal's gait. A remarkable silence and discipline ruled the transport. With only ten officers and gunsmiths as convoy—not a single rifle was visible—the weapons caravan was making a trip of three months through the whole kingdom!" Mannerheim felt few countries in the west could match this.[194]

In Turfan the garrison, made up, it seemed, of prematurely aged men, held an exercise in his honor. Mannerheim compared their movements to a ballet, as they followed signals given by flags and drumbeats "with precision and theatrical effect." From there Mannerheim and his band made the long ride over mountains and desert to Barköl and the oasis Hami. The marches were "long and exhausting." He was fascinated to hear that wild horses could still be seen on the Tien Shan's northern slopes. In the moonlight he spied "a few of these shy creatures" grazing on a field.[195]

The travelers found the pass south of Barköl snowed in. With improvised shovels they managed to open the deep drifts, and get the baggage through and down the mountains, thanks to the marvelous "endurance and brisk work of two thin Chinese from Lanzhou."[196] He describes them as opium smokers. Again and again Mannerheim admires the indefatigable and courageous temperament of the Chinese.

From the oasis Hami to Anxi, where he arrived November 9, was an eleven days' ride through the desert. As usual, he felt for the horses that "must be content with unbelievably poor fodder, and yet manage a stiff piece of work." Colonists from the Honan Province were on their way to Urumchi "usually with no equipment other than the clothes they wear or balance on a narrow swinging board: a blue umbrella, a straw hat with broad embroidered rims . . . Only rarely do they ride a donkey . . ."[197]

Mannerheim made a trip west to Dunhuang, a fruitful oasis where he shot pheasants and gazelles. If he had been able to carry scientific equipment, he could have added to his trophies a priceless thousand-year-old document collection in "the thousand Buddhas' Grotto."[198] He learned of this treasure found by a Chinese priest some years earlier, but thought it beyond his knowledge to examine. The honor of "discovering" it was left to the Hungarian-British archeologist, Sir Aurel Stein.

They left Anxi in late November. After eight days on roads closed by snow, Mannerheim entered a small fortress town where he sought shelter. He rode in through an imposing gate in the Chinese Wall, and into the real Chinese Kingdom. The closing of the gates at night was solemnly announced by cannon shots and trumpets: now all the five iron gates of the ancient Kingdom of China were barred and honest folk were advised to go home. "We were all locked in!"[199]

Mannerheim had hitherto gathered information on political leanings, roads and terrain. Now, inside the old kingdom, he had new duties—to learn the results of political reforms in the kingdom, especially in the military.

On December 1 they reached the district town of Jiayuguan, half way between Kuldja and Peking, a distance as the crow flies of about 1,500 kilometers (about 930 miles). Mannerheim learned that the imperial couriers made the trip in nine days, but often died in the attempt. They offered their lives for an agreed price. It was said that they were laced up to harden their muscles. "Thus wrapped, they were lifted into the saddle and the ride continued to the next station, where the fastest horse was made ready at the sound of the courier bell. When the courier galloped in on his horse, he was lifted into the saddle of the waiting horse, and on he rushed at his top speed."[200] This was a holdover from the days of the Mongol postal system under Kublai Khan in the 13th century, admired by Marco Polo.

Mannerheim made a trip northeast to Chinta where he met a mandarin's son, Cheng, who had studied in Europe when his uncle had been ambassador to Berlin. The young man, himself reform-minded, felt that the old regime would disappear shortly. Mannerheim's Chinese name should be changed, he advised, as one of its three interpretations was a taunt. He hand-printed a hundred visiting cards with "elegant flourishes" which said: "Ma-nu-ör-hei-mu," or "the learned Finn."[201]

Cheng was convinced that the Japanese would play a major role in China. They were already filling teachers' and instructors' positions held by Europeans before, largely because they were cheaper. Cheng felt that China should be run by Chinese with western educations.

As he writes in his Memoirs, while making excursions in the nearby mountains Mannerheim visited the primitive Sarö and Shera Yögur tribes, Turkish and Mongolian peoples who were living isolated from the Chinese.[202] They had never before been studied by anthropologists or scientists. He was fascinated to fill in new information and later published a paper on them, although he was never able to collect documents on their origins or history. These had all been destroyed by fire.

A chieftain of the Shera Yögurs arranged a feast in his honor. One ate with chopsticks, and when the meal had ended, the plates were neatly licked. Mannerheim was entertained by song: two women and two men sang beautiful melancholy Mongolian melodies in subdued voices. "The pairs stood close together, gazing into each other's eyes as if wanting to guess what the next note would be. From time to time one of the singers offered a cup of hot brandy to the guests with both hands and a polite bow. Surprising how daintily they move in their lumpy furs and boots."[203] Mannerheim made his anthropological measurements and notes about the tribe's language, customs and religious beliefs, and said goodbye to them with a real sense of regret.

East and southeast they rode along the big caravan route, the Nanshan mountains on their right, and the Gobi desert on the left. The Great Wall was often near their road. In the northern part of the Ganzhou province Mannerheim made the acquaintance of a fellow cartographer, the Belgian Bishop Otto, who shared with him his notes on the communications system. The Bishop brought with him two Flemish missionaries, Fathers Leo van Dijk and Paul Jadoul. It was through van Dijk's efforts that Mannerheim acquired, in Lanzhou, a rare iconography, a set of 443 Chinese gods drawn in ink, with comments by Father Leo.[204] Mannerheim admired these clergymen's sensitive understanding of Chinese culture; their missionary traditions reached back to the 13th Century. Mannerheim was amused to note the Chinese dress of the prelate and his priests, including pigtail and black skullcap, "an unusual frame around European faces."[205]

Further along the big caravan road was Lanzhou. Mannerheim's words describe the city at a distance "with its threatening dark grey crenellated fortress wall it reaches the water bed . . . Between the river's banks barges loaded to the gunwales with crowds dressed in black and blue are constantly crossing. Here the barges and streets teem with people."[206] This was an important place to make judgments as to future Russian occupation in a push eastward.

Viceroy Shen, governor of Ganzhou, Sinkiang and Shanxi provinces, was a man who had a liking for "wine, cigars and other luxuries."[207] He had known Europe from his diplomatic post in St. Petersburg and so was not hostile to reforms. A corpulent man, he had fully mastered the "goose-waddle so dear to the Chinese heart" and lived a life of comfort, Mannerheim noted in his diary.

The Viceroy honored the Europeans in the city with a large dinner, which Mannerheim looked forward to with some anxiety, for as the guest of honor he might have to give a speech in Chinese. "One must express oneself so beautifully that only the initiated can understand." It was the most elegant dinner he would have in China. Served in a great temple hall decorated with rugs and lanterns, it was prepared by a Belgian dignitary's cook and set in European fashion, wines, table cloth and all appointments borrowed from the Belgian's house. Mannerheim's father, on seeing the photo, remarked with his usual ironic humor that "all are in formal attire, with decorations. Gustaf in tired traveling clothes looks like a tramp."[208]

Real leadership was not reflected in Lanzhou, where Mannerheim arrived January 29, 1908. The military exercises were ancient—slow marches "with bent knees," outmoded weapons, and no tactical instruction.[209] The railroad was far from finished, and without it the products of mines and industry could not be increased. As to the use of opium, the Viceroy proclaimed "Europeans make fun of us [opium smokers] as we have been emasculated and weakened."[210] Officials and soldiers were warned of dismissal and opium forbidden. In actual fact, nothing happened. Shen and his courtiers, the provincial officials and, in secret, ordinary soldiers, were almost all opium smokers.

But for all the lack of enforced military service by the nomadic tribes, for all the antique weapons in place, Mannerheim warned that the Mongolians could offer the Chinese a cavalry more than able to do battle with the Russian Cossacks. They were richly endowed with marvelous horses, endurance and strategic abilities suited to their vast spaces.

He left Lanzhou in March to visit the cloister city Labrang, less than one hundred miles to the southeast, not far from the border of Tibet. The road was dangerous because of robbers. The Chinese supplied an escort of four soldiers, two with rifles and two with enormous swords carried on the shoulder. Labrang's many gilded roofs and spires gleaming in the sunset surprised him. He had not expected so large a cloister—forty small temples and eighteen large ones, served by three thousand lamas. Gifts on a silk scarf presented by Mannerheim in the correct manner did not result in a visit to the incarnate Buddha. The people whistled, laughed and clapped their hands at him to drive away evil spirits, and stones were hurled in anger. When he went to look at the temples, he was met by a hostile "pack of lamas in red." His nervous guide now saw to it that he could meet a high lama, to whom he instantly complained of his treatment. When the answer was a polite avoidance of the issue, Mannerheim angrily said he would ride away, and from that moment the hostility came magically to an end.[211]

From Labrang's cloister city he followed the right arm of the Yellow River to reach Xian, after more than thirty days of riding. The mountains were of a great height, but "the contours are soft, almost hilly . . . On the heights there are large villages, others on the slopes . . . As far as the eye can see, there is one chain behind another . . . The slopes are terraced irregularly—like giant footsteps leading down to a dizzying deep . . . Everywhere life and movement—one meets scores of coolies balancing heavy loads on their dancing boards."[212]

Passing near another lama cloister he was again surrounded by hostile "swarming throngs" of red-robed lamas, who, when he showed himself, "greeted me with some well directed stones. To bring an end to the spectacle I fired a shot in the air with my shotgun, and shortly thereafter one into the ground near a dignified lama who had just flung a rock at my leg. In a trice, yard and slope were empty. I sent a message to the cloister's oldest lama telling him of the incidents, and a message was returned. The prelate promised to cut the throat of the lama who had hit me with his stone."[213]

In the rich valley of Xian there were "colorful types on the road, gaudily dressed men with the looks of warriors, decorative lamas in gleaming red robes, superstitious pilgrims with whirring prayer wheels and women with all their finery . . . The women I saw were ugly but I'm told there are beautiful ones as well."[214] Gustaf Mannerheim would never lose his appraising eye for the ladies.

For the first time he met Europeans inside the Wall. They were missionaries, many from Sweden. They were unfailingly friendly and sometimes helpful, but he felt their talents and interests were limited. "I've never met so many Swedes outside that country's borders as I have the last two months here in China. Unfortunately all the men are missionaries and the women mostly such examples of the species homo sapiens that one hasn't—in kindness to them—the courage to photograph them . . . Many are Americanized Swedes . . . the Catholic fathers are incontestably more highly educated than the Swedes."[215] He was relieved to have as dinner companions "two gentlemen who are not of the spiritual profession and with whom one can sit at the table without food spiced with prayers read aloud, or even better, sung."[216] He had, however, noted earlier, in Kashgar, that the Swedish missionaries were doing superb work in teaching and medicine.

Xian had been, during the Han Dynasty, the most stately of the courts. Mannerheim was sure the Chinese had described the "spacious gardens and walks, outings with escorts clad in red bearing the Empire's insignia, and temples with their colossal gilded idols," without allowing the reader to guess that the palaces had been simple clay huts, the escorts' clothing rags, the streets a "stinking ocean of dirt and dust."[217]

On his way to Kaifeng in mid-May, Mannerheim climbed Hua Shan mountain, borne in a wooden chair by two bearers, to the temple Nanfeng at the peak. It overlooked vast mountains to the east, south and west, and from the north the "mighty Yellow River flowed in two arms." He described the scene in moonlight and early dawn, "when the sun's golden platter slowly rose behind the mountains, covered in a light fog—the mountains in shifting colors of grey and deep green."[218]

The traveler went the last distance to Zhengzhou by train, its whistle sounding like music in his ears. The sights and sounds of khaki-clad soldiers, rickety rickshaws, Chinese murdering the French tongue and dressed in western clothing, proclaimed that he had once again joined civilization. From there the train took him to Kaifeng, Honan's capital city. On the way he noted the heat—"one melts like butter in a cup."[219] He saw some results of reform here. Opium smoking had lessened. Officials had the choice of smoking opium or keeping their job, and now there were institutions to help cure the addiction. On his way north to Taiyuan, he spent a musical evening in a French railroad administration building with some charming Frenchmen and Italians. The first western song he'd heard in two years was engraved on his memory, and years later he could still hear the Frenchmen's muted voices singing this verse to a guitar:

> "Elle est jolie! C'est la fille
> d'un mandarin très haut placé.
> C'est pourquoi sur sa poitrine
> Elle a deux petites mandarines."[220]

In Taiyuan, Lukanin met him with horses and baggage. After selling most of his equipment, Mannerheim saddled Filip for the last trip on horseback in China. He was to ride to the cloister at Labrang in the Wutai Shan mountains, where the Dalai Lama lived in exile. Mannerheim's first biographer, Kai Donner, comparing his trip to that of a Frenchman to Labrang at about the same time, tells of the dangers this man faced. Major d'Ollone's caravan, with a larger escort than Mannerheim's, also was confronted by stone-throwing, and in addition a violent attack by Tibetan cavalry which left some French officers seriously wounded. The swiftly approaching darkness saved them from death. Donner draws the conclusion that Mannerheim was more than merely lucky. It is not hard to believe, he writes, that his "energetic and decisive appearance" saved his life in this experience, as it would in others.[221]

Mannerheim was fascinated to visit the Dalai Lama and was received by the holy man on June 26, 1908. A platoon of Chinese soldiers met him, and at the entrance his Chinese "shadow." It would be clear how carefully the Chinese monitored the Tibetan, his guests, and all that was said and done. But Mannerheim succeeded in getting an audience for two alone: himself and his interpreter. The "shadow" had tried, but failed, to squeeze himself in.

Mannerheim's Memoirs give the flavor of his audience with the holy man. The Dalai Lama received Mannerheim in a small room, sitting "on a gilded throne-like armchair on a platform covered by rugs along the back wall. He was dressed in a yellow silk robe with light blue sleeve facings, and draped in the traditional lama's red toga. Under his feet he had a low, broad footstool and on his right was a chest decorated with heraldic figures. The side walls were adorned with a number of dazzling images applied to paper rolls. Two older, coarsely built Tibetans, unarmed and dressed in yellow-brown robes, stood with bowed heads on each side of the throne below the dais. My deep bow was answered by a slight inclination of his head."[222]

Gifts were exchanged, and the Dalai Lama broke the silence. How old was the visitor? Which way had he come? What was his title? The interpreter whispered Mannerheim's answers, not daring to look at his master. The Dalai Lama asked about the visitor's homeland, and wondered if he had been given the task of forwarding a message from His Majesty the Emperor of Russia. Clearly he was disappointed when the answer was no, the visitor saying that he had not been able to attend the Tsar before his departure. But his visitor could assure the holy man that the people of Russia had undivided sympathy for the Dalai Lama, exiled from his own country and under the rule of China.

Mannerheim's present was a success, though he apologized that it was not handsomer. Times were such, he said, that even a holy man could better use a pistol than a prayer wheel! The Dalai was delighted with the Browning pistol and laughed with pleasure when his guest demonstrated how seven bullets could be loaded at once. In turn, Mannerheim was given twelve lengths of a Tibetan material and five bunches of incense sticks. The Dalai Lama was careful to make sure the door hangings did not conceal listeners and Mannerheim admired him for not playing the role the Chinese had tried to force on him.

The Dalai Lama promised to receive him next in Tibet if he should come on a new expedition to Asia. Indeed, the holy man did return to Tibet, declaring his country independent in 1912. History sometimes does repeat itself, as we know from the annexation of Tibet by China in 1950.

From Wutai Shan Mannerheim went to Kalgan, the end of his horseback trip. His journal ended on July 20, 1908, two years after the start, just as planned. It was with relief that he took the railroad to Peking, where he bade goodbye to his people. "The stout Lukanin" went home to Russia by train, and before saying goodbye to the cook Chang and the interpreter Chao, Mannerheim wondered if they could find him a hair braid, since the reforms included getting rid of pigtails. Chang came to him with a package. In it was a pigtail of silk. He shyly said that his own was under his cap, and that he had mixed it with silk. Mannerheim remarked that Chang "probably didn't see why the reforms should start with him."[223]

Now he faced the labor of cataloguing his material, cleaning up his maps and making notes on his observations. Finally, he left his horse Filip with the Russian military agent in China, unable to take him along.

He went home by way of Japan, Siberia and Russia. On the way to Japan he wrote his father from a steamer about the six weeks he had spent in Peking, working on his report in the sultry heat. He had felt so listless that he could not judge the worth of the account he had written. Members of the Russian legation had told him it was interesting and well written, but he felt their remarks were merely polite; he himself thought them dry and dull. He wanted more statistical material, but there were "impossible difficulties in finding such in China because partly there aren't any, partly they're kept secret."

He loved his ocean voyage. "After the free life I have led it may be difficult to put on the yoke again. On the other hand, I'm too old for new expeditions and adventures, especially with the lumbago which hurts so much that I moan when I turn around.

"I'm writing in the roads of Tschifu. The surroundings are beautiful. This little town lies squeezed between yellow-grey mountains and the marvelous sea. The American Philippine squadron's white ships grace the roadstead. It's as beautiful as Biarritz. It would be an earthly paradise if one weren't surrounded by bandy-legged, rather impolite Japanese. The complete absence of the female element here and everywhere in the Far East gives an odd character to the environs."[224]

For all his labors, Mannerheim felt he had only achieved a "superficial knowledge of the country, a bunch of statistics, some ethnographic and anthropological information, plus over a thousand more or less faulty maps . . . . I think I've been poking around in things already known, even if they've been interesting and unknown to me until now."[225] Nevertheless, his research in ethnographic and folk-lore history and his measurements and observations on the languages and beliefs of the Sarö and Shera Yögur tribes in the western part of Ganzhou province had not been known earlier in Western scientific circles. Many of the nearly two thousand mile stretches of road he drew had never been mapped before. His rich collection of objects from Tibet—temple banners, pictures of gods, bronze Buddhist images—were rare findings because of the difficulty of access to Tibet and its suspicion of foreigners. The Finnish Ugrian Society published his journal with a selection of his photographs in English in 1936, to reach the scholarly world, and an essay was also published by the Finnish Ugrian Society on "A Visit to the Sarö and Shera Yögurs." The English version is called "Across Asia from West to East in 1906-1908." His archeological findings, impressions of rock carvings, manuscripts, anthropological studies, meteorological observations, manuscripts in ancient languages, and the atlas with his itinerary maps were treated by a number of scientists in a second part of his work.

Back in St. Petersburg he was summoned to an audience with the Tsar. The audience, he was told, might last twenty minutes. As the Emperor showed no sign of sitting down, Mannerheim gave his report standing, something courtiers in St. Petersburg had been trained to do. At the end of an hour and twenty minutes Mannerheim caught sight of a clock and apologized. The Tsar insisted that he, too, had not noticed time passing.

Reading his Memoirs, one is aware that Mannerheim is as much at ease with men of no social pretension, of no high social class, as he is with chieftains and emperors. He understands and respects those who are kings in their own realms: Chao, the 16 year-old interpreter, is a fine linguist; Ismail and Chang are masters of cooking; Numgan, a Kalmuck hunter whom Mannerheim has met and hunted with in the Tekes River valley, is a sovereign of the chase. The old man promises to meet him at a particular spot in this "hunting paradise" in exactly five weeks. Hardly expecting him to keep his promise, Mannerheim finds him exactly on the right spot at the right moment, waiting for him, "crouched like a lurking beast of prey."[226] Mannerheim can hardly believe his hardiness: tipped over with his horse by the force of a mountain river, Numgan does not wade ashore or give up his shaky, dangerous footing in the rushing waters until he has succeeded in remounting the animal midstream. The two men understand one another well. When Numgan is away on his own twenty-five hour hunt in the wilds, Mannerheim fells a large mountain goat, larger than Numgan's. Having made a kill to his great satisfaction, he writes his father: "One can imagine how impressive it was to see these two groups [of mountain goats] galloping on each side of the wild and seemingly bottomless gorge with its vertical walls, and to hear their little hooves clattering against the rock like castanets."[227]

Mannerheim was a happy man on this journey, testing his own limits of physical endurance. Though always loath to admit illness, he had suffered sunstroke, rheumatism and neuralgia. His voyage was also a spiritual exercise. In the awesome terrain of the Tien Shan it was not only his hunter's skill that was called on in pursuing and shooting his mountain creature through the heart. His pen was lyrical when he wrote of this "paradise, not only for hunters but for everyone who loves beauty and grandeur in nature and relishes the exertions of alpine sports."[228] The hunter exults in the beauty of the graceful herds standing on the crown of a mountain, majestic in their remoteness, inaccessible to man's bullets, glancing down from their height to guess what man might try next. He has understood a new concept of time here. He says goodbye as though caught in a dream-like memory, to the marvelous gorges, the lush grasses and rich hunting grounds, the timeless splendor of the mountains.

A summation of his Asian ride with many of his photographs was published for the Finnish Ugrian Society in 1990. Remarks in the text prefacing the photographs refer to the value of his scientific endeavors. "Mannerheim said that it was thanks to a couple of English handbooks for explorers that he was able to do anything at all for the benefit of science. In fact he did so much that his material has not yet been published in toto . . . [He] tended to underestimate his scientific field work and collections, but their real value is becoming more and more evident . . . Mannerheim's activities in Central Asia put him alongside the great explorers of that area . . ."

The editor Peter Sandberg writes of Mannerheim's photographic work. "The collection amounts to a vivid portrayal of a remote, bygone world, of little-known peoples and ways of life that have since passed out of existence." In a passage called "The Cavalryman and the Camera," the quality of Mannerheim's photography is discussed. "In terms of skill, the landscapes must be said to fall short of the narrative. Most of them want depth, the foreground is unstructured . . . But Mannerheim had the use of only a single lens and format, and was unfamiliar with panoramic techniques and professional subtleties of exposure . . . Personal in approach, Mannerheim's neglected reportage proves a sizeable addition of no little photographic merit . . . . The portraits, in particular, still poignant in their fresh spontaneity, reveal the photographer's subtle psychological direction of his subjects, whom he seems to indulge with quiet amusement . . . The act [of photographing] required, however, that the cavalryman dismount and mingle with the people. He may have carried out his chief duties in the saddle, but there is no downward tilt to his lens work."[229] This could be a description of Mannerheim himself, his instinctive liking and understanding of others, no matter what their race or rank.

He did not say goodbye forever to Asia. He made two hunting expeditions to India and Nepal in 1928 and 1937 as the guest of Colonel Bailey, the British Minister to Nepal, and his wife Lady Bailey. In his Memoirs, Mannerheim writes that the Maharaja Jung Bahadur invited him to a tiger shoot with Lord Aylesford, the American lawyer and big game hunter Wilton Lloyd-Smith with his eighteen-year-old daughter Marne. The Field Marshal was impressed with the American girl, a good shot, who had taken a wild buffalo. Marne has written me that she kept falling in love with the various single men and was a "worry to her father." The Field Marshal, she wrote, was very good company, nearly 70 at the time. She remembers that the Baileys had set up a luxurious permanent camp from which they set out on elephants or on foot or by car to do their hunting. [Mannerheim became a Field Marshal in 1933. In 1942, on his birthday, June 4th, the President of Finland raised his rank to Marshal of Finland. June 4th is now a national holiday.]

On his way to the camp for the Maharaja's tiger shoot, Mannnerheim writes that he saw 80 elephants ringing the tiger, famously known as a man eater who had broken out of all earlier ringing attempts. In attendance were 1000 men and 200 elephants, the Maharaja's camp a "city of tents." Mannerheim rode an elephant equipped with an English saddle and a handle to grab, convenient, he thought, given the unusual arrangement. The tiger rushed past at 20 meters, and at 50 exposed himself a moment. Mannerheim raised his gun and missed, followed by 400 pairs of eyes, 160 of them elephants.

The tiger passed the Field Marshal again at a wild pace and he fired. His booty made a few leaps, but then the high grass ceased to sway. The Maharaja advised one more shot: "one can never be sure with a tiger." The noble head collapsed. He was a magnificent specimen, 3.23 meters long, the largest tiger taken in Nepal that year. Marne writes with sympathy for the tiger, "he didn't have a chance."[230] Today his magnificent pelt can be seen on the living room floor in Mannerheim's house, now a museum in Helsinki.

In his Memoirs, at the end of his chapter on the Asian journey, Gustaf Mannerheim quotes an Englishman who had worked for thirty years in the service of the Chinese government. "If one has spent three weeks in China, one is prepared to write a book, after three years a brochure, but after thirty years one understands nothing and keeps silent."[231]

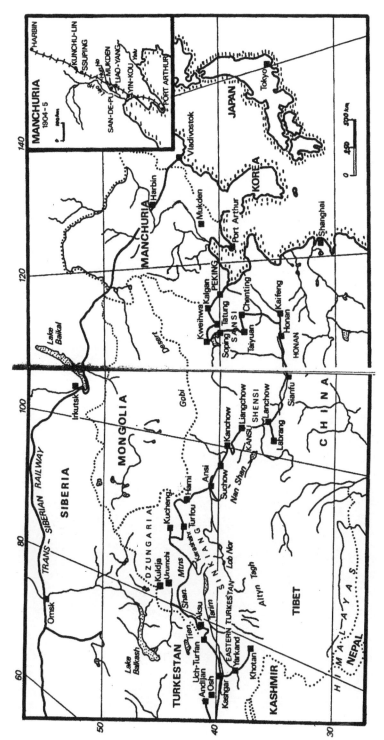

Map of Gustaf's Ride through Asia

265

Shooting Exhibition

Chinese iconography

Chapter 23

THE SPARRES' LAST YEARS IN FINLAND

Eva prepared to take Pehr back to his boarding school in the late summer of 1906, leaving their cottage for the apartment in Helsinki. There, in the beautiful northern summer evening, Eva listened to the noise of cannon shots far out to sea. Probably they were only being fired by Russian ships on maneuvers, though they continued ominously through the night. The next morning they heard the news. Soldiers manning the old fortress Sveaborg had mutinied. From the Porvoo ferry Eva and her boy heard bullets coursing and descending as the men in the island fortress rose against their officers.

Louis, sitting in the lighthouse tower, had watched the bombardment of the fortress and seen the explosion of its ammunition chamber. The mutiny was easily subdued this time, by cannons faithful to the Russian regime. Finnish Red Guards, who had joined the Russians in the mutiny within the fortress, were seized, their lives saved thanks to Finnish justice.

In Helsinki a frightening clash began with workers who interfered with trolley traffic. Defense guards (the Whites) were called out to confront them. Furious, the Red Guards mingled with Russian naval ranks in civilian clothes and with women and children as shields opened fire on the Whites. Seven were killed and remembered.

Both Guards were disbanded, though they would reappear. It was one more foreshock of the Revolution.

Soon after arriving at school, Pehr learned that his father had bought the cutter Svaj with money earned from a portrait. Pehr and Clas were joint owners.

As usual, Eva wrote Pehr about the political events which were changing the old order in Finland. She uncharacteristically mentions her own work, the address cover for the final resolutions, read by the Governor General at the last meeting of the Estates. It was the end of an era:

> "September 19, 1906: Yesterday was the conclusion of Finland's Estates [parliament]. It was beautiful and solemn . . . . I went to a gallery in the Throne Room of the Imperial palace. There I saw the whole elegance. First, the knights and nobility. Leading them was the Marshal with a long staff. The marshal was Baron von Born and he did his duty excellently . . . After the nobility came the clergy, then the burghers, and last the peasants. Next was the Senate's turn and then came the Gov. Gen. with suite. All were so grand and gold-laced . . . the Marshal, and after him the three other Estates' speakers, stepped forward and made speeches . . . [Governor General Gerard] then read the Emperor's answer in Russian. Then he was given the Estates' resolutions in green bindings made by the undersigned and then they trooped out as ceremoniously as they'd come in. The ladies in the gallery stood and watched for the longest time, these men who went never to return. It was like a tale from bygone times and it felt very melancholy."[232]

Historians have characterized it as Europe's most radical parliamentary reform, "carried out in a single sweep: the antiquated Diet of Four Estates was replaced by a democratized system and the number of voters multiplied ten fold. The increase was due not only to the fact that the unenfranchised classes gained voting rights, but also to the extension of suffrage to women."[233] For Eva and many of her class, the departure of the "antiquated Diet" was not welcome. Democracy was not a concept that they fully understood or valued. Something had been lost. The experience in statesmanship of generations of nobles, their best qualities and inherited responsibilities, would no longer have a voice in the governance of their country. It was a confused and dangerous time, although the Diet had been replaced without bloodshed. The nobles with the members of the other Estates had voted themselves out of existence. Civil war had been narrowly averted; the Great Strike was a recent memory and anarchists were active.

It is interesting that one important political development of 1906 is not mentioned in Eva's letters to Pehr, that of women's suffrage. Finland was the first European country to grant women the right to vote. In the U.S. several states granted suffrage within their borders (13 states by 1913), but only in 1920 did the 19th Amendment grant full voting rights for women. It is possible that as a woman who did not feel inferior to men and whose art in a different medium was equal in interest and quality to her husband's, the right to vote was not of major importance to Eva.

Louis officially announced his professional status as a painter by joining the 1906 fall exhibit in which his portrait of Eva, "Summer Evening," would be the centerpiece. Louis rushed to Sweden where he was welcomed by Anders Zorn and Albert Engström, the painter and the writer, two old friends who gave him what he needed at that difficult moment, warmth and the unvarnished truth. Suddenly, as he wrote about it to Eva, his doubts and misery of the last few years gave way to the knowledge that he had made the right move. He had spent "sixteen years sharing with Finnish artists their struggles and exhibits, in and outside the country" and he could see, now, that he did not belong.[234] Louis had for too long lived with illusions. He felt he must truly come home to his own country as the painter he always had been.

The exhibit opened the day of his arrival in Stockholm and was a success. Louis' portrait of Eva and his other paintings were admired by his own painter colleagues. The general public had liked his work, but aside from this and the support of his friends, he had known there was a barrier of indifference, an outgrowth of his own neglect of painting. The Finnish Art Association had never found him worthy to be represented by a single oil, despite the recent exhibit with other artists and his years of work representing Finland abroad. Nevertheless, as a result of the art show, portrait commissions with decisions about price and time came in to assure the beginning of a better new year. He was invited to be a member of the jury for the distribution of prizes, as an apparent soothing of his bitter feelings. Louis declined. In a letter to the Art Association, he refused to sit in judgment on the work of those who felt they were his superiors. The official art was stale and meaningless, he wrote, not fit to fulfill its role of serving to guide good taste. He resigned from the Art Association, returning his share of stock.

With reactionary politics in control once again in Petersburg, it was not surprising that the popular Governor General Gerard did not last long. As Eva reported to Pehr on February 18th of 1907, "the worst is that the Governor General [Gerard] has been dismissed and will leave the country already on Thursday . . . . The air feels heavy and dark. Gerard has been celebrated with song and flowers and telegrams from the whole country. Yesterday evening the workers' organizations arranged a torchlight parade and singing outside his residence. He stood on the balcony and is said to have been very moved . . . Pappa, Aunt Sophie and I were in the crowd to watch." Gerard actually left in 1908. After the Revolution, after Finland's independence had been won, Gerard was invited to be Finland's guest for the rest of his life. His humane rule had not been forgotten.

What Eva apparently wrote nothing about, though perhaps some letters have been lost, was her husband's new undertaking. Louis, ever adventurous, wrote a film script, probably in February, 1907. For the first time, a native Finnish film would be made. A competition was run for a theme, the prize 100 Marks. Louis was script writer; the director was Teuvo Puro, and Albert Engström, artist and author, stood at the camera. The actors came from the National Theater. The theme was a simple one: illicit distillers are busy making schnapps, while a pig serenely eats the mash. A client arrives to taste the brew, and all the others join. They start up a card game and have a fight. The county governor arrives with police, they fire shots in the air to arrest the troublemakers, and the terrified pig flees. Since it's a pig of great value, it must be found before the film can come to a happy conclusion.[235]

The movie was filmed in March, 1907, in the park, Eläintara (Djurgårdsskogen), in Helsinki. It was developed in Paris, with its first showing on May 29, 1907. The author learned from her cousin, Per Sparre, that "in 1949, an attempt was made to restore the film. Since Finland then lacked the facilities to do this, the film was sent to Germany where the best facilities and technology existed for the remastering of film. The ship carrying the film sank on the journey to Germany and the entire film was lost. It sank with the ship."[236]

The Sparres all spent Easter vacation with Louis near Tampere, where Louis was painting a "Little Lord Fauntleroy" portrait of Johan Erik Dahlström, young son of the owners of the great estate of Lielax with its private railroad. Toward the end of April, Eva wrote: "The painting is a good likeness, beautiful in color and painted in a fresh way. The boy stands dressed in a black velvet frock, next to a grey table. Behind him is a yellow drapery and on the table a jar with charming violet rhododendron flowers . . ."

Writing again from home, some weeks later, in May, Eva was at work on important address covers. "[They will] be sent from the university in Helsinki to Uppsala and Stockholm universities in commemoration of Linnaeus' 200th anniversary." [Carl Linnaeus, 1707-78, Swedish botanist and taxidermist, was the founder of the modern scientific classification of plants and animals. He was ennobled as von Linné.]

An invitation to Louis to visit Italy with Hjalmar Linder, his former brother-in-law, came as a boon, especially as it would be during the fall season. The dark autumn days in Scandinavia had always acted as a depressant. Louis soaked up the luscious Venetian evenings, the gaudy crowds, the international exhibits of living artists. Louis found portraits by Zorn and the masterly work of Sargent, and was painting with furious concentration.

Meanwhile, in his absence, Eva wrote Pehr of a remarkable concert, and a new venture. "I've just come home from a wonderfully beautiful Sibelius concert. He conducted the orchestra himself, which played a new composition by him . . . Last night I drew furniture. It was daring of me, now when Papa is away, but I decided to dare. So far everything has gone well. The drawing is approved and being worked out in Borgå [Porvoo] as to suggested expense. If it is ordered, Pappa will be astonished!" Two days later she wrote proudly that the furniture had been ordered.[237]

The story continues after an interval of 90 years. The Director of the Porvoo Museum, Marketta Tamminen, wrote in October, 1996, that she had asked the Curator of the Helsinki City Museum if they had any Louis Sparre furniture. "Nothing much, only a desk, but we have a set of furniture which is said to be designed by Eva

Mannerheim Sparre. But surely there must be a mistake; she did not design furniture as far as we know." Eva's correspondence with her son may be the only evidence there is of her attempt to surprise Louis with her own furniture design. Of the furniture, Marketta Tamminen writes: "They are very elegant, slender chairs, designed by someone who was not well acquainted with carpenter's work."[238] It is delicate furniture, clean-limbed, with the grace of a willow.

Louis sent postcards from Florence and Venice. Unfortunately, a visit to Paris loomed bringing with it the familiar despair. No matter how many visits to elegant restaurants there were with his rich friend Hjalmar, how many theatres and luncheons at the Pavillon d'Ermenonville in the Bois, or his liking for his brother-in-law, nothing could remove the dread of a visit to his father. The old man was experimenting with wood pulp, already in touch with a paper company. Nothing could induce him to leave Paris and live with his son.

Early in November 1907, Eva reported on her new work: "Do you know my little professional school for bookbinders is in full swing. It's very interesting. All places were immediately taken. Twice we've had lessons from 8-10 [in the evening] and then one is tired on coming home. Sunday morning there's also an hour."

In a November letter, Eva described portraits Louis was painting, including one of herself. "From last winter's canvasses he's finishing one nude study, and me by the piano in lamp light. If only once he'd have the satisfaction of feeling that he'd really succeeded."

In January of 1908, Eva wrote of preparations for an exhibit, and a recent book cover "Det Gamla Borgå" ["Ancient Porvoo"], written by Louis. "I think it's the handsomest book I've made," she wrote on January 28, 1908. She was posing for a portrait and Louis had been commissioned to paint a beautiful girl, Miss Fazer, "who looks like a princess . . . Pappa got a proof of his advertisement. It's the St. Nicholas church in the evening, and up in the sky one sees a flock of birds flying away. They are all of us!"

Louis had long planned a retrospective art show of his years in Finland, his paintings and etchings from 1891 to 1907. His and Eva's joint show with 140 oils, etchings and watercolors by Louis and some 20 of Eva's bookbindings and textiles, was well received by the critics. At the time, Eva wrote Pehr there was a "celebratory feeling" Louis sold a good many paintings, although only one small etching represented him in the official art collection of the Ateneum in Helsinki. He refused the official request to purchase two more. (Only in 1912, was a painting of his with a history of exhibits in Paris, Stockholm and Helsinki purchased for the collections at the Finnish Ateneum.) Nonetheless, despite Louis' bitter feelings, the results of his show resulted in many commissioned portraits in Finland.

Pehr received an invitation to their exhibit at the Ateneum, on February 9th. A news clipping from the Helsinki newspaper *Hufvudstadsbladet* describes the show as "a rich exposition of tastefully exhibited, interesting and beautiful works. Among those present was the Governor General Gerard . . . In the exquisitely fine collection [there are] some twenty book bindings and different techniques, as well as textile works, such as curtains, table spreads, quilts, etc. She [Countess Sparre] further establishes her reputation as one of the most gifted artists in the North in the practice of her art's domain . . . The Sparre couple's exhibit is among the most interesting which have come our way in recent times."

Eva wrote on February 23, about the departure of the Governor General. "[He] left the day before yesterday, honored as no one has been in this country. Torches lined his road from his home to the station. Shouts of hurrah were heard during the whole trip. He's been hailed with songs and flowers every day. So many flowers that the Residence looks like a garden. I was there for a large dinner of 400 people. Pappa had drawn the menu with G's portrait. Pappa has received the charming man's photo with signature. The family is still here and yesterday came for tea. It feels so melancholy again for this poor country that there will be a change for the worse."

His successor, Eva wrote, was "a General Bäckman who is supposed to be a very cruel and bloodthirsty man. We'll see if we can keep calm here so he won't have occasion to shoot. Masses of Cossacks have come here and ride daily on the streets screaming and making noise. This must be to inspire fear." Louis wrote proudly to Pehr about the show, with 2600 visitors. He sold a dozen paintings and as many etchings, and Eva 15 books.

A letter from Eva to Louis in March shows the easy, loving relationship between them—whatever their differences might have been earlier. "My Bi [his nickname was Bibi]: The hour just struck nine and already I'm on my tummy in my bed. It was so empty and sad without you here. Getting going with the books just isn't working.

The sun is shining outside! . . . Kisses and more kisses from your longing [illegible nickname]."

In April there was news of Gustaf. He had sent "a letter with a Chinese menu for the dinner given him by the Viceroy, after which he felt so ill he had to postpone his trip several days . . ." At home in Finland, the moving vans arrived although there was no certainty about the future. But Louis was busy with his portraits, which insured a bit of financial stability.

Ambjörn had followed the events with excitement, pleased that Louis and Eva had the sense to move to Sweden. He was working on another gold mine, a machine for refining wood pulp. "I can't earn 100 sous now, but as soon as my affairs are in order, I'll be able to get any sum I want!"[239] Paris was the only place for him, and hardships were merely temporary inconveniences. His faithful Marie had become hopelessly blind, although she to the last believed that he would invent a cure. His head full of dreams, he took Marie out for walks in the Parc Monceau.

Eva did not continue her biography of Louis beyond the move to Sweden in 1908-1909, though there is a hint that she intended to do so. That she herself continued her work in leather is clear from a book on Venice, dated 1911, *Raccolta delle vere da pozzo in Venezia* dedicated to J. Pierpont Morgan, "Mecenato Dell'Arte", published by Ferdinando Ongania. Another is one of twenty of the "de luxe edition" of Bruno Liljefors: An Appreciation, dated 1929, by K.E. Russow, bound in leather with an inlaid plaque on the front cover.[240]

Eva is described as continuing to refine her style and experiments with leather coloring, although after she moved to Sweden she evidently did not develop her style further. The director of the Porvoo Museum observed that Eva continued with her bindings until 1936, when an automobile accident ended that activity, though she recovered her health. She could no longer trust her eye or the steadiness of her hand for the demanding work.

Eva was the first in Finland to develop leather tooling as book art. The bookbinding itself was left to professionals. In a trip to Finland in 1996, I was shown the collection of Eva's sketches for her book designs and photographs of them by Marianne Roos, Curator of the National Board of Antiquities. The following year, in May, an exhibit had been mounted by the Porvoo Museum's director, Marketta Tamminen, for a show of Eva's book art and her tapestry work. Private owners of her books—as many as could be traced—loaned their treasures, and the Kremlin Museum, after much red tape, allowed the Coronation Address of 1896 to be exhibited. Somehow, it had been preserved through the decades of Communist rule.

Eva both engraved and embossed the leather, often in the style of Art Nouveau, based on swirling lines of plants and flowers, thorns and thistles; a stylized "whiplash." It was sometimes illustrative of the content: a medieval church motif, an English hunting scene, a rising flock of birds. On one cover, there is a portrait of a gentleman in the Japanese style of Sharaku, the satirical artist. Sometimes the leather has metal fittings. One binding, ordered by William Morris's Kelmscott Press, shows a symbolic heart covered in a thicket of thorns with a medieval hand in armor pointing toward a rose. The back cover is adorned by a sword and rose spray. One of the most beautiful bindings was found damaged and faded, though the green morocco is still preserved inside in its original color. Its ornaments are in leather mosaic and gold, with purple clematis and carved bunches of gold lines and sinuous leaves. Eva had every book photographed. The National Museum has photos of her albums, books, and address covers. Her books are in Denmark, Russia, England, Sweden (at Upsala and Stockholm Universities, and the Royal Library in Stockholm), in Switzerland, in Finland also at the Åbo Academy Library, and in the U.S. at Bryn Mawr College.

Toward the end of her book Eva writes a sketch of Louis's and her last visit to Ambjörn in Paris in 1920, after the convulsion of wars and revolutions that had separated them. Ambjörn had never given in to despair, not even when he was seriously injured by a car, and the doctors wanted to amputate his mangled leg. "Absolutely not! Get me home—I will take care of this myself."[241] And so he did, even though he had to use crutches.

When Eva and Louis came into his apartment (five floors up, no lock on the door) the old man, stone deaf, was unaware of his visitors. Eva describes the scene: "He sat crouched before a smoldering fireplace . . . Suddenly he looked up and saw us. The handsome wavy hair, the bushy eyebrows, his dark blue penetrating eyes and strongly hooked nose were as before, but he was thinner and had let his beard grow. The sparsely furnished room, a bed, large work table and some chairs, was filled with all sorts of rubbish, machine parts, jars and glasses, the kerosene lamp his only illumination. The other four rooms held the assemblage of the latest invention, a machine for removing bark from logs . . . . 'My little boy,' he said, 'what can you earn with your little hand-work? I can't earn five sous, but the millions will come. I can rest when I'm old!'"[242] He was 92.

Eva ends her biography with her final move from Helsinki to Stockholm in 1908. Louis would come later in the new year. His Finnish portrait commissions alone represented their security. Eva summoned the moving vans with no real sense of what lay before them. But they were both young, full of energy and hope. At the beginning of the new year in 1909, after a trip to Spain, Eva and Louis were ready to set out on the next adventure, and start the rest of their long lives together.

Hunting in India in 1937

Field Marshal and Maharaja

Field Marshal, Wilton Lloyd-Smith, and
Marne Lloyd-Smith (at right)

Endnotes

1   Berta Edelfelt: Sophie Mannerheim, *En Levnadsteckning (A Sketch of her Life)*
    Holger Schildt, Helsinki, 1932 p.53
2   Letters from Eva Mannerheim to her brother Carl, from Stockholm, Sept. 16,
    Oct. 15, 1885; Feb. 12, 1886; National Archives, Helsinki
3   Letters from Eva Mannerheim to Louis Sparre, Mar. 27 and Mar. 30, 1893, Eva
    and Louis Sparre archive.
4   Condensed from Ingrid Qvarnström, *Ett Legendomspunnet Liv, Aurore Karamsin
    och Hennes Samtid (A Legendary Life, Aurore Karamsin and her World)* Holger
    Schildt, Helsinfors, 1937.
5   Information about Swedish noble families is from the volumes of *Svenska
    Adelns Ättartavlor, [Genealogies of the Swedish Noble Families]* Gustaf Elgenstierna,
    Stockholm. P.A. Norstedt 1925-36.
6   *Sveriges Ridderskap och Adelskalender 1992 (Sweden's Knighthood and Nobility)*,
    Norstedt, Stockholm, 1991
7   From *Svenska Adelns Ättartavlor (Genealogy of the Swedish Nobility)* Ed. Gustaf
    Elgenstierna, P.A. Norstedt, Stockholm,1932,Vol.VII; and Erik Hornberg,
    Sverige's Historia (History of Sweden), Bonniers, Stockholm 1941 pp. 107-136.
8   Article in *Arte et Marte*, 1993
9   Carolina Sparre's journal, *Mina Reseminnen sedan 1863 (My Travel Memoirs of
    1863)*, in the author's archive
10 Letters from Teresita and Ambjörn [Aug.1862-Nov.1867], in the Eva and
    Louis Sparre archive, given by my cousin Baroness Christina Klingspor to the
    library in Göteborg. I have edited portions of Teresita's letters by correcting
    spelling, adding punctuation for clarity, but not changing her style or syntax.

Occasionally I have substituted English words for her French usage. In 1960, I visited Gravellona and the old Villa Teresita with my husband and daughter Teresita. We were shown its magnolia garden by the grandson of Corsico, Teresita's gardener. He regretted that he could not show us the interior. The painting by Pehr Georg Sparre is an accurate representation of how it still looked outside.

11 Harrison, *Principles of Internal Medicine*, 12th ed. 1991, pp. 639-40.
12 Eva Mannerheim Sparre, *Konstnärsliv [An Artist's Life]*, Helsinki, Schildts 1951, p.28. Other references to Ambjörn's work are also taken from this volume.
13 *Svenska Dagbladet*, June 12, 1955.
14 Lönnrot later became a professor of the Finnish language at the University of Helsingfors, publishing his work between 1835 and 1849.
15 Eva Mannerheim Sparre: *Bröllopsresan, Beskrivning av en Resa i Fjärrkarelen Sommaren 1893 (Wedding Trip, Description of a Voyage to Eastern Karelia the Summer of 1893)*, Konstvärlden, Stockholm, 1945, p. 34.
16 Ibid. p. 37.
17 Ibid.
18 Ibid. p. 45.
19 Ibid. p. 49.
20 Louis Sparre: *Bland Kalevala Folkets Ättlingar, (Among the Descendants of the Kalevala Peoples)*, Werner Söderström Osakeyhtiö, Borgå, 1930, p. 17.
21 Sparre: *Bröllopsresan*, p. 54
22 Heikki Kirkinen and Hannes Sihvo: *The Kalevala, an Epic of Finland and all Mankind*, Finnish-American Cultural Institute and the Finnish Cultural Foundation, 1985, p. 20.
23 Sparre, *Bröllopsresan*, p. 63.
24 Ibid., p. 67
25 Stig Jägerskiöld, *Den Unge Mannerheim (The Young Mannerheim)*, Stockholm Bonnier, 1964, p. 52
26 Ibid. p. 50
27 Ibid.
28 Ibid. p. 51
29 Ibid. p. 58
30 Veijo Meri, *C.G. Mannerheim, Marskalken av Finland*, translated into Swedish by Ulla Ruuhusulehto, Borgå, 1989, p. 120
31 G. Mannerheim, *Minnen, Del I 1882-1930 (Memoirs, Part I, 1882-1930)*, Helsingfors, Schildt, 1951 p.16
32 Jägerskiöld: *Den Unge Mannerheim*, p. 58.
33 Ibid. p. 64

34   Ibid. p. 78
35   Ibid. p. 77
36   Joint letter from Carl and Gustaf Mannerheim to Annicka, undated; probably late December, 1884; National Archives, Helsinki
37   Meri, *C.G. Mannerheim . . .* , has a somewhat different perspective: p.131
38   Mannerheim, *Minnen, Del I*, p.16
39   Letter of May 20, 1886, in the Eva and Louis Sparre archive
40   Jägerskiöld, *Den Unge Mannerheim*, p. 82
41   Ibid. p. 106
42   National Archives, Helsinki
43   Leonid Vlasov, *Mannerheim i Petersburg, 1887-1904* (*Mannerheim in Petersburg, 1887-1904*), originally written in Russian, translated to Swedish from the Finnish translation by Henrik Ekberg, Gummerus, Helsinki, 1994, p. 28
44   Jägerskiöld, *Den Unge Mannerheim*, p. 111
45   Vlasov, *Mannerheim i Petersburg 1887-1904*, p. 64
46   Stig Jägerskiöld, *Marskalken av Finland: Gustaf Mannerheim 1941-44* (*Marshall of Finland: Gustaf Mannerheim 1941-44*), Holger Schildts förlag, Keuru, 1979, pp. 79-80.
47   Pp. 122-123
48   J.E.O. Screen, *Mannerheim: the Years of Preparation*, London, C. Hurst & Co., 1970 p. 36
49   Jägerskiöld, *Den Unge Mannerheim*, p. 188
50   Qvarnström, *Ett Legendomspunnet Liv*, p. 208
51   Jägerskiöld, *Den Unge Mannerheim*, p. 192
52   Baron Gustaf Erik Adolf Nordenskiöld, geologist, arctic explorer, discovered Northeast Passage 1878-79
53   Jägerskiöld, *Den Unge Mannerheim*, p. 199
54   Vlasov, *Mannerheim i Petersburg*, p. 82
55   Jägerskiöld, *Den Unge Mannerheim*, pps 165-6
56   Vlasov, *Mannerheim i Petersburg, 1887-1904*, p. 113.
57   Veijo Meri: *Marskalken av Finland C.G. Mannerheim*, p. 166
58   Finland's National Archives, Dec. 11, 1900
59   Finland's National Archives, Dec. 22, 1901
60   Finland's National Archives, May 18, 1903
61   Finland's National Archives, April 1, 1904
62   Jägerskiöld: *Den Unge Mannerheim*, p. 207
63   National Archives, Helsinki. Letter from Sotkamo, dated May 31, 1894.
64   Sparre, *Konstnärsliv*, p.136

65 I am indebted to Riitta Konttinen's book *Konstnärspar*, (*Artist Couples*) Schildts, Helsinki 1991, Schildts Keuru, 1991, for the information in this chapter on Carl and Karin Larsson, and the attitudes of and about women artists.

66 Letter of April 22, 1991 from Marketta Tamminen to author.

67 Letter of Dec. 15, 1993, from Marketta Tamminen to author.

68 Konttinen, *Konstnärspar*, p. 145

69 Sparre, *Konstnärsliv*, pp. 160-161

70 Ibid., p. 165

71 Berta Edelfelt: *Sophie Mannerheim, En Levnadsteckning* (*A Sketch of her Life*), Holger Schildt, Helsinki 1932, p. 39.

72 Ibid. p. 42

73 This and the other quotations in this chapter from Carl's correspondence come from a letter written to Carl by his grandmother, old Countess Eva Mannerheim, in the National Archives, Helsinki.

74 Ibid.

75 Tyyni Tuulio, *Friherrinnan Sophie Mannerheim, Människan och Livsgärningen* (*Baronness Sophie Mannerheim, The Person and her Life Achievement*), Söderström & Co., Helsinki 1948, p.76-77.

76 Edelfelt: *Sophie Mannerheim, En Levnadsteckning*, p.63

77 Letter from Sophie to her brother Carl, National Archives, Helsinki

78 Sparre: *Konstnärsliv*, p. 179

79 Tuulio, *Friherrinnan Sophie Mannerheim*, pp. 76 and 79

80 Jägerskiöld: *Den Unge Mannerheim*, p. 16

81 Tuulio, *Friherrinnan Sophie Mannerheim*, p. 76

82 Jägerskiöld: *Den Unge Mannerheim*, p. 170

83 Tuulio, *Friherrinnan Sophie Mannerheim*, p. 78

84 Jägerskiöld: *Den Unge Mannerheim*, p. 213

85 This and the subsequent quotations come from letters from Sophie to her brother Carl, National Archives, Helsinki

86 Letter to author from Elsie Mannerheim Uggla, undated, between 1995-1997

87 Tuulio, *Friherrinnan Sophie Mannerheim*, p. 84

88 Ibid., pp 19-20

89 Marita Munck and Marketta Tamminen, *Furniture by Louis Sparre*, Porvoo Museum publication nr. 3, Porvoo, 1990, p. 62

90 Sparre: *Konstnärsliv*, p. 185

91 Ibid. p.188

92 Ibid. p.200

93 Ibid. p.205

94 Munck and Tamminen, *Furniture by Louis Sparre*, pp. 83 and 93
95 Sparre, *Konstnärsliv* p. 220
96 Munck and Tamminen, *Furniture by Louis Sparre*, pp. 65-66
97 Ibid. p. 67
98 Ibid. p. 68
99 Sparre, *Konstnärsliv*, p. 203
100 Letter from Marketta Tamminen to author, Apr. 22, 1991
101 Heikki Kirkina and Hannes Sihvo: *The Kalevala, an Epic of Finland and All Mankind*, Finnish American Cultural Institute, 1985, p.10
102 Eino Jutikkala with Kauko Pirinen: *A History of Finland*, Dorset, N.Y. 1988, p.189
103 Carl Erik Mannerheim (1759-1837), *Memoirs*, Ed. by Bruno Lesch
104 Jägerskiöld: *Den Unge Mannerheim*, p. 222
105 Ibid. p. 224
106 Ibid. p. 226
107 Eino Jutikkala with Kauko Pirinen : *A History of Finland* (translated by Paul Sjöblom), Dorset, N.Y. 1988, p. 197
108 Ibid.; Sparre, *Konstnärsliv*, p. 212
109 Jägerskiöld, *Den Unge Mannerheim*, p. 231
110 This detail recounted by Carl's niece, Elsie Uggla, in a letter to the author.
111 Letter, May 1903, in Finnish National Archives, Helsinki
112 Sparre, *Konstnärsliv*, p. 258
113 Letter, February 1904, Finnish National Archives, Helsinki
114 Letter, March 1904, Finnish National Archives, Helsinki
115 Jägerskiöld, *Den Unge Mannerheim*, p. 227
116 Letter, Finnish National Archives, Helsinki
117 Ibid.
118 Jägerskiöld, *Den Unge Mannerheim*, p. 232
119 Stig Jägerskiöld, *Gustaf Mannerheim 1906-1917*, Holger Schildt, 1965, p. 306
120 All quotations in Chapter 16 are from Johan Mannerheim's letters to Palaemona Treschow, and her letters to him, in the Finnish National Archives, Helsinki
121 Konttinen, *Konstnärspar*, p. 162
122 Sparre, *Konstnärsliv*, p. 235
123 Ibid. p 247
124 Ibid. p. 250
125 Ibid. pp. 251-2
126 Ibid. p. 253
127 Ibid. Pp. 254-5

[128] Konnttinen, *Konstnärspar*, p. 147 and 163

[129] Elsie Mannerheim Uggla, letter to author, March 18, 1994. (Jeanne died single at 47 in 1910, after a struggle with what was said to have been Parkinson's Disease.)

[130] Edelfelt: *Sophie Mannerheim*, p. 113

[131] Letter, February 15,1904, Finnish National Archives, Helsinki

[132] Jutikkala and Pirinen, *A History of Finland*, p.204

[133] Letter, February 15, 1904, Finnish National Archives, Helsinki

[134] Sparre: *Konstnärsliv*, p. 283

[135] Letter, January 23, 1905 (missdated 1904), Finnish National Archives, Helsinki.

[136] Letter from Marketta Tamminen to author, April 22, 1991

[137] Sparre, *Konstnärsliv*, p. 293

[138] This and all other citations in this chapter from Eva Mannerheim Sparre's letters are in the author's archive, unless specifically noted.

[139] Jutikkala and Pirinen: *A History of Finland*, p. 205

[140] Sparre: *Konstnärsliv*, p. 298 and Jägerskiöld, *Den Unge Mannerheim*, p. 326

[141] Sparre: *Konstnärsliv*, p. 300

[142] Ibid., p. 301

[143] Sophie Mannerheim's role as the founder of modern nursing in Finland carried on the legacy of her distant cousin Aurore Karamsin, who had founded the deaconess's institute in Helsinki in 1867, a year of famine. She has appointed a remarkable woman of her time, Amanda Cajander, as the institute's head. Cajander was the wife of a doctor and had become interested in nursing. She educated herself at the deaconess's institute in St. Petersburg. "She was the first educated woman in Finland who chose nursing as her calling . . . The new institution pursued many sorts of philanthropic activities, but during the epidemic of the famine year, care of the sick became of necessity the principal preoccupation. The care offered by the deaconess's institution was definitely superior to other contemporary nursing care . . . in this institution deaconesses began to be educated as a goal . . . most of the doctors did not yet understand the need of educated nurses." (Tuulio, *Friherrinnan Sophie Mannerheim*, pp. 19-20). Both Sophie Mannerheim and Aurore Karamsin were honored by Finnish postage stamps in 1992.

[144] Cecil Woodham-Smith, *Florence Nightingale*, McGraw-Hill Book Company, New York, 1951, p. 41

[145] Edelfelt: *Sophie Mannerheim*, p. 83

[146] Ibid. p. 120

[147] Ibid.

148 Ibid. p. 129
149 Woodham-Smith, *Florence Nightingale*, pp. 68-9
150 This and other unattributed citations in this chapter are from letters in Finnish National Archives, Helsinki
151 Meri, *C. G. Mannerheim, Marskalken av Finland*; see also Tuulio, *Sophie Mannerheim*, pp.160-161
152 Meri, p. 257
153 Letters from Helene Mannerheim to Hanna Lovén from February to November 1876, in the Eva and Louis Sparre archive
154 Edelfelt, *Sophie Mannerheim*, p. 150
155 Ibid. pp. 146-7
156 Ibid. p. 141-2
157 Jägerskiöld: *Den Unge Mannerheim*, p. 251
158 Mannerheim: *Minnen Del I*, p. 34
159 Jägerskiöld:*Den Unge Mannerheim*, p. 251
160 This and all other correspondence in this chapter comes from letters in the Finnish National Archives, Helsinki.
161 Ibid. p. 273
162 Denis and Peggy Warner: *The Tide at Sunrise: A History of the Russo-Japanese War 1904-1905*, Charterhouse, New York, 1974. p. 20

These recent historians of the war have a different view of Kuropatkin. They find him often prescient and "bedeviled by incompetent officers like Grippenberg" (quoted under illustration of General Kuropatkin following p. 308.) They misspell Gripenberg; they call him "Oscar Casimorovitch Grippenberg" in the Russian fashion, misspelling Casimir, whereas his Finnish name was Oskar Ferdinand Gripenberg. He was a much honored and experienced soldier.

The Warners say that "Grippenberg" was a veteran of the Crimean War and an epileptic. This and other physical disabilities attributed to him by the Warners have not been mentioned by the noted historian, Stig Jägerskiöld. This Professor of History at Uppsala University, in his 8-volume biography of Gustaf Mannerheim, and particularly in the chapter devoted to his service in the Russo-Japanese War, writes extensively of Gripenberg's command and background.

The facts are that Oscar Ferdinand Gripenberg was, at 16, a warrant officer with the Finnish Grenadier Sharpshooter Battalion in 1854, at the time of the Crimean War, in which he is not said to have served either by Prof. Jägerskiöld or an official genealogy reporting on his military career. Gripenberg rose in the sharpshooter battalion to the rank of Captain, then joined the Russian campaigns in Turkestan, where he was several times rewarded for valor in storming a fortress and taking one although wounded. In the Turkish campaign of 1877 he distinguished himself in battle, and in a brave defense prevented Turkish advances and drove them back. For this he was given a decoration never before achieved by any Finn. He was promoted to the rank of lieutenant colonel, and in 1901 a general of the infantry. In 1903 he became adjutant general to the Tsar.

Professor Jägerskiöld writes (as also appears in the genealogy) that General Gripenberg accused Kuropatkin of denying him support. General Gripenberg requested and was granted a recall to St. Petersburg and thus departed from the war theatre. [Stig Jägerskiöld, *Den Unge Mannerheim*, pp. 275-276, 289 and Gustaf Elgenstierna, *Svenska Adelns Ättartavlor*, Norstedt & Söners Förlag, Stockholm 1927, Vol III p.132]

[163] Jägerskiöld: *Den Unge Mannerheim*, p. 278
[164] Hannes Ignatius: *Från Ofärdsår till Självständighet* (*From Years of Oppression to Independence*) Söderström, Helsinki 1927, pps 43-46
[165] G. Mannerheim: *Minnen, Del* I, p. 38
[166] Jägerskiöld, *Den Unge Mannerheim*, p. 293
[167] Ibid.
[168] Ibid.
[169] Ibid. p. 294
[170] Ibid.
[171] Ibid. pp. 302-304
[172] Letter, September 9, 1905, author's archive
[173] G. Mannerheim: *Minnen Del* I, p. 42
[174] Ibid., p. 42
[175] Ibid p.43
[176] Ibid.
[177] Jägerskiöld, *Den Unge Mannerheim*, p.309
[178] Information in this chapter comes from various family letters: Helene Mannerheim to her sister Hanna Lovén in Stockholm, 1877; August's letters to his brother Johan and sisters Sophie and Eva 1904 and 1910; Johan's letter to Gustaf (presumably 1894); Carl's letters to August of 1905; and from an informal biography of August, written by August's widow Elsie Nordenfelt Mannerheim in 1956.
[179] C. G. Mannerheim, *Till Häst genom Asien* [*Across Asia on Horseback*], Shortened Version, Söderström & Co. Helsinki, 1942; Editor Kaarlo Hildén
[180] Letter of May 21, 1906, Finland's National Archives, Helsinki
[181] Letter of July 14, 1906, Finland's National Archives, Helsinki

182 K. Donner: *Fältmarskalken Friherre Mannerheim* (*Field Marshal Baron Mannerheim*), Helsinki, 1934, pp. 29-30

183 G. Mannerheim: *Minnen, Del I*, pp. 51-2

184 Ibid. p. 59

185 Stig Jägerskiöld: *Gustaf Mannerheim 1906-1917*, Helsinki 1965, p.41

186 Ibid. p. 46

187 Ibid. p. 51

188 Meri: *Marskalken av Finland C.G. Mannerheim*, p. 208-9

189 Jägerskiöld, *Gustaf Mannerheim 1906-1917*. p. 54

190 Ibid. p. 55, footnote, and 56

191 Ibid. p. 57

192 Ibid. p.61

193 Ibid. p. 63

194 G. Mannerheim: *Minnen, Del I*, p. 90

195 Ibid. p. 92

196 Jägerskiöld: *Gustaf Mannerheim 1906-1917*, p. 67

197 Ibid., pp. 67-68

198 Ibid., p. 68

199 G. Mannerheim: *Minnen, Del I*, p. 95

200 Ibid.

201 Ibid. p. 96

202 called Saryg Yugurs and Shira Yugurs in *C.G. Mannerheimin Yalokuvia Aasian-Matkalta 1906-1908* (*Photographs by C.G.Mannerheim from his Journey across Asia 1906-1908*), edited by Peter Sandberg, Otava, 1990 p. 11. The text is in Finnish and English.

203 G. Mannerheim: *Minnen, Del I*, p. 100

204 From a pamphlet describing C.G. Mannerheim's Chinese Pantheon, *Materials from an Iconography of Chinese Folk Religion*. By Harry Halén and Bent Lerbæck Pedersen, Finno-Ugric Society, Helsinki 1993

205 Ibid. p. 101

206 Jägerskiöld, *Gustaf Mannerheim 1906-1917*, p. 70

207 Ibid.

208 Ibid. p. 71

209 G. Mannerheim: *Minnen, Del I*, p. 104

210 Jägerskiöld: *Gustaf Mannerheim 1906-1917*, p. 98

211 G. Mannerheim: *Minnen, Del I*, p. 111

212 Jägerskiöld: *Gustaf Mannerheim 1906-1917*, pp. 72-3

213 G. Mannerheim: *Minnen, Del I*, p. 112

214 Jägerskiöld: *Gustaf Mannerheim 1906-1917*, p. 73

215 Ibid. p. 74
216 Ibid. p. 75
217 G. Mannerheim: *Minnen, Del I*, p. 114
218 Ibid. p. 115
219 Jägerskiöld: *Gustaf Mannerheim 1906-1917*, p. 76
220 G. Mannerheim: *Minnen, Del I*, p. 118 The verse translates as follows: "She is pretty, she's the daughter/of a high ranking mandarin;/that's why she has on her chest/two little mandarins [tangerines]!"
221 Donner, *Fältmarskalken Friherre Mannerheim*, p. 59
222 G. Mannerheim: *Minnen, Del I*, p. 121
223 Ibid. p. 124
224 Letter of Sept. 13, 1908, Finland's National Archives, Helsinki
225 Letter to his father, quoted in Jägerskiöld, *Gustaf Mannerheim 1906-1917*, p. 108.
226 G. Mannerheim: *Minnen, Del I*, p. 80
227 Jägerskiöld: *Gustaf Mannerheim 1906-1917*, p. 106
228 Ibid. pp. 59-60
229 C.G. Mannerheimin *Valokuvia Aasian-Matkalta 1906-1908*, pp. 5, 9, 13, 16
230 Letter to the author from Marne Lloyd-Smith Hornblower, March 7, 1996, and G. Mannerheim: *Minnen, Del I*, p. 424- 428
231 G. Mannerheim: *Minnen, Del I*, p. 128
232 This quotation and others in this chapter from the correspondence of Eva and Louis Sparre are from letters in the author's archive.
233 Jutikkala and Pirinen, *History of Finland*, p. 207
234 Sparre, *Konstnärsliv*, p. 319
235 Dr. Helge Miettunen, *Filmerna och Filmproduktion i Finland*, Porvoo 1959, translated into Swedish by Anna Maria Reinilä
236 Letter to the author.
237 Letter of September 25,1907.
238 Letter from Marketta Tamminen to the author, October 14, 1996
239 Sparre, *Konstnärsliv*, p. 333
240 Both books are now in the Rare Book Collection of the Bryn Mawr College Library
241 From a Swedish newspaper, probably *Svenska Dagbladet*, of unknown date
242 Sparre, *Konstnärsliv*, p. 334

Lightning Source UK Ltd.
Milton Keynes UK
UKHW041025291219
355996UK00006BA/1059/P

9 781425 785956